O.J. Unmasked

"By combining common sense, logic, and thorough research, Ms. Rantala dissects the ambiguities, cotions of the Simpson trial. She places proper perspective by extracting th flights of fancy. Her analysis of the DNA evidence is particularly brilliant, finally disposing of the arguments raised by the defense. *O.J. Unmasked* would make a great textbook in courses teaching rational and critical thinking."

—George Schiro
Forensic Scientist,
Louisiana State Police Crime Laboratory

"A valuable and scholarly book on the Simpson case."

—Vincent Bugliosi
Prosecutor of Charles Manson
Author of *Helter Skelter*

"M.L. Rantala has produced a highly readable and illuminating analysis of the O.J. Simpson case, including some of its seemingly unapproachable aspects like the DNA evidence. With a careful assessment of the facts and scrupulous attention to the standards of inductive reasoning, Ms. Rantala makes logical mincemeat of the Simpson defense theories and thereby challenges the verdict to which they gave rise.

"This is a welcome work for those who value an understanding of the case which goes beyond the often incoherent and superficial accounts presented by the mainstream media and their 'legal experts'."

—Ray Perkins, Jr.
Associate Professor of Philosophy, Plymouth State College,
Author of *Logic and Mr. Limbaugh*

An excellent job. *O.J. Unmasked* is a fascinating, educational, and impressive book.

—Marilyn Harris
Owner of "Courtroom", an Internet group
devoted exclusively to discussing the Simpson case

"Ms. Rantala does a terrific job of presenting the evidence, reviewing the key testimony, and explaining the jury's verdict. Mr. Simpson and the jurors ought to be having many sleepless nights. I find it difficult to imagine any reader of *O.J. Unmasked* who would not be driven to conclude that O.J. got away with murder."

—Robert Haselkorn
Distinguished Service Professor of Molecular Genetics
and Cell Biology, University of Chicago

"Combining meticulous logic with a witty and entertaining writing style, Rantala provides a gripping, and utterly convincing, analysis of the evidence in the Simpson case. I cannot imagine how anyone could possibly do a better job."

—David Detmer
Associate Professor of Philosophy, Purdue University Calumet
Author of *Freedom as a Value*

"A superbly readable and provocative book, chock-full of information from the evidence and witness lists to the trivia quiz. Cuts to the core of the Simpson evidence and its use, misuse, disuse, and abuse by both sides."

—Howard Coleman
Forensic Scientist,
Author of *DNA in the Courtroom*

"Juries, unfortunately, are drawn chiefly from people who are generally ignorant of how scientific merit can be assessed. *O.J. Unmasked* would be useful for anyone who might be in the position of having to weigh evidence in a court of law or anywhere else. It exposes ways in which expert testimony and statistics can be used to twist the truth."

—Dr. Damon Chase Shutt
Department of Biological Sciences,
University of Iowa

O.J. Unmasked

O.J. Unmasked

The Trial, the Truth, and the Media

M.L. Rantala

CATFEET
P
PRESS
Chicago

CATFEET PRESS™ and the above logo are trademarks of Carus
Publishing Company.

© 1996 by Catfeet Press™
First printing March 1996
Second printing May 1996

Printed and bound in the United States of America.

Library of Congress Cataloging-in-Publication Data

Rantala, M.L.
    O.J. unmasked : the trial, the truth, and the media / M. L.
Rantala.
      p.   cm.
    Includes bibliographical references and indexes.
    ISBN 0-8126-9328-0 (alk. paper)
    1. Simpson, O.J., 1947- --Trials, litigation, etc. 2. Trials
(Murder)--California--Los Angeles.
KF224.S485R36 1996
345.73'02523'0979494--dc20
[B]
[347.30525230979494]
[B]   96-11127
                                 CIP

For my grandmothers

Contents

Preface

I disapprove of murder.

—Hercule Poirot

Commentators are regularly asked "why all the interest in the O.J. Simpson case?" The answers generally include: Simpson's wealth, fame, and widespread popularity prior to the murders; the strangely compelling nature of the June 17th Bronco chase; the hideous brutality of the murders; people's interest in how justice may differ when defendants are black rather than white, or celebrities rather than unknowns; and a certain suspicion of police in general and the LAPD specifically. These factors do explain much of the initial interest in the case, but they are insufficient to explain a voracious attention spanning the nearly sixteen months between the murders and the not-guilty verdict at trial.

While the trials of Lorena Bobbitt, William Kennedy Smith, and the Menendez brothers were fascinating to millions, they differed in one crucial aspect from the O.J. Simpson case: dismemberment, sexual intercourse, and killing by shotgun were not denied by these defendants. Rather, they all attempted to provide an explanation which made them either legally not guilty of any crime at all, or guilty of something far less than what the prosecution alleged.

I think the biggest factor which explains the enduring interest in the Simpson case is that people want to decide for themselves what the evidence shows. The complicated defense offered by Simpson's lawyers has been given serious attention by the public, even those who ultimately concluded that O.J. Simpson murdered Nicole Brown Simpson and Ronald Goldman.

Scrutinizing the case carefully, people on either side of the O.J. fence have found many puzzling little facts hard to explain by their own theories. This is of course typical of any case based entirely on circumstantial evidence where the accused denies guilt, and Simpson did not hesitate to proclaim himself "absolutely, one hundred percent not guilty."

This leads to two basic approaches to the events: an explanation of the evidence against him which is consistent with innocence or an explanation consistent with guilt.

Mysteries attendant upon the first approach include: Why did Simpson make so many demonstrably false statements to police only fifteen hours after the murders? If one concludes that the testimony of defense expert Dr. Henry Lee supports the theory that blood was planted on swatches, why is the blood on these swatches significantly degraded when the source of plantable blood is a robust, preserved sample? How could a partial footprint, consistent with the Bruno Magli shoes which left bloody shoe impressions walking away from the bodies, have been made by Detective Fuhrman when the evidence is clear his shoes were nothing like Bruno Maglis? Why did the defense show the jury only four of the five pieces of luggage O.J. had the night of the murders and what happened to the mysterious fifth piece? Is O.J. the most unlucky man in the world, accidentally cutting himself at home more or less at the time of the murders and then finding himself unable to remember how it happened?

While the second approach (guilt) does explain far more of the evidence, even here there remain several small puzzles still gnawed at by O.J. junkies: Why did Simpson leave the location of the bodies, seemingly hide in the bushes, and then return to the murder scene without collecting the glove and the hat? How did Simpson come to lose the glove found behind Kato Kaelin's guesthouse? How did Simpson dispose of the bloody clothes and murder knife? What was in his Louis Vuitton garment bag, taken away by his friend and lawyer, Robert Kardashian, on the day after the murders? What happened to the mysterious knapsack that Kato Kaelin testified Simpson insisted on carrying himself?

In addition, there are some facts of the case which are equally well explained by either theory. People want to understand for themselves which explanations should be accepted and which rejected. So they drank in the trial coverage and commentary in hope of answers.

Part of the thirst for trial coverage was the need to have

everything explained. While this book attempts to explain many of the important issues, it cannot be emphasized enough that in virtually every crime there are loose ends which are never tied up. If people wait to have every single question or anomaly explained before drawing conclusions about a case, then they should stock up their cupboards for a long wait indeed. Some things remain forever unknown. Vincent Bugliosi, the famed Charles Manson prosecutor, explains:

> In literature a murder scene is often likened to a picture puzzle. If one is patient and keeps trying, eventually all the pieces will fit into place.
>
> Veteran policemen know otherwise. A much better analogy would be two picture puzzles, or three, or more, no one of which is in itself complete. Even after a solution emerges—if one does—there will be leftover pieces, evidence that just doesn't fit. And some pieces will always be missing.[1]

We should chew on this for a time before rushing to agree with Johnnie Cochran that "if it doesn't fit, you must acquit."[2]

In a court of law Simpson was not required to present a complete or even internally consistent theory rebutting the prosecution case against him, let alone prove his innocence. And the prosecution was not required to explain every detail of Simpson's movements before, during, and after the murders. Nor could they reasonably be expected to do so.

Nonetheless, I believe that many issues left still cloudy after the trial was over can be elucidated more fully. This book is an attempt to examine many of the important issues of the trial and provide reasonable conclusions, based on the evidence, facts, and logic.

In spite of the continuing supply of "O.J. Analysis", many of the interesting questions go unanswered and important issues remain unexplored. This is primarily due to the fact that media discussions, and especially the TV commentary programs all suffer from various defects.

First, the individuals invited to give their views are nearly always lawyers. Many lawyers, when discussing the competing testimony on a given issue, have simply said "it's up to the jury to decide". They assumed that what interested people most was the verdict and since legally the facts of the case are decided by the jury, any detailed analysis by a lawyer is beside the point. The verdict was certainly received with rapt attention, but there can be no doubt that, as with the Kennedy assassination, discussion of the facts of the case will go on and on. Most people have decided for themselves on Simpson's guilt or innocence. The jury verdict did not affect those decisions, nor should it.

Second, in-depth discussion of particular issues was eschewed in favor of short, snappy commentary on a large number of topics. Just as a viewer or reader gets interested in a particular issue, the article ends or the commercials come on.

The public was often referred to as the thirteenth juror. This book addresses in detail many of the issues raised at trial which, in their deliberations of less than four hours, could not have been considered in any depth by the jury. I attempt to discuss the issues in the way an intelligent and conscientious jury would. In a few cases my discussions are not limited to evidence or argument actually put before the Simpson jury. A book of this length cannot possibly cover every important issue of an eight month trial, but all major issues in dispute are given some consideration.

I decided to write this book when the trial was nearly over. My editors told me they wanted to go to press in March of 1996. Because of the pressure to publish speedily, imperfections may have crept in for which I apologize in advance.

Acknowledgments

I am grateful to many people who read a draft of this book and provided helpful comments and suggestions: Howard Coleman, forensic scientist, GeneLex Corporation; Professor David Detmer, Department of Philosophy, Purdue University Calumet; Professor Kristina Detmer, Mercer University School of Medicine; Tracie M. Jenkins, Ph.D., Research Professor in Genetics, Mercer University School of Medicine; Marilyn Harris; Professor Robert Haselkorn, Department of Molecular Genetics and Cell Biology, University of Chicago; Rob Keister, forensic scientist, Orange County Sheriff–Coroner Department; Dr. Margaret Morgan, Department of Molecular Genetics and Cell Biology, University of Chicago; Richard F. Porter; Raymond R. Rantala; George Schiro, forensic scientist, Louisiana State Police Crime Laboratory; and Dr. Damon Chase Shutt, Department of Biological Sciences, University of Iowa.

I am grateful to specialists in many areas who have provided advice and who have read drafts of some of the technical portions of this book: Peter D. Barnett, Forensic Science Associates; Professor John W. Farley, Department of Physics, University of Nevada, Las Vegas; Roger Kahn, Ph.D., Metro-Dade Police DNA Unit, Miami, Florida; Norah Rudin, Ph.D.; Toby L. Wolson, M.S.,

Metro-Dade Police Crime Laboratory Bureau, Miami, Florida.

Some of the topics covered in this book were discussed in "Courtroom", an Internet group devoted to discussion of the Simpson case. I am indebted to the members of "Courtroom" for their insight and lively debate.

I was assisted by members of the Internet forensic discussion group "Forens-L". Several forensic scientists on this list provided helpful information and useful references to the forensic literature.

I also appreciate the assistance of Andrys Basten, Hal Bogner, Mark Brady, Judith Lawrence, Jeff Marschner, Judith Milgram, Diane Prendiville, Eric Schiller, Tero Valkonen, and especially Dionne Rantala.

I am exceedingly grateful to my editors, David Ramsay Steele and Kerri Mommer, who contributed immeasurably to this project and who made working on it a pleasure.

I could not have written this book without the assistance of my husband, Arthur J. Milgram, who found time while working on his Ph.D. dissertation to compose appendix 2. His scientific expertise and unflagging support were indispensable at all stages of my work.

None of these people are responsible for the content of this book and I alone am responsible for any errors which may remain.

M.L. Rantala
Chicago, February 1996

CHAPTER 1

Facts and Theories

For when the knife has slit
The throat across from ear to ear
'Twill bleed because of it.

—A.E. Housman

Around midnight, as June 12th, 1994, became June 13th, Sukru Boztepe and Bettina Rasmussen learned what had agitated a stray dog which had come into their possession. Following the dog, they were led to the front of 875 South Bundy Drive in the Los Angeles neighborhood of Brentwood. One look up the pathway was enough for them to discern a very dead woman and rivers of blood.[1]

It was so dark that the first policeman on the scene didn't find the second body until he approached the murdered woman from the sidewalk. Officer Riske touched the eye of the second victim to confirm that he was dead.

Police descended on the quiet street. The woman was identified as Nicole Brown Simpson, resident of the Bundy condominium. The second victim was not identified until hours later. He was Ronald Lyle Goldman, Nicole's friend. Both were the victims of multiple knife wounds. Nicole's throat had been deeply slashed. Ron had been stabbed all over his body.

An envelope was found near the bodies. It contained eyeglasses belonging to Nicole's mother. They had been lost earlier that evening in front of the restaurant where Ron worked. On his way to spend an evening on the town with a friend, he had come to Nicole's condo to drop off the glasses. Also found on the ground was Ron's beeper. The last person to leave a message on his beeper was the friend he never got a chance to meet that night.

The Facts

In the hours after the murders, police and criminalists would identify important evidence at the scene. Bloody shoe impressions led away from the bodies toward the back alleyway. Several drops of blood appeared to the left of these footprints. Although the door to Nicole's condo was ajar, there was no evidence whatever of blood inside her home, neither was there any sign of ransacking. Numerous officers saw blood on the back gate, leading to the alley—this blood would become an issue hotly disputed later.

A glove and knit hat were found on the ground near the bodies.

The first two detectives on the case, from the local station, were quickly replaced by two detectives from the central Robbery/Homicide division of the LAPD. All four of these men would become central figures in the case.

The four detectives left the Bundy murder scene and traveled a few miles to 360 North Rockingham Avenue. They had been ordered by a superior, according to their testimony in the legal proceedings which followed, to notify the ex-husband of the female murder victim. The ex-husband was the father of Nicole's two children, who had both been found sleeping and unharmed in the condominium at 875 South Bundy Drive.

The ex-husband would become the most famous man of his generation to be tried for murder.

Nicole's ex-husband was O.J. Simpson, a man who had achieved considerable success in spite of humble beginnings in a poor San Francisco neighborhood. As a college football player at U.S.C. he won the famed Heisman trophy. As a professional player for the Buffalo Bills he set NFL records for rushing, which eventually led to his induction into the NFL Hall of Fame. He served as a pitchman for many companies, most visibly the Hertz rental car agency. He worked for two major networks as a football commentator. He had roles in many films, including the successful *Naked Gun* cop spoof movies.

Rich, handsome, popular, and successful, when O.J. Simpson became a suspect in the murders, the public was shocked and fascinated.

Blood was found inside and outside Simpson's white Ford Bronco, including what appeared to be a bloody shoe impression in the carpet. Blood was in his driveway, his foyer, and his bathroom. He had a deep cut on one of his left fingers when he spoke to police some fifteen hours after the murders. He could not recall exactly how he had come to have that cut.

And in an obscure location on his property was a blood-drenched glove which matched the single glove found at the murder scene.

The Prosecution Theory

In the wake of the murders, investigators learned of a history of abuse of Nicole by O.J. Simpson—abuse which spanned their seventeen-year relationship. While the abuse notably included brutal beatings, prosecutors contended that it was more than that: it was an obsession which included verbal attacks, humiliation, and financial control. The worst episodes were followed by periods of acute contrition and attempts by both of them to try again. In arguing before the judge on the admissibility of such evidence, prosecutor Scott Gordon argued that "what must be recognized is that this murder took 17 years to commit."[2]

The prosecutors believed that the murder of Nicole was a premeditated act born out of Simpson's obsession with her and his final realization that he could no longer have her. Ron Goldman had the disastrous bad fortune to appear on the scene and become the second victim, so that the murderer could escape without a witness.

Along with motive, the prosecution had other evidence of Simpson's guilt:

- The blood found at the murder scene, to the left of the bloody footprints, was identified by DNA tests as Simpson's.

- The shoes leaving the bloody footprints were identified as Bruno Maglis—expensive and rare Italian-made shoes. The prints were made by size 12 shoes, O.J. Simpson's size. Such shoes were sold in only forty stores in the U.S., including Bloomingdales, a place Simpson regularly purchased size 12 shoes.

- A hat found at the murder scene had hairs in it consistent with Simpson's.

- The blood on the back gate (observed by many on June 13th but not collected until July 3rd) was identified by DNA tests as Simpson's blood.

- Simpson's white Ford Bronco had blood of the victims on the center console. On the driver's side carpet was an impression in Nicole's blood which was consistent with the Bruno Magli shoe pattern left by the killer at the murder scene.

- A trail of Simpson's own blood led from Simpson's Bronco into Simpson's house.

- Socks found in Simpson's bedroom contained his own blood and Nicole's blood.

- One glove (the Bundy glove) was found at the murder scene; another glove (the Rockingham glove) was found on Simpson's estate. These gloves were a pair. Not only were the gloves Simpson's size, they were expensive and rare, sold only by one store. They were the same size and brand that Nicole had purchased the week before Christmas in 1990. The prosecutors argued that the gloves were purchased for Simpson as a Christmas gift.

- Several photographs and videos of Simpson wearing gloves of the same make and model as those found at Bundy and Rockingham were located.

- The day after the murders police observed a serious cut to one of the fingers on Simpson's left hand, a cut which could have left the blood trail at Bundy and at Rockingham. Simpson told police he could not recall how he had initially received the cut.

- Simpson was observed the night of June 12th wearing dark blue or black clothing. Blue-black cotton fibers were found on the victims. The dark clothing Simpson was wearing that night has never been found.

- When the limo driver arrived at Simpson's home to take him to the airport, there was no reply for twenty minutes. The limo driver then saw a tall, 200-pound black person enter the house and only then were the driver's buzzes finally answered by Simpson. Simpson told the driver he had been sleeping.

- When he approached 360 North Rockingham, the limo driver did not notice any Bronco.

- Brian "Kato" Kaelin, who lived in a Simpson estate guesthouse, heard three thumps behind his room the night of June 12th. He left his room to investigate. At the same time Kato reached the front of the house from one direction, Simpson approached his own door from a different direction. The prosecution argued that Simpson had come from the general direction of the thumps. In spite of Kaelin's great concern over the thumps, the fact that Simpson was about to leave town so that his main house would be unoccupied, and that Simpson's own daughter resided in her own quarters on the premises, Simpson did not investigate himself, did not call the police, did not alert his private security service, and uncharacteristically forgot to turn on his security alarm before he left for the airport.

- The Rockingham glove was discovered behind Kato's room, near the place where the thumps had occurred.

- The Rockingham glove had on it fibers from Ron Goldman's shirt, hair from Nicole, carpet fibers matching the carpeting in Simpson's Bronco, and the blood of Nicole, Ron, and Simpson.

- Loading up the limousine, Kato Kaelin offered to fetch one of Simpson's bags from the pavement. Simpson insisted on carrying the bag himself. By the next morning, that bag was gone. It has not been seen since.

- The night after the murders, Simpson told friend Ron Shipp that he had previously had dreams of killing Nicole. He asked how long it took for DNA tests to yield results.

- A doctor hired by the defense to examine Simpson less than seventy-two hours after the murders found multiple cuts and abrasions on his left hand.

- Simpson had no alibi.

This, and still more evidence, led the prosecution to believe they had a strong case for murder. But none of the numerous prosecuting attorneys had ever seen a defense like the one waged on behalf of O.J. Simpson.

The Defense Theory

Simpson employed a battery of defense attorneys, often referred to by the media as the Dream Team. They ranged from the well-known and flamboyant F. Lee Bailey to the obscure and mild-mannered Robert Blasier. Key players in the multi-million dollar legal array were Robert Shapiro (original lead attorney), Johnnie Cochran (lead attorney by the beginning of the trial),

Barry Scheck and Peter Neufeld (DNA legal experts), and Alan Dershowitz (who sent faxes to the courtroom and held court himself on television).

In his opening statement, Johnnie Cochran told the jury that the evidence against Simpson was "contaminated, compromised, and ultimately corrupted".[3] The DNA evidence implicating Simpson was contaminated with the blood Simpson voluntarily gave to the police. The investigation of the crime was so bungled that conclusions could not be trusted. And the bloody glove found on Simpson's estate, along with much of the other evidence, was placed there by dirty cops interested in convicting Simpson at all costs.

The defense argued that Simpson didn't have time to commit the murders and that he was too infirm to have accomplished them. The murders were committed by two men, not one. Simpson was a happy man who had no reason to murder Nicole or anyone else.

While Simpson regretted the fact that he had struck his wife in 1989, he had not been physically violent with her after that incident.[4]

Members of Simpson's family denied that Ron Shipp ever had a private conversation with Simpson the evening following the murders. In the hours between the murders and the time Simpson was notified by police, he showed no agitation and was in fact his usual, affable self.

Rather than scrutinizing the seemingly incriminating evidence against Simpson, defense attorneys urged the jury to judge the police. Detective Mark Fuhrman was accused of finding two gloves at Bundy and taking one to Rockingham in order to frame an innocent man. Before depositing the glove behind Kato's room, he rubbed it inside the Bronco to connect Simpson to the murders. Detective Vannatter used the blood Simpson had voluntarily given to the police the day after the murders to plant more evidence against Simpson.

Blood found on the back gate at Bundy and on the socks in Simpson's bedroom contained a preservative, clearly showing that the blood, while it was indeed Simpson's, had first spent time in a purple-top test tube, just like the test tube used by the jail nurse who took Simpson's blood the day after the murders.

The murders happened later than the prosecution suggested, leaving Simpson no time to have committed them.

It wasn't true that Nicole had purchased the accoutrements of her own murder. The gloves found at Bundy and Rockingham were not those given by Nicole to her husband as a Christmas gift three-and-a-half years earlier. In fact, these gloves had nothing to do with O.J. Simpson.

They didn't even fit him.

CHAPTER 2

A School of Red Herrings

The flowers that bloom in the spring,
Tra la,
Have nothing to do with the case.

—W.S. Gilbert, *The Mikado*

It is the stuff of TV courtroom drama. The eagle-eyed attorney pounces on some inconsistency or misstatement in the witness's responses. The witness hesitates, nonplussed, then comes up with some rather lame-sounding explanation. The attorney pursues the matter further, and the witness begins to look as if his ulcer is giving him trouble. The attorney's tone of voice suggests that he has exposed a serious anomaly in the witness's story. The attorneys on the other side try to conceal their discomfiture.

At this point, in the old Perry Mason TV series, the witness usually breaks down, at five minutes to the hour, and emotionally blurts out that he, and not the accused, did the murder. In real life, and in the original Perry Mason novels, this hardly ever happens. But what may occur is that the casual or half-awake onlooker, who may be on the jury, assumes that a really damaging point has been made, and at the very least, that the witness has been somewhat discredited.

But wait a moment! Is this newly uncovered anomaly really relevant to the issue of the guilt or innocence of the accused? Or is it just a red herring? Even if it is relevant, is it only very marginally relevant? And is there a simple and innocent explanation?

Defense attorneys who know that their client is in a tricky spot, because there is so much evidence against him, resort to various standard tricks to distract the jury's attention from the sheer strength of the prosecution case. The defense will try to find issues on which the prosecution witnesses can be tripped up, *even if these issues have very little bearing on whether their client committed the crime.* The more complicated the arguments become, the more opportunities for the defense to cloud the issues.

What protection do we have from defense attorneys' distractions, diversions, or smokescreens? First, a prosecution which understands the need to keep the whole case as simple as possible, and resolves not to be drawn into the endless exploration of minutiae. Second, a judge with backbone, who will not permit lines of questioning which are immaterial or for which no foundation has been laid. Third, a jury which deliberates and which has one or more members who are open-minded and critical, who will insist, in case the other jurors have overlooked it, that such-and-such a point can be answered, or has nothing to do with the issue being tried.

All these safeguards were absent in the Simpson trial, so the Dream Team was able to cast its net widely, and inevitably they netted a number of red herrings, some of which I look at in this chapter.

The Unsoiled Socks

The defense argued that the person who murdered Ron Goldman was engaged in a pitched battle in a small area with lots of loose dirt. The lack of dirt on Simpson's socks indicated that those socks and Simpson himself weren't at that murder scene.

This argument is inconsistent with other evidence in the case, never challenged by the defense. The bloody footprints leading away from the murder scene contained only Nicole's blood. This was demonstrated by tests on Item 56, one of the bloody shoe impressions leaving the Bundy scene. The bloody shoe impression in the Bronco was also Nicole's blood—none of Ron's.

The murderer was in a small box-like area struggling with Ron Goldman and inflicting several wounds after the cut to the jugular vein which produced great amounts of blood. Thus, whoever the killer was, he didn't struggle enough with Goldman to get a significant amount of Goldman's blood on the bottom of his shoes, so why should we expect dirt on the socks? The shoes, after all, *had* to touch the ground near where Goldman was and there was no blood from Goldman leading away from the scene. It is hardly surprising, then, that there is no dirt on the socks, which might well have been covered by pants.

Too Little Blood

In their closing argument, the defense emphasized that only 0.07 milliliters of blood was found in Simpson's Bronco. They suggested that such a small amount was inconsistent with Simpson being a brutal double murderer. But the small amount of blood found in the Bronco is actually highly incriminating:

Since Simpson did not know Ronald Goldman, *any* amount of Goldman's blood in Simpon's vehicle is damning. To dismiss it by saying "there's not very much" is hardly persuasive.

One defense explanation of the blood was that Detective Mark Fuhrman put it there, or at least some of it. The defense suggested that there were really two gloves at Bundy. Fuhrman took one of them, rubbed it in the victim's blood, and took it to Rockingham to incriminate Simpson. If this were true, why would he plant such a remarkably puny amount in the Bronco? The amount of blood found was not only very small, but much of it was Simpson's. Since the defense contends that Simpson's blood was deposited there innocently, then what was planted, according to the defense theory, was *even less than 0.07 milliliters*. What kind of a frame-up is that?

The small amount of blood is not only inconsistent with a theory of a racist cop who wanted to frame Simpson (such a man would make sure there was lots of blood), but is highly suggestive of someone taking great pains *to keep blood off the Bronco surfaces*—precisely as a murderer would do.

In the hours following the murders, only one stain collected from the Bronco was identified as being consistent with Ron Goldman. The defense even questioned the validity of the DNA tests which formed the basis for this conclusion, because to identify Ron took careful interpretation. In August, more blood was collected from the Bronco and several stains were identified as containing Ron's blood. The defense suggested that Ron's blood wasn't in the Bronco in the hours following the murders, but was only planted later. This, of course, contradicts the other defense theory that Fuhrman planted the victim's blood in the Bronco on June 13th. But this claim that Ron's blood only appeared in the Bronco much later does not explain the presence of a shoe impression on the Bronco carpet in Nicole's blood. That shoe impression, cut out of the Bronco less than two days after the murders, linked Simpson to the crime scene and was never disputed during the evidentiary part of the trial. In closing argument, with no evidence to support it, the defense claimed the shoeprint was made by Fuhrman. But if no blood of Ron Goldman was planted in the Bronco in the hours after the murders, what defense explanation can account for Fuhrman's footprint in the Bronco?

The defense maintained that the murderer of Ron and Nicole would be covered in blood. Since there was so little blood in the Bronco, Simpson could not be the murderer. But even the defense's own experts disagreed with this argument. Bloodstain expert Dr. Henry Lee, called as a defense witness, testified under cross-examination:

Q Now, with respect to the amount of blood that we are going to expect to find in an item such as the Bronco, do you agree with the idea
   that we can only interpret the bloodstains that are physically present
   and that no one should speculate as to why a defendant was not
   blood stained except in the most unusual cases?
A Yes, in general. …
Q Isn't there a lot of forensic science literature out there that generally
   cautions the forensic scientists who are involved in blood spatter that
   you can't really say that someone didn't participate in a crime just
   because they are not covered in blood even if it is something like a
   stabbing?
A Yes, sir.[1]

Another defense blood expert, Herbert MacDonell, wrote about this subject in a paper entitled "Absence of Evidence is not Evidence of Absence". Judge Ito read into the record the relevant paragraph from this article at a sidebar conference:

"The complete absence of bloodstains on a defendant or his clothing
is frequently assumed by many to be definitive evidence that the
defendant did not directly participate in a violent act. This is a misconception fostered and exploited by those who have insufficient knowledge and experience in bloodstain pattern interpretation or by those
who hope that such an opinion would aid in their client's defense.
Explanations for the lack of bloodstaining on an individual who has
actively participated in a violent act are innumerable. These include the
assailant cleaning up prior to his being apprehended, removal of his
clothing prior to committing the act or simply not being stained because spattered blood was intercepted by some intermediate target."[2]

The prosecution theory for why Simpson did not transfer large amounts of blood to the Bronco was that he attacked his victims from behind. Marcia Clark was able to bring some of MacDonell's relevant analysis before the jury during cross-examination:

Q   You have previously testified, sir, that the absence of blood on a perpetrator does not indicate non-participation in a violent act, correct?

A   That is correct.

Q   And when we discussed this before, you indicated as well that although attorneys may want to argue that the absence of blood on a— on their client indicates that he did not commit the bloody act, you have advised them that that is not the case, that that is a misconception, have you not?

Mr. Neufeld: Objection, argumentative and irrelevant as to what he advised other lawyers.

The Court: Overruled.

A: I have said that there are exceptions to every rule. It is possible to commit a crime and not get blood on you. Most often you will see clothing that has no blood on it and assume that the person did not participate, but we would rather explain seeing the blood and trying to establish the mechanism it got there and speculate why it did, not but that is the basis of that article ["Absence of Evidence is not Evidence of Absence"].

Q   Which is that you must interpret what you see and not what you do not see?

A   Correct.[3]

Rockingham Blood Trail

The defense claimed that the trail of blood at Rockingham was inconsistent with Simpson being the murderer. There was blood in the Bronco, the driveway, and the foyer but no blood anywhere between the foyer and Simpson's bathroom, where another drop was found. There was no blood on the door to the Rockingham house or on any of the light switches or carpet.

Since the bloody shoe impressions at Bundy faded out completely before the Bundy carport, there is no reason to expect bloody shoe impressions at Rockingham on surfaces like the brick driveway or the foyer where the floor is bare wood. It's possible that the blood still in the crevices of Simpson's shoes (which made the impression in the Bronco carpet) would have dried by the time he went up his own carpeted stairs, explaining the lack of blood there. Or perhaps he took off his shoes as soon as he entered his house.

The defense explanation for Simpson's own blood in his Bronco and at Rockingham was bleeding from an innocent cut he incurred the night of June 12th. The jury learned this from defense witness Dr. Michael Baden. Simpson himself told police that he had cut himself that night before leaving for Chicago, when he gave his statement to police the next day, although this statement wasn't introduced to the jury. So the defense explained that Simpson's blood in and around his own home was due to some cut (never explained), perhaps resulting from a mishap with a cellular phone in his Bronco.

This means that an innocent man can bleed in his vehicle, driveway, and foyer without leaving any blood on his front door or his light switches, perhaps because he operated these with his uncut right hand. An innocent man, by the defense theory, can also drip blood in his foyer and in his bathroom without leaving any drops of blood in between. So why does a guilty cut have to bleed differently? If an innocent person can stop the bleeding between the foyer and the bathroom, so can a murderer. The pattern of Simpson's own blood at Rockingham in no way rules him out as the killer.

Tarzan's Grandfather

The defense suggested that Simpson was too infirm to have committed the murders. Dr. Robert Huizenga examined Simpson on June 15th, less than seventy-two hours after the murders. Huizenga told the jury on direct examination that while Simpson had the body of Tarzan, he walked like Tarzan's grandfather. But he also admitted that Simpson had seven abrasions and three fresh cuts (one in two parts) *on his left hand*. On cross-examination he conceded that despite the arthritis Simpson suffered, he would have been strong enough to have killed two people with a single-edged knife. Another defense witness, Richard Walsh, had worked on an exercise video with Simpson two weeks before the murders. He admitted that Simpson was able to perform all the exercises required, even after twelve hours of hard work.

A Misspoken Word

Defense partisans routinely pointed out that during his preliminary hearing testimony Detective Fuhrman used the pronoun "them" in answer to a question about the Bundy glove. This, they said, shows that there were two gloves at Bundy and supports the proposition that Fuhrman absconded with one glove and transported it to Rockingham in order to frame O.J. Simpson. Fuhrman explained that his use of "them" referred to the single Bundy glove and the knit hat, because both of these pieces of evidence were lying together.

The "Them" Defense

F. Lee Bailey's cross-examination of Fuhrman's use of the word "nigger" became one of the most talked-about aspects of the trial. Bailey also bestowed great attention on the word "them", trying to convince the jury that Fuhrman did find two gloves at Bundy. Bailey was delighted to question Fuhrman about this for three days running, beginning on March 13th:

Q When discussing this event in the preliminary hearing and talking about the glove, your tongue slipped and you said "them," didn't you?
A Yes.
Q And you have examined that in the transcript, haven't you?
A Yes.
Q And you know it has been played on video to the jury? The word "them" is clear?
A Yes.
Q That is a slip of the tongue?
A No.
Q It was not? Okay.[4]

It wasn't really okay for Bailey, who could not resist returning to the subject the next day, reading to Fuhrman some of the questions he had been asked at the preliminary hearing:

"Question: When did you first observe it [the Bundy glove]?
"Answer: We had flashlights. We were looking at the female victim. We looked at the male victim. I noticed the glove when I walked around to the—after I exited the residence the first time and walked around to the side or the north side, north perimeter of Bundy of 875 Bundy, there is an iron fence and through that iron fence you can get very close to the male victim, and looking there I could see them at his feet."
Did you use the word "them" in your answer on July 5th?
A Yes, sir. Yes, sir.
Q And was the last item to which "them" could have applied in your narrative the word "glove"?

A Singular, yes.

Q I'm simply asking whether glove, line 14, was the item you were talking about just prior to saying "I saw them at his feet"?

A "Them," I was referring to the knit cap, the glove.

Q Show me anywhere on that page where the knit cap is mentioned? Can you?

A That page, no.

Q All right. All right. Do you see anything on the prior page, Detective Fuhrman, about the knit cap?

A Do you want me to look at that prior page?

Q Sure. I don't know how you can answer the question without looking at it. 63.

A (witness complies.) I do not.[5]

Bailey returned to "them" the next day with more of the same sort of questions and Fuhrman provided the same answers.[6]

Dershowitz Needs a Do-Over

Fuhrman's contention that "them" referred to the glove and the hat is by no means fantastic. But just suppose that Fuhrman had made a verbal slip. What would this show?

If all slips of the tongue are proof of some underlying fact, then Alan Dershowitz let the cat out of the bag as to who owned the gloves in evidence. Speaking before the judge the day after Simpson tried on the murderer's gloves in front of the jury, Dershowitz said:

> If the prosecution had a second opportunity, if they could do what we when were [sic] kids we called a do-over, obviously they would try this case rather differently. I doubt that we would see O.J. Simpson being asked to try on his gloves. I doubt that we would see Dennis Fung being called as a witness.[7]

Dershowitz refers here to "*his* gloves". So Dershowitz agrees that the murder gloves are indeed Simpson's! Marcia Clark glee-fully offered to stipulate for the record that the gloves did belong to Simpson. Dershowitz came back (perhaps wishing he himself could have a do-over and expunge his earlier remarks from the record) and humbled himself:

> May I formally correct the record, when I referred to "his gloves," obviously I was talking about the prosecution's theory that they are his gloves. The evidence yesterday proved dramatically that they are not his gloves.[8]

Scheck Slips Up, His Hood Fuming

Barry Scheck, too, showed how easy it is to make a mistake with terminology, even when his whole point was to differentiate between two particular things and show that the prosecution experts didn't know how to make this important distinction. He asked Dr. John Gerdes a long series of questions about two kinds of hoods used by scientists. A hood controls the air flow around a scientist and the samples. Different kinds of hoods channel the air differently. His line of questioning ended like this:

Q   Are laminar flow hoods used in forensic labs?
A   Yes.
Q   This—knowing that you have a laminar flow hood, as opposed to a chemical hood, is this a fundamental piece of information in terms of DNA laboratory practices? ... *Is it a fundamental fact, be it in terms of DNA laboratory procedures, to know if a hood is a laminar flow hood as opposed to a chemical hood?...*
Q   Are they [LAPD Scientific Investigation Division witnesses] correct in their statement that it is a laminar flow hood?
A   No. ...
Mr. Scheck: We also have a printout with the laminar flow hood that I would mark 1303-a.
The Court: Chemical hood. You see, it is an easy mistake.[9] [Emphasis added.]

It is true that Fuhrman testified at the preliminary hearing under oath, and Simpson's attorneys are not testifying at all. But Dershowitz and Scheck make their living presenting subtle points in front of judges and juries, where the issue of a single word can matter. Dershowitz is also no stranger to the camera and microphone, appearing frequently on national and even international television, walking the tightrope in terms of what he can and cannot say about his ongoing cases. In spite of this, both these Simpson attorneys misspoke. It's not surprising—we all do it.

The problem for the defense, if they want to suggest that Fuhrman's use of the word "them" is a slip revealing that he actually saw two gloves, is that so many people claim to have witnessed precisely one glove. Some fourteen officers were at the Bundy murder scene before Fuhrman and not one of them saw two gloves. Every officer who testified on this issue swore under oath that there was only one glove. The defense maintained in closing argument that the conspiracy against Simpson could have proceeded with only Fuhrman and Vannatter taking an active role while other cops merely remained silent. If this were true, we would expect the other police officers to say they didn't observe the hat-and-glove evidence at all or to say that they couldn't tell how many gloves were there. By testifying to a single glove at Bundy, if we accept the defense theory, they are all committing perjury in a double-murder case. This goes far beyond simply keeping quiet.

So Furhman's original claim, that the word "them" referred to the hat and the single glove makes sense when examined in light of the corroborating evidence and the widely observed fact that it is easy to misspeak a word.

Gate Stain DNA Content

The DNA content of the stains collected from the Bundy back gate was much higher than the DNA content of the blood drops leading away from the scene. Two of the gate stains had fifteen times as much DNA in them as the first Bundy blood drop. The defense argued that this supported their claim that the back gate stains were planted with high-quality blood stolen from Simpson's reference vial, because if the blood had been on the gate since the time of the murders it would be as degraded as the Bundy blood trail stains. But California Department of Justice scientist Gary Sims told prosecutor Rockne Harmon that the difference could probably be attributed to the collection and drying process:

> No, again, I don't think it is the amounts of DNA that are significant. I think the significance is probably in the collection, the drying process.[10]

It should also be noted that not all the samples degraded exactly the same way. Both Item 6 (one of the blood drops at Rockingham) and Item 48 (one of the blood drops at Bundy) although collected on the same day, degraded to different degrees, according to Sims, with Item 48 having significantly less DNA than Item 6.[11]

Sims told Harmon that he saw no evidence of bacterial degradation in the back gate stains. Sims explained that the absence of bacteria on the sample explains why the DNA content was so high:

> A   Well, the significance that I see in this is that there's no evidence of the kind of massive bacterial contamination of these samples that was seen in some of the other Bundy samples. So in other words, I don't see the evidence of that. So it's not surprising to me that we

recovered a good amount of DNA out of these samples to work with.

Q   And if 115, 116 and 117 were in fact there on June 13th and there was no bacterial-induced degradation, would you expect to see what you saw when you analyzed those samples?

A   Yes. That's a reasonable expectation.[12]

Serological Tests Show Age of the Stains

Sims then discussed some of the serological tests conducted on the back gate stains by LAPD serologist Greg Matheson. One serology test, called PGM analysis, tests for genetic variations of a certain enzyme in the blood. Blood at room temperature, prepared by a laboratory worker, would show the presence of the PGM marker for a month or more, according to Sims.[13] Yet the back gate stains, when tested, did not show the presence of the PGM marker. Sims explained what could have caused this:

A   Well, with time, any stain would—and not—unpreserved, in other words, left in the environment, the ambient environment, it will get to the point where it's no longer typeable.

Q   What about sunlight?

A   Yes. Sunlight could have an effect on something like that.

Q   Well, what kind of effect?

A   Well, again, it would no longer be—be typeable.[14]

Thus, the PGM test corroborates the prosecution claim that the blood *was* out on the back gate since June 12th, 1994. Other serological tests showed the same thing.[15] Sims then testified that the tests he conducted as well as the tests Matheson conducted showed results consistent with blood having been on the gate for two or three weeks:

Q   Is there anything about your observations, the testing of those three stains that your lab did as well as your review of Mr. Matheson's test results, which is inconsistent with those stains being on the gate for the same period of time?

A   I found nothing inconsistent.

Q   And same question, but let's make that same period of time begin June 13th.

Mr. Scheck: Objection to that.

The Court: Foundation.

Q   Mr. Sims, is there anything in your—that you've seen in your review of Mr. Matheson's test results on June—on 115, 116 and 117 combined with the actual testing and review of those three stains yourself which is inconsistent with those stains being on that gate for a period of two to three weeks?

Mr. Scheck: Objection.

The Court: Overruled.

The Witness: I found nothing inconsistent with that.[16]

Thus, the prosecution established that the back gate stains did degrade, *exactly as experts would expect if these stains were made at the time of the murders*, even though the DNA did not undergo bacterial degradation. Blood proteins degrade quickly, while DNA in blood remains typeable for three weeks, even when left outside and exposed to sunlight.[17]

The Unusual Journey of Simpson's Blood Sample

The defense established that Detective Vannatter did not immediately book into evidence the vial containing the blood which Simpson volunteered at Parker Center. Instead, Vannatter took the vial to Rockingham a few hours later and gave it to the criminalists. The defense argued that this was indicative of wrongdoing and tended to establish a conspiracy against Simpson.

But this explanation doesn't accord with the facts. By the time the blood was given, Simpson had already told Vannatter that he had been bleeding at his Rockingham home and in his Bronco the night before. So Vannatter had no need to plant *Simpson's* blood at Rockingham or in the Bronco. The defense theory also explicitly claimed that planting on the Rockingham bedroom socks and the Bundy back gate happened days or even weeks after the murders. So Vannatter, by the defense's own theory, did not use those few hours with the vial to plant any blood.

Failing to Act Out a Conspiracy

So what is the significance of his keeping the blood for that time? If he was going to abscond with blood to use at a much later date it hardly requires hours. Only a few minutes—which no one would have noticed—would have been enough.

If Vannatter planned a diabolical scheme to frame Simpson, why would he maintain custody of the blood for so much longer than he needed it? Even Dennis Fung, so often at a loss for explanations for what was done on June 13th, was able to explain the unusual route that the blood vial took. Fung testified that he had never known the police to obtain a blood sample from a possible suspect so very early in the investigation. Usually by the time such a blood sample has been taken, the criminalists have already booked the crime scene evidence and the detective could be confident that normal booking channels would ensure that the booking number assigned would accord with the other evidence in the case in question.

No Sneakiness with the Sneakers

The defense argued that the unusual, improper treatment of the blood signaled conspiracy. But the blood wasn't the only evidence treated this way. Simpson's lawyers also established that Vannatter's partner, Detective Lange, took Simpson's Reeboks home overnight. This, too, was a violation of procedure. But where's the conspiracy? What is Lange supposed to have done with these sneakers overnight? Those shoes were never shown to have been used for illicit purposes, nor was any specific malfeasance even suggested.

In closing argument, Christopher Darden pointed out to the jury how the defense had made a big issue out of Lange taking the shoes home, but at no time could they ever make even the slightest argument about the relevance of this action:

> And let me tell you, they made a big deal out of those white Reebok tennis shoes. They were all over Detective Lange about taking those shoes home. Remember? Remember that? They were all over him. They were trying to make him look like a fool for taking those white Reebok shoes home.
>
> Did you hear in this trial at any time that there was any forensic evidence, that there was any forensic value to those shoes? Did you hear anything about hair and blood and fiber or anything having to do with those white Reebok tennis shoes? They sent Detective Lange off on a wild goose chase and when the goose got to the witness stand they tried to roast him.[18]

Again we have a simple and complete explanation for these two anomalies: the detectives violated usual procedures simply because it was more convenient. The defense theory of planting blood from the Vannatter vial must be considerably more convoluted. It needs to explain why Vannatter would keep it for over two hours when he could steal blood in just minutes, why he didn't plant blood on the back gate immediately, why there is a separate, nonconspiracy explanation for Lange taking the Reeboks home before booking them, and why this explanation for

Lange doesn't apply to Vannatter. Never were there any such explanations attempted by the defense.

When Batterer Turns Murderer

One of the curious red herrings spawned by the defense was not placed before the jury, but was for public consumption. In March, Alan Dershowitz pointed out on national television that only about one-tenth of one percent of batterers murder their wives. This statistic was meant to suggest that the prosecution evidence of O.J.'s abuse of Nicole was not particularly probative in a murder case. Statistician Jack Good, of Virginia Tech, examined Dershowitz's claim and concluded:

> His statement, though presumably true, is highly misleading for the woman in the street. A probability of greater relevance for legal purposes would be based on the knowledge that the woman was both battered by her husband and also murdered by somebody.[19]

Professor Good computed this more appropriate statistic and found that the probability that a woman battered by her husband *and then found murdered* was killed by her husband exceeds fifty percent.[20]

No Sign of the Real Killer

The defense argued that tests done on the blood under Nicole's fingernails provided evidence of a killer who was not O.J. Simpson. Nicole's fingernail scrapings were tested using both conventional serology and PCR tests. The PCR result matched Nicole but the serological marker EAP did not. Nor did it match Simpson. The defense said that the EAP test revealed the blood of the real killer. Both Nicole and Simpson have EAP type BA. The blood under her fingernails had an EAP type B.

Since Nicole's hands were resting in a pool of her own blood when her body was found, it seems incontrovertible that at least some of the blood under her fingernails was her own. The prosecution introduced evidence that the EAP marker can degrade and when a type which is BA degrades, the A degrades first, leaving only the B. This claim is supported by the fact that PCR testing is much more sensitive than EAP testing. If there were two types of blood under Nicole's nails—her own and the killer's—then the PCR test would have identified them both. But the PCR tests only revealed Nicole's own blood.

Further evidence that the EAP test was measuring Nicole's

own degraded blood comes from another crime scene sample. Blood on the back gate was identified as O.J. Simpson's. The defense conceded this, arguing that it was planted by police. But this back gate blood, similarly, had an EAP result of B, even though Simpson like Nicole is a type BA. Since there was no dispute that the back gate blood was Simpson's, then this is further evidence that degradation can explain EAP readings which on first blush seem inconsistent.

The Adventure of the Misplaced Staple Holes

One example of just how absurd some of the defense red herrings were concerns Barry Scheck's misadventure with staple holes. At the very end of his cross examination of Dennis Fung, Scheck produced page 4 of a crime scene checklist. He accused Fung of destroying the original for nefarious reasons:

Q   5:20 is the time that you wrote on the gray envelope you received it from Detective Vannatter?
A   Yes, it is.
Q   If there were something filled in there that said 5:15 as to the time leaving scene, that would be inconsistent with what you wrote on the gray envelope you received from Detective Vannatter?
Mr. Goldberg: Argumentative, your honor.
The Court: Overruled.
The Witness: If there was that time there, yes, it would.
Q   And that is why you destroyed the original page 4, Mr. Fung?
A   That is not true.[21]

Fung then examined the pages of the crime scene checklist and Scheck proceeded with his questioning:

Q   One of those pages doesn't have staple holes in it, Mr. Fung?
A   That's correct.
Q   That is page 4, isn't it?
A   Yes, it is. ...
Q   That is because you got rid of the original page 4; isn't that true, Mr. Fung?
A   That is not true.
Q   That is because it had the wrong time on it; isn't that true?
A   If it had wrong time—no, that is not true.[22]

By the time re-direct examination was conducted, the true original of page 4 was located. Fung had examined his own notebook, usually containing only photocopies, and found the original page 4. Goldberg had the real page 4 marked as an exhibit and then proceeded to have criminalist Fung, an expert in analyzing tool marks, look for the staple holes and compare them to the other originals used by Scheck during his cross-examination: "I can form a preliminary conclusion. ... They appear to have—this appears to be the document that was missing from this set of originals."[23]

What followed was a brouhaha extending over two days. First, at sidebar, prosecutor Goldberg told the judge that if Scheck looked bad before the jury it was his own fault:

> Well, this is what I think counsel refers to as an attempt to achieve a Perry Mason moment where he wants to spring something on the witness that they didn't disclose to us which he is entitled to do that in this instance. ... They have been hoisted [sic] on their own pitard [sic] and they tried to do something for dramatic effect, it seemed to work for a few moments, but as a result of holding back they have produced a situation on their own. ... They have made representations and predicating it on a line of cross-examination to the jury that isn't true. That is not my fault.[24]

Judge Ito, after examining the issue, made two findings: first, that the failure to turn over the original page 4 before trial was inadvertent; and second, the failure to immediately inform Scheck when the true original was located was a violation of the Court's order to provide this information to the defense.

But Ito also described for the record what both the original and photocopied documents looked like:

> And in examining the two items, both the—what was originally—let's make sure I have the precise terminology here—the original page 4 that was disclosed as and purported to be an original and then the late discovered original—in examining the two forms, the court finds that they are identical except for a poor Xeroxing of one of them, that there is no information contained, they're essentially blank forms ...[25]

Thus, Scheck's suggestion that Fung destroyed the original page 4 because it contained incriminating information makes no sense. That page 4 was never a page which had information about Simpson's blood vial is clear. It never had any information on it at all. It was always irrelevant.

What could Scheck's theory of a destroyed original document possibly mean? If the original had contained incriminating timing information, wouldn't Scheck's illicit replacement theory require that a new time be placed on page 4? If the defense theory is that after the fact Fung lied and put an inaccurate time on a previous sheet, why would Fung replace page 4 at all instead of just throwing it away and saying there never was a page 4?

CHAPTER 3

Dogs that Didn't Bark: What the Defense Didn't Say

"Is there any other point to which you would wish to draw my attention?"
"To the curious incident of the dog in the night-time."
"The dog did nothing in the night-time."
"That was the curious incident," remarked Sherlock Holmes.

—Arthur Conan Doyle, "Silver Blaze",
The Memoirs of Sherlock Holmes

The case for the defense centered around a conspiracy against O.J. Simpson orchestrated by the police. Some officers, like Vannatter and Fuhrman, were accused of actively participating in evidence planting and tampering. Others, both officers and members of the LAPD Scientific Investigation Division, were accused of a more passive role. Some of these passive participants knew that something was wrong, Simpson's lawyers argued, but refused to tell anyone about it, even when testifying under oath. The defense dubbed this latter aspect of their theory the "conspiracy of silence".

There does seem to have been a concerted effort to avoid many specific issues in the case. But it was not the investigators who were mute. The real conspiracy of silence seems to have been perpetrated by Simpson's attorneys, who again and again failed to challenge or expose prosecution witnesses when they had a chance to do so.

Additionally, defense attorneys regularly made out-of-court statements that not only was O.J. Simpson an innocent man, wrongfully accused, but that they expected to establish him as innocent in the minds of the public. Simpson's attorneys had no legal duty or obligation to prove Simpson innocent. But in light of these claims, one would have expected the defense to do many elementary things—such as produce the knapsack used by Simpson the night of the murders. After all, the defense put on an elaborate case of their own, calling nearly five dozen witnesses.

Simpson's June 12th Luggage

It was the defense who arranged to have the luggage Simpson used on the night of June 12th, 1994, collected and introduced into evidence. But the defense was unable to produce the crucial knapsack which Simpson insisted on fetching and carrying himself. Not only was it not produced, but the trial record suggests that the defense tried to introduce an imitation evidence knapsack in place of the real thing. On March 29th, 1995, in open court outside the presence of the jury, Christopher Darden told the judge:

> We have no objection to the defense presenting to the witness the golf club bag, the Louis Vitton [sic] bag or the duffel bag enroute [sic] from the grand jury; however, the other two bags, the black garment bag and the small brown leather bag with the blue trim, we do have objections to bringing those to the witness.
>
> And no witness has described either one of those two bags during their testimony. And as the Court noted in chambers, the smaller bag appears to be brand new and it has the keys still attached to it, as well as the tag.[1]

Johnnie Cochran tried to explain this knapsack, which the *judge* had observed to be brand-new, including keys and tags attached:

> With regards to the other bag and the newness of the bag, Mr. Simpson has not been able to go back out and pick out which bag or whatever. He has been in custody.
>
> With regard, however, you will notice even the golf clubs still have the labels. That is of no moment. And the golf clubs have obviously been used, so the fact that it looks new or has some keys on it I think

is not of any moment.

The question is can this witness describe these? Because after all, we were not out there and we can't put our judgment in this. We have to ask the witness who was there.[2]

Pretty feeble excuses. Does the defense expect anyone to believe they haven't got the resources to locate the correct knapsack if it is still in Simpson's or Kardashian's possession? The cost of producing Polaroid photographs of every piece of luggage in either Simpson's home or Kardashian's is negligible compared to the expense incurred by the defense for numerous other matters. Simpson could identify the correct bag from the county jail based on such photos. But why would even that sort of effort be required? Is anyone really expected to believe that Simpson doesn't know where the bag is?

Production of this bag would be an important rebuttal to the prosecution contention that it contained the murder weapon and yet the defense flailed around forever unable to produce the bag.

Christopher Darden tried to get the defense to take a position on the knapsack: were they contending it was used by Simpson the night of June 12th or not? Cochran refused to answer the question:

Mr. Darden: We have heard a lot this morning about good faith and I would ask the court to inquire of the defense. Is it their contention that that small leather bag, the one with the blue tag, is the bag Mr. Simpson carried?... If not, they are acting in bad faith. Why introduce it to the witness? This is supposed to be a search for the truth and we shouldn't be trying to trick witnesses to get to them [to] say something that might affect their credibility.
Mr. Cochran: Nobody is trying—
Mr. Darden: That seems to be what they are trying to do.
Mr. Cochran: Nobody is trying to trick anybody. With all their search warrant powers and all the things they did, they never even tried to find these bags, just talk about it and throw all these theories up. Let's not try and talk about tricking anybody. *We are the ones, with the court's indulgence and help, who brought these bags in here.*[3] [Emphasis added.]

While Cochran attacked the prosecution because they did not search for Simpson's luggage, his claim that it was the defense who located the bags makes the absence of the knapsack all the more damning. The prosecution, it could be argued, had an incentive not to find the bag. But the defense had not only the incentive to find it, but confidential access to the man who carried it that night. And still the defense was unable to produce this crucial piece of evidence.

Judge Ito refused to let the defense introduce the brand-new bag into evidence. Ito's ruling addressed specifically Cochran's desire to have the witness identify the bag—Allan Park could *not* identify it:

> I'm going to sustain the 352 objection for this reason: the offer of proof was this could possibly be and the statement by Mr. Park with counsel at side bar "that does not look familiar," but he couldn't tell, you have—it is too speculative at this point and the danger of misleading the jury is apparent.[4]

By closing argument, the defense argued that the missing bag was of no moment and simply contained golf balls:

> If you look at everything in a cynical fashion you heard this morning, aha, there was a knapsack over or nap bag or some little bag they were talking about over on the driveway.
>
> Well, if you are golfer, isn't it reasonable to assume there is golf balls in there? And if you put that in your golf bag, what is the big deal? Because they have got to try to theorize and try to explain everything, which they can't explain.
>
> They weren't there, they rushed to judgment and it leads to this kind of wild speculation. You have to do that when you don't have a case. That is all you have seen them do time after time after time.[5]

Cochran accused the prosecution of speculating about the bag, yet immediately before this accusation he himself speculated that the missing knapsack contained golf balls and further speculated that the knapsack was put in the golf bag. There was never a scrap of evidence to suggest this. Cochran used a deflecting tactic, designed to suggest that the bag is of no particular importance. But the defense brought the golf bag to court and it did *not* contain the knapsack, clearly suggesting that Cochran's speculations are unfounded.

Cochran mentioned the bag again, later in his closing argument, "Then, of course, you remember we talked about the knapsack bag, which we think logically had golf balls in it, was inside the golf bag."[6]

But now the defense has really done too much. It is certainly reasonable to suggest that a golfer traveling to a golf tournament will take golf balls with him and perhaps even put a bag of golf balls in the case along with his clubs—although this was never proven during the trial and amounts to speculation, which Cochran professed to hate. But if such a golfer returns home without having played golf, and has no time to play after he gets home because he has to attend the funeral of his young children's mother, and concern himself with the fact that the police suspect him of murder, *why isn't the knapsack with golf balls still in the golf bag?* Why did the defense produce all the luggage except this one piece which they claim is so innocuous and which based on their own theory should still be in the bag containing the golf clubs? Cochran accused the prosecution of being unable to explain things, but he could never explain the absence of that supposedly innocent bag.

Related to the missing knapsack are the dark clothes which both Allan Park and Kato Kaelin testified were worn by Simpson that night. (It was only after the trial that Simpson admitted that it *was* he whom Park had seen entering the Rockingham house just before he finally answered Park's repeated buzzes. Simpson stated this in a phone call to the *Larry King Live* show.) The prosecution maintained that Simpson disposed of the clothes because they were stained with incriminating blood of the victims and could be linked to the fiber evidence left at the murder scene. A photograph of Simpson dressed partially in dark blue-black clothing was even introduced by the defense: it depicted Simpson and his daughter Sydney at the recital which took place in the early evening hours of June 12th. Why didn't the defense produce this clothing and authenticate it by comparing it to what Simpson was wearing in that photo? This would have been powerful evidence in opposition to the prosecution theory, and yet the defense was conspicuously silent about what happened to that clothing.

Playing Around with Gloves

The defense engaged bloodstain expert Herbert MacDonell to work on several blood-related aspects of the case. MacDonell refused to specify exactly how much he would charge O.J. Simpson for his work on the case. He testified that normally, if he were out of town overnight for a client, his fee would be $3,000, but that he would not be charging the defense that much in this case. Even at, say, half his normal fee, MacDonell costs hundreds of dollars an hour.

The defense employed MacDonell, among other things, to conduct a glove-shrinking experiment. MacDonell concluded that new Aris Leather Lights coated with blood will not shrink to any appreciable degree. But this experiment failed to address the actual circumstances of the case, since it was established that the gloves in evidence were well-worn and not new. Additionally, glove expert Richard Rubin explained that the materials used in leather gloves to keep them elastic and stretchable wear away with repeated exposure to moisture. (I discuss the gloves in chapter 5.)

A far less expensive and far more relevant attack on the prosecution glove evidence would have been to produce the gloves Simpson was seen wearing in the numerous photographs introduced by the prosecution in rebuttal. This simple and inexpensive approach was never attempted by the defense.

The defense never had an obligation to produce these gloves or the knapsack and clothes discussed earlier. But their failure to produce them is strange if their client is innocent. After all, by engaging MacDonell to conduct the glove-shrinking experiment they were actively choosing to dispute the prosecution glove evidence when they could have simply argued that the prosecution hadn't proved its own case.

Moreover, when the defense had actual physical evidence to rebut the prosecution claims, they were very interested in producing it. The most dramatic example is the so-called 'mystery envelope' first made public during the preliminary hearing. An important part of the prosecution's case during the preliminary hearing was testimony from Ross Cutlery witnesses. Ross Cutlery is a store which sold Simpson a knife about a month before the murders, a knife the prosecution originally contended might have been the murder weapon. After the prosecution had learned that the mystery envelope contained a knife like that described by the Ross Cutlery witnesses (and which it is rumored was forensically tested and determined to be entirely clean), they completely abandoned this line of attack against Simpson, which had at first seemed so damning. The defense could have similarly scotched the knapsack attack, the dark clothes attack, and the football game gloves attack by merely producing these items the same way they produced the Ross Cutlery knife.

The Hair at the Crime Scene

The defense waged a double-attack on the hair found at the crime scene which was identified as consistent with Simpson's. First, they argued that it could have been introduced into the crime scene by the blanket taken from Nicole's condo (although they never established that any of Simpson's hair was in fact anywhere inside Nicole's condo). Second, they claimed it wasn't Simpson's hair, since there was no dandruff in the hat but there was dandruff in the exemplars taken from Simpson. But the defense had at their disposal an expert in hair analysis, who did not offer any testimony challenging the prosecution's evidence that the hair was consistent with Simpson's. On cross-examination, criminalist Dr. Henry Lee told the jury how powerful hair evidence could be:

Q ... with respect to trace analysis, would it be your position that in some cases regarding hair comparisons that identifications can be made with a high degree of certainty and can often establish partial individuality of a specimen with confidence?
A Yes, sir.[7]

Conspiracy Evidence

By the time of closing arguments, the defense was fulminating in full force regarding the supposed police conspiracy against their client. But their willingness to pursue this conspiracy theory with witnesses on the stand was lukewarm at best. Many aspects of the conspiracy theory were never once brought up in the course of testimony, only to magically appear in closing arguments unsupported by any evidence.

The Bronco Shoe Impression

One defense claim in closing argument, completely unsupported by any evidence, was the assertion that the bloody shoe impression in the Bronco was made by Detective Fuhrman. Not only was no evidence put forward to support this claim, the defense conspicuously failed to challenge FBI shoe impression expert William Bodziak in two of his central claims for the prosecution: first, that the Bronco carpet impression had characteristics of the Bruno Magli shoe sole which left the bloody footprints at Bundy; and second, that Mark Fuhrman's shoes left impressions completely unlike that of the Bruno Magli shoe. Neither of these important aspects of Bodziak's testimony were touched upon by F. Lee Bailey in his cross-examination. He failed to ask a single question regarding the elimination of Detective Fuhrman as having left any shoe impressions even remotely resembling a Bruno Magli shoe and Bailey's only question concerning the carpet impression identification was the following:

Q With respect to your examination of the photographs of the Bronco which you enhanced in two ways I believe, but the second time you photographed in daylight inchoata [sic]?

A The carpeting you're referring to?

Q My understanding is, there was insufficient detail present to call it one way or the other as to those marks, whether they're a footprint or not, in the Bronco?

A I couldn't associate them with the sole to sole, yes.[8]

Why didn't the defense challenge Bodziak's claim that the "Silga design is totally different than any of the designs of these officer's shoes",[9] including Mark Fuhrman's? One possibility is that the defense did not believe that Fuhrman turned in the shoes he was wearing the night of the murders for comparison by Bodziak. But the defense never had to trust Fuhrman. Early on in the trial, a photograph of Fuhrman at Bundy was introduced into evidence, a photo which clearly showed his shoes. Johnnie Cochran knew about this photograph because he cross-examined Officer Riske about it not once but twice. His second reference to this photograph was on February 14th:

Q Yeah. With regard to that area [where the bodies were found], while you were there, now you saw in one of the photographs that Detective Fuhrman, you saw his shoes and footprint in there when he was pointing at something under some of the foliage. You recall that, right, that one picture?

The Court: I think that—I don't think there was any testimony that Detective Fuhrman's footprints were at the scene.

Mr. Cochran: Let me rephrase it, your honor.

Q You saw a photograph, did you not, of a detective or some individual in a shirt and some pants pointing down at—toward the foliage. Do you recall that?

A That's true.

Q Do you know who that person was?

A Detective Fuhrman.

Q And did you see that person's shoe also?

A Yes, I did.

Q   And the shoe was uncovered? It had no booties or anything on that shoe, did it?

A   That's correct.[10]

So the defense had a photograph of Fuhrman's shoes right there at Bundy which they could have used to challenge Bodziak's elimination of Fuhrman. But they still failed to do so. Unfortunately for the defense, this evidence photo also shows Fuhrman very close to much of the blood of Nicole and Judge Ito makes it clear for the record that Fuhrman did not step in that blood. If he avoided stepping in the blood then, when he was so close, just when did he step in that blood which later the defense claims was deposited in the Bronco, but nowhere else?

Not only did the defense fail to challenge Bodziak's crucial testimony, but when they called their own shoe impression expert, again there was silence concerning the bloody Bronco carpet. Conspicuously absent from any of Dr. Henry Lee's footwear impression testimony, which included a failed attempt to show that there were shoe impressions of more than one killer at Bundy, was any mention of the Bronco.

The defense also failed to elicit the simple information of what size shoe Fuhrman wears, either from Fuhrman himself or from Bodziak. In closing argument, Cochran used the standard trick of asking the jury a question and hoping they would assume an answer beneficial to the defense. "Are his shoes size 12?" Cochran wondered.[11]

The defense remained mute on the issue of that bloody imprint in the Bronco until the time of closing argument, when Fuhrman's racism alone apparently explained how he *might* wear size 12 shoes and how he *might* have made a bloody impression with S-like squiggles when his shoes did not have S-patterns on the soles.

Nicole and Ron's Reference Blood

The defense conspiracy theory required that the police have some of both Ron's and Nicole's blood to plant. Ron's blood was purportedly planted in the Bronco—a second time even after Fuhrman supposedly rubbed the glove there, and Nicole's blood was planted on the socks. But when Shapiro cross-examined Detective Vannatter he never asked a single question about how Vannatter had treated this blood after he received it at the Medical Examiner's office. Far more damning than O.J.'s blood found in his own home, was the blood of the victims found in Simpson's Bronco and on his socks. Yet how this highly incriminating blood found its way into the Bronco or onto the socks, or even just to the LAPD, was never the subject of cross-examination.

EDTA

The prosecution was anxious to try to directly rebut the defense claim of planted evidence. One means of doing this was to test the blood on the socks and the Bundy back gate for EDTA. But when the prosecution first suggested such a test, the defense actively argued *against* it. On February 14th Rockne Harmon told Judge Ito:

> I made a proposal about a week and a half ago that we do this jointly, your honor, the whole EDTA thing so they can have their people watching it, kind of looking at it, checking it out and actually watching the whole EDTA test. That was one possibility, if they wanted to find out if there's really EDTA in there. I mean it would be a tremendous accomplishment for them to find EDTA in this blood on the sock. And they keep hedging about it or avoiding it like a dirty diaper pail here.[12]

For the defense, Robert Blasier answered Harmon by—quite falsely—claiming that EDTA testing wasn't necessary because most blood isn't put into such vials.[13]

Harmon pointed out that Blasier was incorrect as a matter of fact, that the LAPD routinely did use EDTA-treated containers. But even in theory Blasier's claim makes little sense. Generally referred to during the course of the trial as a preservative, in blood EDTA actually serves as an anti-coagulant. It is a chemical which keeps blood from clotting. Without EDTA or another anti-coagulant, the sample blood would clot and become much harder to work with in a laboratory. If Blasier had been correct and Vannatter had smeared non-EDTA blood on the back gate, the planting of gloppy, clotted blood would have been evident even to the hapless criminalists of the LAPD, not to mention the defense experts who visited the Bundy scene before the blood on the gate was collected.[14]

The defense posturing on the EDTA issue becomes clear when you remember that the entire defense theory of planting on the socks requires a *wet* transfer. Non-EDTA blood—clotted blood which is no longer liquid—is completely incompatible with such a theory. So why did the defense continue in their efforts to thwart

EDTA testing, rather than embracing the idea for themselves? One of Barry Scheck's first arguments was a standard complaint generally applied to forensic DNA testing:

Mr. Scheck: ... I know that the court may have looked at something about EDTA testing, but I'm not fully satisfied I understand exactly what is involved, whether—

The Court: Nor am I. But there are some tests out there that are relatively simple, at least as far as the scientific community is concerned, and gas chromatography is a relatively well-accepted chemical testing process.

Mr. Scheck: We are talking about forensic testing. That technology, something that's done on food additives, is extremely different.

The Court: Don't you think if it is good enough for the FDA, it's good enough for us?

Mr. Scheck: These are different kinds of samples.[15]

Of course when it suited him, Mr. Scheck was happy to let the jury know that the FDA had approved one of the kits which defense witness Dr. Gerdes uses in his lab, even though the relevance of Dr. Gerdes's testimony was to "different kinds of samples".[16]

The following day, Scheck had further complaints about EDTA testing:

Last night I looked at the submissions that Mr. Harmon made to the court about EDTA testing, which had to do with discovering EDTA in time release cold capsules, in mousse, food substances where you already know it is there. That is an entirely different proposition than testing a sample when you don't know whether or not it should be there. And—and this is really the most critical point I think, is that Mr. Harmon was indicating yesterday that they have no idea how much sample is necessary to perform this test, even assuming that it could get past Kelly-Frye and it's reliable on a forensic sample.[17]

The defense had made the blood missing from Simpson's reference vial an important element of their opening statement. Yet when the prosecution accepted the challenge to actually find out if the blood from that vial was on the evidence, the defense balked and prevaricated. Nor did they ever undertake themselves the task of analyzing the blood they argued was planted. They relied instead on an expert who simply challenged the solid findings of FBI Special Agent Roger Martz. Martz's testing concluded that the blood on the gate and the socks did not contain

EDTA-preserved blood and therefore refutes the claim that the blood was planted.

Miscellaneous Omissions

Why did the defense promise to call Simpson's regular arthritis doctor, one who knew about Simpson's long-term physical condition, but called instead a doctor who had never seen Simpson before the murders? With so many people at Simpson's home the evening after the murders, why did they rely on his closest family members—people who could honestly misremember events of that evening in favor of Simpson—to establish that Ron Shipp might have been intoxicated? Why did Cochran tell the jury that Lenore Walker, an expert in battered women's syndrome, had examined Simpson but then not present her testimony to the jury?

CHAPTER 4

The Beast with Five Fingers

[Simpson] seems to have been exceedingly careless with that awful bloody glove, which has since turned into a beast with five fingers, accusing him.

—Arn Lesikar

Shortly after the murders occurred, news of a bloody glove found on Simpson's property became public. It was publicly denied by defense lawyers, including Alan Dershowitz who hadn't even been retained by Simpson at the time. But of course the reports about the glove proved to be true. At the preliminary hearing, Detective Mark Fuhrman described finding this incriminating glove. He was generally viewed as a cool, professional cop who testified to damning evidence in a cool, professional way.

So strong was Fuhrman's testimony and presence on the witness stand during the preliminary hearing that the defense fought quickly to neutralize it. Soon rumblings were heard that the glove had been illicitly placed on Simpson's property by Fuhrman himself. Jeffrey Toobin broke the story in the *New Yorker* in July of 1994[1] and the snowball continues to this day to career down the mountain, gathering size and speed, but no evidence.

The defense theory was that Mark Fuhrman saw two gloves at the Bundy crime scene. He picked one of them up, took it with him to Simpson's Rockingham home, wiped it inside the Bronco (thus explaining some of Ron Goldman's blood found there) and then dropped it behind Kato's room.

The smear-and-then-drop-the-glove theory was repeated frequently by defense attorneys and their supporters. Yet several simple, obvious questions about the theory were unanswered—some strangely unasked—even when the case was over.

The Itsy-Bitsy, Teeny-Weeny Flashlight

How did Fuhrman even notice this second glove at the murder scene which none of the fourteen officers at Bundy before him had observed? It was Officer Riske who had the high-powered flashlight. Fuhrman had a small penlight that F. Lee Bailey variously characterized as "little", "little tiny", "little teeny", "little bitty", and generally "rather inadequate for the task". Bailey even asked Fuhrman once why he didn't make use of one of the "grown-up" flashlights his colleagues had.[2]

Neither F. Lee Bailey nor any of the other defense attorneys could ever glean even the slightest bit of evidence supporting the possibility that there were two gloves at Bundy. For example, all Bailey learned when cross-examining Lt. Frank Spangler was the following:

Q   Okay. Did you direct anyone to see if there was another glove around, since they normally come in pairs?
A   When I was looking at the crime scene I illuminated the area with a flashlight and there was never any other glove there. That was only that one that I could see by an oblique illumination of the crime scene and a horizontal illumination. I only ever saw the one, sir.
Q   Did you look around the body?
A   Yes, I did.
Q   Where?
A   From two perspectives. Actually three, excuse me. From the doorway inside the condominium you could look down and have a limited view. From the south side of the bodies, when we walked through the planted area, and then from the north side of the bodies when we walked up on the outside of the fence. I looked at it three different angles.[3]

Then Lt. Spangler described for Bailey the three perspectives from which he examined the crime scene. Other officers testified under oath that there was only one glove. The defense theory seemed to be not only that Fuhrman was a remarkably strong racist, but that he had unusually strong eyesight too, including the ability to see things numerous other officers couldn't.

The defense theory also assumed that even before Fuhrman

arrived at Simpson's home, when he knew nothing whatever about where Simpson might be, he nonetheless picked up the glove in order to frame Simpson. What was he going to do if the evidence at Bundy exculpated Simpson?

Questions, Questions, Questions

The first part of the Fuhrman-frame theory maintained that he entered the Bronco and used the pilfered glove to plant blood. Why would Fuhrman plant blood in the Bronco at all? According to the defense theory, the Bronco was not parked askew and the tiny stain above the driver's door handle looked as much like dried taco sauce as blood.

There are two different sub-theories about *why* Fuhrman planted the glove. The first suggests that Fuhrman planted the glove because he believed Simpson to be guilty and he was thus just helping things along. (The defense shied away from this sub-theory because the defense was uncomfortable with why Fuhrman would believe this—the defense wanted to stay as far away as possible from Simpson's violence in the past, some of which Fuhrman had observed.) So why should Fuhrman assume that the Bronco, with only teeny-tiny amounts of blood in it, was the vehicle that had transported Simpson from the terribly bloody murder scene? Fuhrman and the cops could easily see the Bentley and Arnelle's Saab through the Rockingham gate. Why would Fuhrman plant blood in a vehicle that might be the wrong one? And what about the garage? At the time of the supposed glove smearing, Fuhrman didn't know if the garage could contain a blood-laden car either.

The second sub-theory, the one the defense clung to, was that Fuhrman had no reason to believe that Simpson did the crime. Fuhrman wanted to frame an innocent man. But again, the cars inside the compound would provide better grist for the planting mill than one sitting outside the gate. Why didn't Fuhrman use the small bloodstain on the outside of the Bronco to convince the other cops that they should jump the fence, and then create *lots* of bloodstains in a vehicle inside the compound? The closer to the house, the more secure the car, the more damning would be the planted evidence. Neither sub-theory can explain why he would choose the *inside of the Bronco* for his bloody Jackson Pollock imitation.

Ignoring the Sure Thing

Fuhrman didn't plant the glove in the Bronco, although that was a sure thing since according to the planting theory he has already broken in. How would he know at that point that he would even get inside the grounds of Simpson's estate? Not only is planting the glove in the Bronco a sure thing, it places the glove in a far more logical place than it was eventually 'planted'. If Fuhrman's plan was to make the Bronco appear to be the murder vehicle, why not place the glove inside this murder vehicle instead of the remote location unrelated to the blood he alleged planted in the Bronco?

Why So Little Blood?

The Rockingham glove was extremely bloody. The planting theory argued that it was still moist. So why when coming from such a terribly bloody murder venue with such a notably bloody glove did Fuhrman plant such minute quantities of blood in the Bronco? Why didn't he really rub it around extensively so as to ensure his deed accomplished its end, that is to make the Bronco unquestionably an extension of a terribly bloody murder scene? Trying to frame someone with almost no blood at all makes no sense.

If Fuhrman broke into the Bronco to leave blood stains, why not leave them on the dashboard which could easily be reached without going into the Bronco itself? Entering the vehicle risks leaving trace evidence that might be connected back to Fuhrman. (No trace evidence *was* linked back to Fuhrman.) A dashboard plant would also be more easily visible to the other cops when he shows them the Bronco, as the dashboard is much closer to a window than the console where the blood was actually found. The blood of Ron Goldman is primarily on the console, including the side of the console which is most distant from the driver's door, quite a reach from outside the Bronco. Why plant there?

The 'Real Thumper' Angle

Instead of planting the glove in the Bronco, the defense theory is that Fuhrman chose to plant it behind Kato's guest-house. Kato told Fuhrman that the night before he heard loud thumps on his wall. Fuhrman went to investigate the possible source of the thumps and found the glove there. But many questions remain unanswered about the glove-and-thump theory.

How could Fuhrman know that the thumps Kato heard

wouldn't be readily attributed to something completely unrelated to the murders? Perhaps neighborhood teenagers were climbing trees and fell down, hitting the air conditioner, making the thumps. Perhaps the Salingers were burglarized that night and the criminal made his escape by climbing the fence at that point. Perhaps a neighbor's dog (Brentwood is flush with dogs) was chasing a small frenzied animal which jumped the fence or dropped from a tree and used the air conditioner to break its fall before it ran further away, all in full sight of the later-famous Rosa Lopez. How could Fuhrman be sure an explanation such as these wouldn't be forthcoming? According to the planting theory, he *knew* that the frightening sounds had nothing to do with O.J. dropping the glove at all—he was just putting the glove there to wrongly establish that O.J. himself was there. What did Fuhrman think actually caused the thumps? If Fuhrman planted the glove there, then he knew there was a true explanation for the thumps which might and almost certainly would exculpate Simpson, so why did he take the chance and plant the glove there of all places?

Since the defense believed he was smart enough to use the glove to smear the Bronco, why didn't Fuhrman smear anything near where he allegedly planted the glove? Fuhrman had just come from a very bloody murder scene and had no way of knowing whether or not very bloody clothes will be found. Failure to smear the air conditioner or Kato's wall is clearly inconsistent with his previous, ingenious use of the glove inside the Bronco. While Henry Lee observed some blood on the air conditioner, neither the cops nor the LAPD criminalists observed it. Whatever blood was there was hardly commensurate with an evidence planter enacting an all-encompassing evil scheme.

After questioning Kato, Fuhrman brought him to the main house. Fuhrman *walked through the house* before allegedly planting the glove. The house had been locked! Leaving the glove in the house would have been far, far more damning than leaving it outside where any defense lawyer could argue the real killer might have deposited it to make O.J. look guilty.

The Guiltiest Place of All

If Fuhrman was concerned that no search warrant would issue, so that planting the glove in the house might be for naught, why not use his already established 'wiping technique' somewhere in the house and *then* plant the glove outside? This would provide in-house evidence if a search warrant is forthcoming but if not, still ensured that the glove would come into evidence when he 'found' it outside. This would provide a devastating link to the murder victims inside a locked house—far more incriminating than a glove found outside the house, where any defense lawyer could argue someone else had planted it. (If Fuhrman planted it, he had to know that a defense attorney would be bound to consider arguing that the police had planted it.)

If the other cops were in on the conspiracy, why didn't they move the glove into the house where it would be so much more damning and wouldn't require any peculiar explanations, which the cops clearly didn't have? (It wasn't until closing argument that any complete explanation for the glove's location was made which was consistent with the blood trail from the Bronco, up the driveway, and into the foyer with no blood trail leading to the glove itself.)

Failing to Use Kato for Information

Why didn't Fuhrman find out whether Kato had already been back there? If Kato had gone all the way back to check things out, he might have testified that there was nothing there at all. While it was dark when Kato made his two abortive attempts at examination, Fuhrman could not have known whether Kato had in fact gone back there with a strong flashlight and made a thorough examination. The testimony clearly shows that Fuhrman made no such attempt to find out if Kato had made a detailed search behind his wall, even though the conversation between Fuhrman and Kaelin skirted the issue. Fuhrman, when questioned by Marcia Clark, testified about Kato Kaelin, "He said he saw a limo in the driveway and then he proceeded towards the area where he was going to investigate, but he didn't describe anything any farther."[4]

Similarly, the questioning of Kato Kaelin by Marcia Clark revealed that Kato never told Fuhrman that he had investigated the thumps:

Q   Okay. Did you tell him [Detective Fuhrman] that you had gone out to that walkway area twice earlier that night to investigate the thumps?
A   No.[5]

Not only didn't Fuhrman know whether or not Simpson had an alibi for the time of the murders, but he didn't even try to find out when he had a chance. Why didn't he ask Kato about a possible Simpson alibi before planting the glove? He questioned Kato outside the presence of the other detectives and could have asked Kato anything he wanted. Since there was circumstantial evidence that Simpson wasn't currently at home (no answer to repeated buzzes and phone calls), Fuhrman must have considered the possibility that not only was Simpson away, but might have been away at the time of the murders. Why didn't he ask Kato the simple question "Do you know when Mr. Simpson left?" Kato testified that he hadn't told Fuhrman when Simpson left before Fuhrman went to investigate the thumps:

Q   Okay. Did you ever tell him what time the defendant left the house?
A   I don't think I did at that time. No.[6]

Fuhrman didn't know whether Simpson had an alibi or if eyewitnesses to the murders might emerge. He didn't know the time of death for the victims. So he had to have known there was a possibility that some development might completely exculpate Simpson. That being the case, why would he plant the glove in a location pointed out to him by a non-police officer—who could not possibly be expected to adhere to the so-called code of silence—and who is a friend of Simpson's to boot? Kato would be able to point to their conversation, Fuhrman's interest in it, Fuhrman's subsequent disappearance, and the finding of the glove. The planting would be transparent. Fuhrman had a large estate on which to plant this incriminating evidence; why select a place which Kato, friend of Simpson, might later say Fuhrman was quite interested in? There are numerous places completely unrelated to Kato and anything Kato said. Fuhrman could have planted the glove in any one of those places without ever having to worry about what Kato might say later. Fuhrman knew that this case would have more than the usual amount of scrutiny, not just from the defense, but from the public as well.

A Grave Disincentive

Perhaps the most compelling unanswered question is *why would Fuhrman risk his own life to plant this evidence?* The California penal code has stiff penalties for planting evidence. In a murder case, the penalty may include death. Did the defense really believe that Fuhrman would risk his own execution just so he *might* contribute to the conviction of O.J. Simpson for murder?

CHAPTER 5

If the Glove Fits ...

Reasons are not like garments, the worse for wearing.
—Robert Devereux, Earl of Essex

Then up he rose, and donn'd his clothes.
—William Shakespeare, *Hamlet*

On June 15th the jury watched (once) and the world watched (over and over and over again via videotape) O.J. Simpson put on the gloves used in the commission of the murders of Nicole Brown Simpson and Ronald Goldman. He appeared to struggle with them and even audibly claimed, "they're too small". The most significant manifestation of the demonstration was Cochran's repeated refrain in his closing argument, "If it doesn't fit, you must acquit."[1]

Can this glove demonstration be reconciled with Simpson's guilt? There are at least four reasons which explain why the gloves didn't fit and there is the notably ignored possibility that the gloves did not fit Simpson but that he used them to murder Nicole and Ron anyway.

The glove demonstration was widely-regarded as a defense victory, but Cochran's cross-examination of the glove expert on the stand at the time of the demonstration provided much material beneficial to the prosecution. As with so much of the more subtle evidence, this was never analyzed by commentators or even reported as significant.

The Gloves Shrank

Both Richard Rubin, former Aris vice president and general

manager, and Brenda Vemich, former men's glove buyer for Bloomingdales, testified that the gloves in evidence were Aris Leather Lights, size extra large. Rubin testified that Simpson's hands were "in some styles, size large, in most styles, extra large".[2] Darden showed Rubin three golfing gloves from the golf bag Simpson took to Chicago the night of the murders. All three gloves were size extra large.

Rubin examined the gloves found at Bundy and Rockingham and he concluded that "at one point in time, those gloves would be actually I think large on Mr. Simpson's hand."[3] The second time Rubin testified (he was sworn in a record four times), he said "the gloves in the original condition would easily go onto the hands [of Simpson]."[4]

Rubin estimated that the gloves had shrunk approximately 15 percent from their original size. He explained that at the time of purchase gloves are in their largest possible condition. Over time—as they get wet then dry, get wet again, then dry—they shrink. Wearing the gloves will stretch them out again, but they won't ever be as large as when they were purchased. Rubin testified:

> Traditionally in the normal use of a dress glove, the glove might be exposed to some snow or rain or a car handle, something like that where it would get wet, and then it would gradually dry and it might lose two, three percent of its size. It wouldn't be a tremendous amount of size, but if you were to drench the gloves and have them dry naturally, that is where you would get the 10 to 15 percent shrinkage.[5]

Both the prosecution and defense seemed to assume that the gloves incurred a single great act of shrinkage. The defense suggested this could have happened at a time long before the murders. In that case, Simpson could not have worn them that night because they were already too small and so he wasn't the murderer. The prosecution seemed to imply that the gloves were full-sized until the blood of Nicole and Ron gushed over them. But these two aren't the only possibilities. If the gloves were purchased in 1990 and worn several times in rainy and snowy weather, the moisture on the gloves would absorb the fat liquor in the leather. It is the loss of the fat liquor which reduces the leather's elasticity so that they shrink. If they contained little or no fat liquor the night of June 12th, 1994, then this might explain the great shrinkage observed by Rubin. This is precisely the situation which defense blood expert Herbert MacDonell did not consider in his experiment. His blood-and-glove-shrinkage experiment used spanking new gloves loaded with fat liquor in the leather.

Even Judge Ito mentioned some of the problems with MacDonell's experiment, as he told Peter Neufeld outside the presence of the jury:

> ... in establishing the materiality of your glove drying experiment, obviously those experiments were conducted upon the new gloves, the Aris Lights, if I'm not mistaken, that the Aris Corporation was kind enough to provide to the Court. The knowledge issue being that obviously for cross-examination purposes I could do this cross-examination in ten questions, one of which would be did you use new gloves, did you take into consideration shrinkage that occurs over a period of time, did you take into consideration the tanning method, the silicone impregnation of leather to prevent moisture problems, that sort of thing, and then show a picture of the defendant wearing gloves in winter. I mean, that is pretty simple, wouldn't you say?[6]

After some argument by Peter Neufeld and Marcia Clark, Ito repeated that factors not taken into account by MacDonell's experiment were clearly relevant issues for cross-examination:

> Counsel, I think that if you bring in evidence regarding this experiment as to how these gloves did not shrink under your experiment, the prosecution is entitled to cross-examine on factors that were not taken into consideration during the course of the defense experiment, such as the age of the gloves, other weather exposure, particular materials that were involved in this—with this particular glove, the nature of the—how the leather was manufactured, what kind of water repellant [sic] treatments were placed on it, whether or not any of these things were taken into consideration. I think that is fair game for cross-examination.[7]

When Marcia Clark cross-examined MacDonell, he admitted, "certainly if there's a treatment that's put on anything to prevent something, as the chemical, whatever it may be, is worn away or leached away for whatever reason, then the purpose it was put in there is going to be most achieved when it was fresh ..."[8]

MacDonell's experiment seemed clearly irrelevant to rebutting the prosecution argument that Simpson committed the murders with a pair of gloves which were three-and-a-half years old, regularly worn in wet weather, and then drenched in blood the night of June 12th.

The defense did not even challenge the fact that the evidence gloves were old. Peter Neufeld told Judge Ito, "We are not disputing, Your Honor, that the gloves in question are older gloves and they are not new gloves. The jury has seen the gloves and they know they are older gloves." [9]

Additionally, Johnnie Cochran inadvertently lent some support to the prosecution claim that the gloves had already been subjected to environmental insults. Cochran himself suggested that the gloves might have been exposed to rain or snow long before the murders, during his questioning of Rubin:

Q ... Assume hypothetically these gloves were purchased in 1989 or in 1990, and let's assume they were worn during the winter, during that time, rain and snow. You can't tell this jury how much those gloves shrunk during that period of time, can you?

A I cannot.

Q You have no way of knowing that, do you?

A I have no way of knowing how much liquid or rain or snow or whatever, you know, elements went onto the product and actually how they were dried.[10]

The Latex Gloves Impeded a Proper Fit

Even before the most replayed part of the trial took place, the prosecution was aware of the potential of latex gloves to interfere with a proper fit. The following discussion took place at sidebar on June 15th, shortly before Simpson tried on the gloves:

Mr. Cochran: Are you going to allow them to have the defendant try these gloves on? [referring to a new pair of Aris Leather Lights]

The Court: I think it would be more appropriate for him to try the other gloves on.

Mr. Cochran: That was exactly my point. So—

The Court: I mean the real gloves that were found.

Ms. Clark: The only problem is, he has to wear latex gloves underneath because they're a bile hazard [sic. Surely Clark said "biohazard"] and they're going to alter the fit.[11]

When the time came, Darden recklessly decided to take the plunge notwithstanding the latex layer that Simpson would have on his hands. The latex gloves greatly increased friction, making it more difficult to get the gloves on. Following the glove demonstration, Rubin testified to this difficulty after trying on his own leather gloves over latex gloves: "I had more difficulty in getting the personal gloves on my hand with the latex glove on my hand than I normally would."[12] Darden suggested that the latex gloves themselves were the wrong size for Simpson (large instead of extra large) further exacerbating the problem. If Simpson's hands weren't properly covered with latex gloves, for example leaving latex webbing between his fingers, this would obviously impair his getting the leather gloves completely on his hands.

Unfortunately for the prosecution, the latex gloves also altered the *perception* of fit. The latex gloves were much longer than the leather gloves, extending significantly past the wrist. This made the leather gloves appear all the more peculiar, since it is natural, but wrong, to assume that the second glove would completely cover the first, even though their designs were different. This perception was important to the defense, even though such an unconscious comparison was inappropriate. With a jury predominantly composed of women, it was surprising that Clark didn't argue in closing that trying on those gloves over latex to assess fit was like trying on a bra over a blouse.

Simpson Manipulated the Demonstration

After viewing the glove demonstration, Richard Rubin testified about Simpson, "his hands should be able to fit into that pair of gloves."[13] Darden suggested that Simpson didn't put the gloves on as a person would normally do. His question to Rubin, "could you tell whether or not he was intentionally holding his thumb in a certain position so that he couldn't put the gloves on?" was ruled by Ito to be argumentative. Others have observed that Simpson arched his hands in such a way as to impede getting the gloves on.

Vincent Bugliosi, in analyzing the glove try-on, pointed out how inappropriate it was to let Simpson himself control the demonstration. The brilliant writer and former prosecutor said that the better course of action would have been to have a third party put the gloves on Simpson. Would June 15th have been reported completely differently if Richard Rubin had put the gloves on Simpson's hands? It seems very likely, since Rubin was convinced that those gloves found at Bundy and at Rockingham should have fit Simpson that day in court.

Forensic scientist Rob Keister has suggested that a cast might have been made of Simpson's hands, via a court order. A mannequin similar to what you see in department stores—with hands identical to Simpson's—could have been brought into courtroom and the gloves placed on it. This would have eliminated the possibility of interference by the defendant who had an obvious motive to make the gloves not fit. The model could have been passed around to the jurors and they could have judged for themselves whether the gloves fit. (The gloves and model would also have been available during deliberations.) The expert who made the cast could have testified regarding the authenticity of the model.[14]

In addition, Simpson exhibited a strange demeanor when he tried on the murder gloves, looking more like the hapless Nordberg character he played in the *Naked Gun* films than the man on trial for double-murder that he was. Some Simpson supporters tried to explain this, saying that because he was innocent, he knew the gloves would not fit, so he approached the demonstration with no fear. But surely an innocent man's greatest fear in a situation like this would be that someone else's gloves would by chance fit him. Could Simpson's demeanor be better explained by the fact that he knew he could manipulate the fit of the gloves?

One commentator on the Internet concluded: "Master illusionist David Copperfield earns a comfortable living by appealing to our perceptions and creating doubts about what we thought to be 'real.' Stop focusing on what O.J. couldn't seemingly do in the courtroom and direct your focus on what he could have done at home."[15]

The Gloves Were Always a Tight Fit

The photos of Simpson wearing both black and brown Aris Leather Lights introduced by the prosecution during rebuttal showed Simpson repeatedly in gloves which were very tight and sometimes even showed the base of his palm exposed. By no stretch of leather or imagination could the gloves in the photos be called a generous fit. More than documenting that O.J. wore two different pairs of Leather Lights after Nicole's purchase of two pairs of Leather Lights, these photos clearly showed that Simpson was in the habit of wearing gloves which are a tight fit as well as a bit short.

Stretching a Point

Relevant to any of these preceding four explanations is the

fact that the gloves in evidence could still be stretched to make them bigger. Surprisingly, the prosecution did not exploit this fact. They concentrated on the possibility that blood at the Bundy murder scene is what caused the gloves to shrink, but missed the importance of the fact that whoever wore those gloves could himself stretch them by wearing them for several minutes and flexing his hands. This important aspect of 'fit' was not incorporated in the glove demonstration, because Simpson took off the gloves—quite easily—as quickly as possible.

Rubin testified that the evidence gloves could be expanded by flexing to about 90 percent of their original size. And important testimony about how glove stretching takes place was brought out not by Darden, but unexpectedly by Cochran when questioning Rubin about Aris Leather Lights in general:

Q   ... if a big person ... puts their hands in some of these gloves, an extra large glove, they would tend to stretch those gloves, don't they?
A   Not initially. They would have to wear them some time before they would actually stretch. They would have to open and close their hand quite a few times. This is what really stretches a glove. When you open and close your hand, your knuckles become quite broad. That is what creates the stretch.[16]

If the prosecution had realized the importance of such a fact, they could have asked the judge to require Simpson to flex his hands several times over a few minutes and then try to pull the gloves on further. This aspect of glove 'stretch' is known to most glove wearers, but is generally part of their unconscious knowledge. Only after the fateful glove demonstration did Darden explore this issue with Richard Rubin:

Q   And with time would you expect those gloves to loosen up, that is, if the defendant wore them for more than the brief moment he wore them here in front of the jury?
A   They wouldn't change in two minutes, but over time, *if someone were to move their hands back and forth, drive a car, do something with the gloves on,* they gradually would get a little looser initially, yes.[17] [Emphasis added.]

The importance of this testimony is that Simpson could have put on the gloves at Rockingham and loosened them as he put things in his Bronco or as he drove to Bundy. The fit of the gloves at the time he put them on is not as important as how they fit several minutes later after he had been moving his hands.

The Fret over Fit

Even the question of fit itself may be entirely off the point. If one concludes in spite of all the arguments that the gloves simply do not fit (as juror Brenda Moran pointedly concluded in her remarks to the media after the verdict), does this really mean one must acquit? One can reasonably conclude that the murderer wore these gloves so as not to leave any fingerprints or other evidence anywhere near the murder scene. Whether they are tight or short is irrelevant. As long as they cover the hands and permit their wearer to wield a weapon, they meet their purpose. Even with unlubricated latex gloves under them, these gloves covered O.J.'s hands and permitted him to grip a marking pen, Christopher Darden's suggested surrogate for a knife. When selecting gloves for the commission of murder, does a man consumed with malice fret over fit? Availability and utility are what matter and no matter how ill-fitting the gloves may appear to be, they would still be seen by a prospective murderer as functional.

The fact that Simpson struggled to put the gloves on in court doesn't exclude him as the murderer, even if the struggle was unfeigned. Perhaps he similarly struggled with these gloves on the night of June 12th, 1994. And similarly got them on his hands. Richard Rubin testified that Simpson could even get size medium gloves on his hands.

If the gloves fit his hands badly on the night of June 12th, this would mean that how, when, and to what extent they shrank is irrelevant, and so too the defense experiment on shrinkage.

Poor Fit Actually Explains Use

If they were a bad fit before the murders maybe that was the very reason Simpson chose them: he wouldn't mind disposing of them afterwards. And a bad fit would help to explain how the left-hand glove was dislodged during the murders—an ill-fitting glove may be more likely lost in a struggle.

This idea that poor fit actually explains the choice of the brown Aris Leather Lights is supported, unexpectedly, by the testimony of William Bodziak, the FBI shoe impression expert. He testified that the specific Bruno Magli shoes which left the bloody impressions at Bundy were imported into the U.S. during 1991 and 1992. Only 299 pairs came into the U.S.

One possibility is that the murderer acquired his pair at the beginning of this period meaning that they were three-and-a-half years old at the time of the murders. (Interestingly, about the same age as the gloves purchased by Nicole.) Another possibility is that the shoes came into the murderer's possession at the end of the distribution period, meaning that they were one-and-a-half years old at the time of the murders. Whenever they were acquired, Bodziak concluded that the shoes worn at Bundy had very little evidence of wear:

A   All of the impressions that I examined from the Bundy scene which you could see the design clearly reflected a shoe that was in a relatively unworn condition. Umm, unworn to the extent that the design had not yet started to change.

Q   So was it either new or relatively new then, in your judgment?

A   It could be anywhere from new to moderate wear to where the shoe design was still pretty much intact and hadn't begun the change.

Q   By "new" I should probably clarify, are you talking about when it was purchased or just the wear, how frequently or often it was worn?

A   Well, when you are talking new, to me that means the shoe is relatively unworn. It could be a shoe that is several years old that just was never worn.[18]

So the man wearing those shoes on the night of June 12th had not worn them extensively before that, and might have had them as long as three-and-a-half years. This could suggest that the owner never really cared for the shoes, making them a perfect choice for murder because he knew he might have to throw them away. The gloves may have similarly been selected for the same reason: they were getting old (the right-hand glove was very worn) and didn't fit very well so the killer didn't mind that he'd have to get rid of them forever after the crime.

It is conceivable that the Bruno Magli shoes might have been on a store shelf for a year-and-a-half and purchased only shortly before the murders. But then one must ask the question: why would anyone commit murder in such an expensive pair of brand new shoes which would have to be immediately thrown away? A rich man, with nothing but expensive shoes in his closet might do this, but does this fit the profile of an 'ordinary' killer?

The Accoutrements of Her Own Murder

The defense also tried to deflect the power of the glove testimony by suggesting that the sales receipt from Bloomingdales, signed by Nicole, was not proof that she had in fact purchased the accoutrements of her own murder. But the Aris Leather Light glove was manufactured for and sold exclusively by Bloomingdales. Both Richard Rubin and Brenda Vemich testified that the Aris Leather Light glove was distinctive: The leather was nearly paper thin, the stitching was brossier—a very refined whip stitch, the glove had a V-shaped vent on the palm side, and the glove was lined in cashmere. They both identified the gloves from Bundy and Rockingham as Aris Leather Lights.

These gloves were quite rare. About 200 pairs in brown and extra large were sold in 1990. Many fewer were sold the following two years and then the glove was changed. Very small numbers of these gloves were also sold in the years between 1982 (when it was introduced) and 1989 (just before Bloomingdale's made its large order from which Nicole's purchase was made).

The defense questioned whether or not the Bloomingdales sales receipt was actually for Aris Leather Lights. This was because the receipt contained the style number 70268 and the style number for Aris Leather Lights was actually 70263. However, the rest of the information on the receipt was undisputed:

- The purchase made was category '55' which means the items bought were gloves.

- The vendor number was 953, which means that the items were manufactured by Aris.

- The total price of the two pairs of gloves was $77. This price reflected a 30 percent discount. A $77 purchase for two pairs of gloves meant that without the discount the two pairs would have sold for $110, or $55 a pair. The only Aris gloves which sold for $55 a pair in December of 1990 were Aris Leather Lights.

Mistaking a 'three' for an 'eight' is an understandable human error. Bloomingdales did not use scanners in 1990. Bloomingdales *never* sold a glove or any other item with the style number 70268. Under cross-examination, Brenda Vemich replied to Johnnie Cochran: "I'm indicating that that [70268] is not a style number that existed at Bloomingdales ever."[19]

Cochran for the Prosecution

Christopher Darden was universally criticized for asking Simpson to try on the evidence gloves. But Cochran himself asked several questions regarding the gloves which turned out to be quite damaging to the defense, yet much of this testimony was ignored because commentators were so fascinated with the glove fashion show.

It was in answer to a question by Cochran, not Darden, that Richard Rubin told the jury just how small the quantity of Aris Leather Lights manufactured actually are: "The quantity that was manufactured in [sic] this glove was minuscule in the scheme of the amount of leather gloves that Aris produced."[20] While Cochran wanted to suggest to the jury that there were lots of brown gloves floating around the country, it was Cochran's question which permitted Rubin to report that, as the numbers of Aris Leather Lights ordered by Bloomingdales went up over the years, the percentage of brown gloves fell significantly: "Actually, the mix of black to brown gravitated dramatically, more toward black as we went farther into the '80's."[21] And while the defense was always free to argue that the Bundy and Rockingham gloves were not a pair, since it hardly takes an expert to suggest such a thing, Cochran couldn't resist asking the question. He got stung by the answer:

Q   But you can't say they're the exact same gloves that were sold at the same time, can you?

A   When I was looking at—when we looked at the gloves earlier—was the grain of the leather, the way these gloves were manufactured, just looking at them in this condition, they appear to be a pair that was cut out of approximately half of a skin, and that's what I was looking at. They appear to be a pair.[22]

Darden later further bolstered this claim by Rubin, by having him compare cutter numbers on the inside of the leather:

Q   You told us that the first glove was XL cutter 359 sequence 9; is that correct?

A   Yes.

Q   And the second glove?

A   It is the same. This is a pair.[23]

The defense might have at one point been able to argue that the gloves in evidence were not actually a size extra large—since they were about 15 percent smaller than a brand new extra large—but in reality a size large. However, Cochran himself elicited testimony further strengthening the claim that the gloves are Simpson's own size, extra large. He suggested that Rubin relied on the size label inside the glove to determine the glove size and that this was just an assumption:

Q And that's the assumption because you saw an extra large tab in there; is that correct?
A Yes.[24]

Mr. Cochran might have stopped here to good effect, but he then asked a question to which he clearly did not know the answer:

Q Okay. And that could have been wrong in the first place, couldn't it?
A Well, in this particular glove, it's not wrong because inside the glove, when the lining was torn away, I did see the "XL" stamping that I had mentioned yesterday along with the other markings.[25]

Perhaps the strongest prosecution point Cochran educed from Rubin was never again mentioned by the prosecution. During Rubin's last appearance as a witness, it was revealed that he had written a letter to Darden mentioning a future prosecution victory party, which he would be happy to attend. Suggesting bias, the defense danced this evidence in front of the jury with delight. In closing argument Cochran even described Rubin as "a soldier in the prosecution's army".[26]

But isn't it possible that Rubin, more intimately familiar with the gloves than any other party to the trial, was only predicting with reason what he supposed the inevitable outcome would be? In one of his earlier appearances on the witness stand, he was questioned by Cochran and Simpson's own lead attorney brought before the jury the fact that Rubin had shown no bias against Simpson and in fact had spoken kind words directly to the defendant:

Q As you were leaving yesterday, did you say something to Mr. Simpson?
Mr. Darden: Objection.
The Court: Overruled.
The Witness: I wished him the best of luck.[27]

CHAPTER 6

Vannatter and the Vial

A very good blood-and-thunder fiction.

—Robert Henry Newell, *Orpheus C. Kerr Papers*

T he defense argued that there was something sinister about Detective Philip Vannatter bringing O.J. Simpson's vial of reference blood to Rockingham, where he gave it to Dennis Fung, instead of booking it into evidence himself. In closing argument Barry Scheck said:

> I think there's something really wrong here, but, you know, you don't even need it, really, if you think about it, because in terms of access and opportunity, all that really matters is what nobody can deny, and that is Detective Vannatter is walking around with a May 10th envelope [Scheck pointed out earlier this mistake in the date on the envelope] that he should have sealed and he should have booked for three hours, at least, unaccounted for.
>
> What is going on? There's something wrong. It's not coincidence. There's something wrong. Terribly wrong.[1]

Scheck said all that really mattered was that Vannatter was walking around with the vial. Of course what matters is whether or not Vannatter used that purple-top tube to create evidence against Simpson. Since Scheck had *no* evidence that Vannatter had done anything of the kind with the reference sample, Scheck asserted that access was enough. Vannatter's failure to book the vial immediately was described as unprecedented, but what the defense ignored was Fung's explanation of this:

Q   And in your experience is it not the ordinary practice that after detectives get a blood sample from a suspect that they take it to the evidence control unit and book it there?

A   In my experience I have never had a detective obtain a blood sample that quickly.[2]

Just what malevolent action *could* have taken place during the time Vannatter had the vial and particularly after the vial reached Rockingham? Where might Vannatter have planted Simpson's blood?

Rockingham Driveway, Bronco, and Foyer

Simpson gave an interview to Vannatter and Lange at Parker Center about fifteen hours after the murders, on the afternoon of June 13th. Simpson told the two detectives that he had been bleeding at his Rockingham home the night before. "I recall bleeding at my house and then I went to the Bronco," Simpson told them. Tom Lange asked again about this, "Well, there's blood at your house in the driveway, and we've got a search warrant, and we're going to go get the blood. We found some in your house. Is that your blood that's there?" Simpson replied, "If it's dripped, it's what I dripped running around trying to leave." Since Simpson clearly acknowledged bleeding in the driveway, the Bronco, and inside the house, Vannatter had no need to plant Simpson's blood there. Even without serology or DNA testing results, that blood was identified by the man who had dripped it. So there would be no reason for a conspirator to plant Simpson's blood in these places. It's there already.

Moreover, there was no opportunity for Vannatter to do so in the case of the driveway or the vehicle. When Simpson first arrived at Rockingham (before being questioned or giving the blood), television cameras were already trained on the Rocking-ham estate and the Bronco itself. Reporters were so close to the Bronco that at least one of them rested a coffee cup on its hood. Even if Vannatter hadn't been to Rockingham himself that day and seen the cameras—but he *had* been there and he *had* seen the cameras—as a homicide detective working in a unit specializing in high-profile cases he would clearly have anticipated their presence. So why would he even consider planting blood in the full sight of uncountable television cameras? Further, by the time Vannatter arrived at the Simpson estate with the blood vial, the Bronco had already been impounded. It had been removed from Rockingham under the auspices of the police and was miles away from Vannatter and the vial. So neither motive nor opportunity to plant blood was present.

The Socks

A pair of dark socks were found on Simpson's bedroom floor. There was blood on these socks. DNA tests revealed that the blood came from both Simpson and Nicole. The defense's position was that there was no blood on the socks when they were found in Simpson's bedroom and that this blood was planted days or weeks later. So we know that Vannatter didn't use the blood vial on June 13th to plant blood on the socks. The defense theory explicitly stated that the planting occurred sometime later.

Perhaps Vannatter *wanted* to plant blood on the socks and just arrived back at Rockingham too late to accomplish his end. But why would he want to? He had already obtained admissions from Simpson that it was Simpson's blood in and around Rockingham; adding *Simpson's* blood to the socks wouldn't make any difference. If Simpson planned to use a defense like "I innocently cut myself at Rockingham and was never anywhere near Bundy on the night of June 12th", adding Simpson's blood to the socks doesn't diminish or contradict the defense offered.

The truly incriminating blood on the socks would be blood of either or both of the victims, and Vannatter didn't have any of that stashed in the evidence envelope. No blood was obtained from the bodies until autopsy, later in the week. So Vannatter had no reason to plant blood from Simpson's reference vial on the socks on June 13th and by the defense's own theory he certainly did not do it at that time. But, as we have seen, given Simpson's admitted bleeding, Vannatter must have known that planting Simpson's blood on Simpson's socks would be entirely pointless.

The Rockingham Glove

The glove found behind Kato's room had already been collected by the time Vannatter returned to 360 North Rockingham with the vial. We know it was in the evidence truck, because Fung testified that he had showed it to Detective Lange at the Bundy crime scene while it was still in the plastic evidence bag.[3] We also know that media outlets had cameras at Rockingham, which captured Vannatter's return and the trips of Fung and Mazzola to the evidence van. Vannatter didn't visit the evidence van after he returned with the sample vial. So he had no opportunity to plant any of Simpson's blood on the Rockingham glove and he knew that he would have no access: because he knew the glove was already in a plastic bag in the van. Moreover, the defense theory isn't that Vannatter planted blood on the glove, but rather that Collin Yamauchi inadvertently transferred Simpson's blood to the glove when Yamauchi opened the reference vial in the lab. Again, there is neither opportunity for planting of blood by Vannatter, nor is the planting even consistent with the defense theory.

The Rockingham Pathway

One of the biggest curiosities of the planted-glove scenario is the lack of blood found near the site of the glove. The only person who did find blood on the nearby air conditioner was defense witness Dr. Henry Lee, although he only performed presumptive tests. So concerned was Barry Scheck with this testimony, that during a break in closing arguments when the jury was not present, Scheck told the judge:

> And, in fact, as I indicate in the record that Dr. Lee was about to say that presumptive tests on sink traps, metal surfaces like air conditioners, door knobs and on that kind *would always give false positives* because of the nature of the metal surface and the bacteria, et cetera, which was what he was about to testify to and they knew it because in interviews with Dr. Lee that's what he had said.[4] [Emphasis added.]

Surely Scheck must have meant that the tests *could* yield false positives—otherwise why would a defense consultant engage in tests that would necessarily yield misleading results which could only harm the defendant? (It should be noted that a presumptive test was perfect for the Simpson defense because if a positive result were obtained, it could never be entered into evidence against Simpson—Judge Ito had barred the admission of presumptive tests because such tests may yield positive results in some cases when blood isn't actually present.)

If the Rockingham glove was planted and other police officers aided and abetted Fuhrman in this endeavor, even if only after the fact, why was no blood planted leading up to, or in the immediate vicinity of the glove? Even without the vial, since the defense claim was that Fuhrman used the glove to wipe blood in the Bronco, why didn't someone wipe it on the air conditioner *in amounts Fung could find?* It seems to be sheer luck for the prosecution that Dr. Lee found blood. Why didn't someone plant blood on the wall and other places near where the glove is said to have been planted? It can't be argued that the police already had an explanation for this anomaly of missing blood near the glove. It's clear that in the preliminary hearing, the opening statements to the trial, and in the trial testimony of Vannatter, there was no such police-prosecution reconciliation of the fact that the blood trail led from the Bronco to the house foyer and did not point to a detour behind the house. This explanation was provided only in Marcia Clark's closing argument. This pathway behind Kato's room is remote and inaccessible to television cameras. Vannatter could easily have gone down there and dropped some blood. If he took the vial for planting purposes, why didn't he plant it there?

The Bundy Back Gate

The only place left to consider is the Bundy back gate. But by the time Vannatter left Parker Center with the vial, Fung and Mazzola had long finished at Bundy. To plant blood on the gate would mean that it would have to be collected after the crime scene had been broken down. While in fact we know *now* that the blood on the back gate was collected later, how could Vannatter even know that, if he planted blood after the crime scene was released to the family, any of the planted blood would still remain undisturbed?

But there was no need to plant blood here because cop after cop after cop—including Philip Vannatter—had already seen the blood on that gate even before O.J. Simpson returned from Chicago (as discussed in detail in chapter 8).

Announcing a Conspiracy

One of the biggest peculiarities about the theory of blood planting by Vannatter is how well he must be supposed to have covered his tracks. The *only* evidence linking Vannatter to any sort of blood planting is his vial transportation to Rockingham. How could he be so clever at hiding everything else, but not be careful about this? He could just as easily have taken the blood vial from Nurse Peratis, gone to a private location, removed a small amount of blood in a few minutes, and then booked the vial as evidence. The few minutes involved could be explained by a trip to the men's room or an important phone call to his wife. Yet the defense theory is that this veritable Houdini of faked evidence managed to plant blood without a single slip, except that he totally unnecessarily drew attention to his possession of the blood by carrying the vial around for three hours.

Withering Weitzman

The defense vial-and-planting theory fails to account for any motive on the part of Detective Vannatter. Why would he want to frame O.J. Simpson? This query becomes even more striking when you recall who Simpson's attorney was during the first forty-eight hours or so after Simpson returned to Los Angeles. His attorney was Howard Weitzman, known to Detective Vannatter on sight:

Q Did you see any lawyers on the property or anyone you knew to be a lawyer on the property at that time [when Simpson first returned to Rockingham]?
A I saw a lawyer by the Rockingham gate, yes.
Q Okay. Did you recognize that lawyer?
A I did.
Q This lawyer was a lawyer you had seen in the past?
A Yes.
Q And who was that lawyer?
A Howard Weitzman.[5]

Howard Weitzman is a famous Los Angeles lawyer who has had many famous clients. Most relevant to Vannatter and the conspiracy theory would be Weitzman's participation in the defense of John DeLorean. DeLorean was charged with drug possession and dealing. The evidence against him was considered strong, including multiple videotapes, the last one showing DeLorean with a briefcase full of drugs in his lap. Weitzman engineered an acquittal in that case by arguing that the case against DeLorean was *created by government agents*.

Even before Vannatter took Simpson to Parker Center for questioning, even before he requested a blood sample from Simpson, Vannatter knew the attorney representing O.J. Simpson was Howard Weitzman. Isn't his DeLorean success going to deter Vannatter from playing around with the evidence, even before he gets any to play around with? Why would anyone contemplate planting evidence if they are going to face Howard Weitzman in court?

CHAPTER 7

The Case of the Bloodstained Bindle

*Merely corroborative details, intended to give artistic
verisimilitude to an otherwise bald and unconvincing
narrative.*

—W.S. Gilbert, *The Mikado*

One of the most eagerly anticipated witnesses of the
Simpson trial was criminalist Dr. Henry Lee. Lee
immigrated to the U.S. from Taiwan in 1965 with only
fifty dollars and just a few words of English. His studies in
America culminated in a Ph.D. in biochemistry from New York
University. Today he is the chief of the Connecticut State
Forensics Science Laboratory and probably the country's most
famous forensic scientist. He has been involved in numerous
high-profile cases, including the William Kennedy Smith rape
trial, the shooting death of Scarsdale diet doctor Herman
Tarnower, and the so-called wood chipper murder of Helle Crafts,
killed by her husband who then chopped her body into pieces
with a chain saw and later shredded these dismembered portions
with a wood chipper.

Long before he took the witness stand, the jury already knew
much about Dr. Lee. Many witnesses were asked about his
writings; the jurors learned that Lee had examined some of the
evidence for the defense, including testimony from Dr. Baden
that Lee had examined O.J. Simpson's body for forensic evidence;
and one prosecution witness even testified that Lee had con-

ducted an examination of the evidence socks without ever changing his gloves. (By the end of the trial this didn't seem to matter—an extrovert manner covers many a Fung-like foible.)

At the end of direct examination, defense attorney Barry Scheck asked Dr. Lee about wet transfer stains made on a paper bindle. A bindle is a piece of paper specially folded to completely contain a sample. Scheck asked about Item 47, the first of the Bundy blood drops, which had already been identified as matching O.J. Simpson. Dr. Lee testified that the paper bindle in which the Item 47 swatches had been wrapped had transfer stains on them, which meant that the swatches were not completely dry when they were placed in the paper. Scheck asked Dr. Lee his opinion about these transfer stains:

Q ... you told us that one would expect that these swatches, having been put in a test tube at 6:30 P.M. on June 13th and removed at 7:30 A.M. on June 14th, to [sic] be dry.
A Yes.
Q Given that fact—
The Court: Given that opinion.
Q By Mr. Scheck: Given that opinion, what is your opinion about the existence of these transfer stains?
Mr. Goldberg: Overly broad, no foundation, calls for conclusion.
The Court: Overruled.
The Witness: Only opinion I can giving under this circumstance, something wrong.[1]

This "something wrong" testimony was widely hailed by defense partisans as supporting a conspiracy theory. If the swatches had thirteen hours to dry, they should have been completely dry by the time they were put in the bindles. If they were dry, there would be no wet transfer onto the paper they were wrapped in. Conspiracy theorists suggested that the evidence of wet transfer shows that someone engaged in skullduggery in the night and the proof of their planting labors shows up in those wet transfer stains: the planted evidence didn't have sufficient time to dry and was the direct cause of the wet transfers.

Degraded Argument

The enthusiasm for the proposition that the blood on the swatches in Item 47 was planted is very odd because the blood here (as for all of the other Bundy blood drops) was highly degraded. The defense argued that the very fact that blood on the back gate at Bundy was *not* degraded supported their claim that the back gate blood was planted.

Barry Scheck repeatedly made the point throughout the trial that the back gate stains had far more DNA than other pieces of evidence.[2]

This means that Vannatter, the man who carried the blood, has discovered something thus far unknown to science: how to reverse the decomposition process of DNA. Blood from his magic vial is degraded in June (when the transfer stains on Item 47 occurred) but rejuvenated by July (when the Bundy back gate stains were collected). Call the Nobel committee.

The Goldilocks Factor

So there is a terrible inconsistency in this planting theory: if the source of planted blood is the high-quality stuff from the EDTA tube prepared by Nurse Thano Peratis and turned over to Detective Vannatter, why is the blood in Item 47 so seriously degraded? Perhaps the person planting the blood purposely did something to encourage degradation. Maybe he heated the swatches or rubbed them in dirt. But why would someone go to the trouble of planting useful evidence and then engage in activity to destroy that very evidence? And how could the blood on those planted swatches be manipulated in such a way as to closely match the degradation of the other blood drop samples from Bundy? The DNA content of the other swatches can't be discerned by simply looking at them, so how does a conspirator know how degraded they are? Assuming he had this information, the evidence planter-and-degrader then has to walk a fine line in his efforts to destroy some of his evidence. Too few insults to the planted swatch and it will stand out from all the others because of its high DNA content, signaling that it has been planted. Too many insults to the planted swatch and all the DNA will be destroyed and the planting will be for naught. As one commentator observed, "The postulated mistreatment has to be done in Goldilocks fashion, that is, *juuuust* right!"[3]

The Bacteria Did It

Another possibility is that the blood said to be planted on the swatches from Item 47 was actually high quality, undegraded blood. In this scenario, blood from Vannatter's vial was placed on the swatches created by criminalists Fung and Mazzola and the nasty bacteria which had already eaten up the blood of the real killer went after the planted, fresh blood of Simpson for dessert.

Adding wet blood to the swatches would provide the moisture bacteria require. But it was the heat and overall humidity in Dennis Fung's van which contributed to the degradation of the DNA on the swatches. The Scientific Investigation Division's drying cabinet is neither a hot nor humid environment, and that is where Item 47 reposed just before the bindling took place. We have data on just what kind of degradation takes place in that drying cabinet, based on evidence presented at trial on Item 56.[4] Item 56 is blood taken from one of the footprints on the Bundy walkway which was found to be Nicole's blood. There was never any dispute in the trial that these footwear impressions in blood resulted from the killer stepping in the pool of Nicole's blood. No one ever suggested that this evidence was planted or created, so it is an excellent source of information on what actually happened to the blood evidence in this case. Item 56 represents blood collected at Bundy, temporarily housed in the SID van, and then placed in the drying cabinet.

Item 56 was found to be highly contaminated, meaning it was full of the bacteria which break down DNA. The defense argued that the methods used by criminalists Fung and Mazzola contributed significantly to the degradation of the samples. The prosecution argued that the stains were in dirty places at the crime scene, and that degradation occurred before the criminalists got there.

No matter which theory is correct, we can reasonably conclude that much of the degradation of Item 56 took place *before* it was brought to the laboratory. The swatches arrived at LAPD teaming with DNA-hungry bacteria. These swatches were then left for hours to dry. If it were the case that degradation continued at full pace at room temperature, there should have been nothing left of the human blood on Item 56. Yet Dr. Robin Cotton testified that Cellmark was able to obtain a typeable result from this sample. Item 56 suggests that degradation does *not* take place rapidly at room temperature. Thus the claim that simply placing high quality blood on bacteria-rich swatches in the lab can explain the degradation of Item 47 is unsound. Again it seems that the low quality of blood on Item 47 remains strong evidence that this sample was not planted.

This argument is certainly conjectural, but there is some experimental data to support the conclusion. A study of forensic blood samples exposed to high concentrations of bacteria and left at room temperature for five days still contained enough DNA for PCR testing (the same PCR test, in fact, used by the LAPD).[5]

This particular theory that Item 47 represents planted evidence is merely an attempt to replace one discrepancy (wet transfer stains) with another (less effective planting on Item 47 than on the back gate).

The idea of planting new blood upon old has other problems. Since the person planting the blood of O.J. Simpson couldn't know how much DNA was in the swatches already, planting Simpson's blood on top of the original blood would be taking a hideous risk: the DNA tests could show a mixture which would be very difficult for anyone to explain. How could two killers leave a trail of mixed blood in single drops leading away from the scene? If the blood were planted, new swatches are obviously the only method to employ. Sadly they don't come pre-contaminated for the convenience of evidence planters who want less than perfect samples for verisimilitude.

It Doesn't Add Up

Henry Lee testified that there were four wet transfer stains which appeared to come from three swatches—one swatch probably left two stains. If wetness is the proof of planting, then were only three of the seven swatches in that bindle planted? This is too bizarre to even contemplate. Someone smart enough to plant evidence knows that everything in a single bindle needs to be the same stuff. Not just the same level of degradation in the DNA but, by the way, the same DNA itself. Yet the wet-means-planted theory can only account for three planted swatches out of seven.

The fact that not all the swatches were wet was even a puzzle for Dr. Lee. Barry Scheck originally intended to end his direct examination after Lee's "something wrong" answer. But after a break Scheck came back one more time and elicited the following:

Q Dr. Lee, the last answer that you gave this jury with respect to this board is "something is wrong." could you please explain what you mean?

A What I mean—

Mr. Goldberg: Calls for conclusion, Your Honor. His opinion is speculation, no foundation.

The Court: Overruled.

A: What I mean, there are seven swatches, maybe a potential eight swatches, four imprints, wet transfer on the paper. If seven swatches all dry, I shouldn't see any wet transfer. If seven swatches all wet, I should see seven transfers. I only see four. The number did not add up. There may be reason to explain. I don't know.[6]

This is not nearly so powerful for the defense as stopping when Scheck first intended. It's easy to manipulate the un-elaborated "something wrong" answer into support for nefarious planting activity. But Lee's elucidation of his answer is that the number of swatches and the number of wet transfers don't add up. This fails to support any reasonable planting theory, since it is ridiculous to propose that someone would replace only some of the swatches in a bindle but not all of them. It is important to note that when Scheck asked Lee to explain what he meant, Lee had the opportunity to put forward a theory—conspiracy or otherwise—and he explicitly chose not to. He refused to specu-late about what caused the swatches to still be damp.

The wet plant theory also fails to explain why only Item 47 exhibits the tell-tale transfer stains. It makes no sense to plant blood on only three swatches of the eight total swatches for Item 47. What about the rest of the Bundy blood drop evidence, Items 48, 49, 50, and 52, each of which had multiple swatches?

Planting Pointless Evidence?

Henry Lee's "something wrong" response was invoked by Simpson defenders repeatedly until the end of the trial. Com-mentators would use this testimony to suggest that there was something seriously wrong with the prosecution case. Almost completely ignored was the fact that Henry Lee's examination of the evidence bindles also revealed that there were wet transfer stains on the bindle for Item 42. The defense never elicited this testimony. Item 42 was blood from the pool around Nicole's body, later identified as her own blood. Hank Goldberg discussed this with Dr. Lee on cross-examination:

Q Is this [photographs of bindle number 42] one of the items that you examined?
A Yes, sir.
Q And did this also contain some wet transfers?
A In my notes, I did mention this item have wet transfer.
Q And, sir, if the testimony in this case is that the swatches here came from a pool of the victim's blood, Nicole Simpson, would you expect that to play any material role in terms of whether or not we would

Q get a wet transfer? In other words, would her blood be different from someone else's blood?

A I don't know. I did not group that. I can't really tell you whose blood. The transfer in my note refer a bow tie, like a bow tie transfer. I try to find a piece in here have a bow tie (indicating). Whether or not can fit this bow tie, I wasn't too successful.

Q And that could be something twisted; is that correct?

A Yes, sir.[7]

There was absolutely no need whatever to plant any of Nicole's blood at the murder scene, unless the planters knew that the 'real victim' was someone other than Ms. Brown Simpson and wanted to keep this vital fact out of court. The pool around Nicole's body was never suggested by anyone to be other than her own blood. Obviously these swatches were not planted, altered, or doctored in any way. There was no reason for anyone to do that.

Yet the bindle they were placed in contained wet transfer stains. This strongly indicates that there must be an innocent explanation for these transfer stains, which just happens to have affected some swatches incriminating O.J. Simpson and some swatches of the victim's blood incriminating no one at all.

The Innocent Explanation

Under cross-examination, Dr. Lee admitted that a criminalist cannot always explain things after the fact:

Q Dr. Lee, are there many occasions where you said as a forensic scientist where you look at a case or a piece of evidence and you just don't have all the answers?

A That's correct.

Q And there is nothing surprising about that, is there?

A Nothing surprising.[8]

Dr. Lee admitted under cross-examination that the transfer stains on the bindle for Item 47 did not soak through to the outside of the bindle. This suggests that rather than being wet, the swatches were merely damp.

The simple explanation is that the swatches didn't dry completely. Henry Lee dries his swatches in test tubes which are stored vertically. The LAPD criminalists lay their tubes on their sides. This latter method could inhibit drying since vertical convection currents can't then move water vapor out of the tubes.

Perhaps certain areas in the drying cabinet have different air movement patterns and the tubes containing the swatches from Item 47 and Item 42 were in the least efficient areas. Hank Goldberg suggested to the judge that perhaps a 'swatch sandwich' was created, whereby some swatches were closely wedged next to each other. This close contact would mean that air couldn't reach some of them and they never completely dried. This sort of careless handling by Fung and Mazzola hardly seems implausible.

The innocent explanation—incomplete drying—has the advantage of being simple and explaining the wet transfers on both Item 47 and Item 42. The evidence-planting explanation for wet transfer is an incomplete theory. If wet transfer is significant for 47, what is the significance for Item 42 (Nicole's own blood around her dead body)? The planting explanation considers wet transfer significant only when it helps the defense and otherwise ignores it completely.

CHAPTER 8

Blood on the Back Gate

Some circumstantial evidence is very strong, as when you find a trout in the milk.

—H.D. Thoreau, *Journal 1850*

Blood was found on the back gate at Bundy, and this blood was identified as O.J. Simpson's. The defense claimed that this blood was planted. Unless the back gate blood *was* planted, it is difficult to see how Simpson could possibly be innocent.

The claim that the back gate blood was planted is absolutely crucial to the defense. Yet, it turns out, this blood evidence is different from all the other blood evidence identified as Simpson's at Bundy, because the defense's attacks upon other blood evidence (however strong or weak those attacks may be) simply don't apply to the back gate blood:

- More blood was found on the back gate than anywhere else at Bundy, so the back gate blood was tested with numerous RFLP probes—stronger and more discriminating DNA tests than PCR.

- Since Dennis Fung didn't collect the back gate blood the same day as he collected the other blood evidence from Bundy, Barry Scheck's withering attacks, particularly relating to leaving the evidence in plastic bags all afternoon in a hot van, don't apply.

- Of all the blood evidence from Bundy, these back gate stains were the only ones not collected before the defense had a chance to investigate. Both defense witnesses Henry Lee and Michael Baden visited Bundy between the time of the murders and the time this blood was collected. Strangely, they were never asked under oath by the defense whether or not they saw blood.

- If the back gate blood was planted, numerous police officers had to be in on the plot. It is quite impossible for the two evil demons, Vannatter and Fuhrman, to have faked this evidence all by themselves.

By the time of closing argument, Cochran limited his uninhibited, hot-tempered attacks on the police to Vannatter and Fuhrman. But those two men alone cannot account for the blood evidence on the back gate because numerous officers at the scene who were called as witnesses testified to seeing that blood. Thus, if the blood were planted, these officers, too, must have been in on the conspiracy.

So how do we explain the testimony of so many officers who saw the blood on the back gate? This is Barry Scheck's explanation from his closing argument:

> Now, there is another thing. They are going to say, well, you know, Officer Riske, Phillips, I believe, Fuhrman, Rossi, that night when they were entering the premises, the back gate, they had their flashlights and they were looking up and down and they think they saw some blood on the back gate, so they all testified to it, so you know it is there.
>
> Well, first of all, we know—you have been there—that this gate was rusty. There were all kind of darknesses, imperfections. There were berries all over there. There is all kind of discolorations. And what did they really see with their flashlights? It is not clear what they saw with their flashlights.[1]

An examination of the testimony regarding the blood of the back gate, however, does not support Scheck's account. No officer was ever challenged about confusing blood with either berry stains or rust, and no such evidence of the possibility of confusion was ever offered by the defense. And the very first witness to testify that he had seen the blood also testified that he had used a large, powerful flashlight. The testimony is striking not only for its clarity but for the lack of any defense attack on it.

Even the reference to the jury view is pretty feeble, considering that the jury saw the gate six months after the murders, in broad daylight, and after it had been covered in fingerprint dust.

One of Johnnie Cochran's fifteen questions for the prosecution in his closing arguments concerned the back gate, "Why do bloodstains with the most DNA not show up until weeks after the murder, those on the socks, those on the back gate?"[2]

This not only contradicts Barry Scheck, who clearly acknowledged that many officers *claimed* they saw the back gate blood only hours after the murders occurred, but is in direct contravention of the record, which shows again and again that the blood was present and observed in the early morning hours of June 13th. The record is also remarkably devoid of any challenge, by Cochran or any of his colleagues, to the observations of these officers.

Officer Robert Riske

The first officer to testify at trial about the blood on the back gate was Officer Robert Riske, who carried a large, high-powered flashlight with him while examining the crime scene. On direct examination he told Clark about the flashlight he used during the early morning hours of June 13th:

Q   What kind of flashlight do you have?
A   I have a streamline, long black metal.
Q   Long black metal light?
A   Right.
Q   It is very powerful?
A   I think it is rated at 30,000 candle power. It is powerful.[3]

Riske told Clark, more than once, that not only did he see blood on the back gate, but that his partner saw blood, too:

Q   And at the rear gate that you pointed out to us that's now shown in photograph F, did you notice anything unusual about—on that rear gate?
A   There's blood at various locations on the gate, that would appear to be blood.
Q   And did your partner point out any other blood with respect to that rear gate?
A   He pointed out blood on the outside of the gate on the back.[4]

Not only did Riske see the blood on the back gate, he testified that he showed it to other officers:

> We [Riske, Sergeant Rossi, and Sergeant Coon] went—after I showed them the initial crime scene, we went down to Dorothy, went around to the rear. I showed them the jeep, the change on the ground, the blood on the driveway. I took Sergeant Rossi to the gate, showed him the blood on the gate and we went approximately halfway down the walkway. I showed the bloody footprints.[5]

Riske didn't show the back gate blood to other people just once, but many times:

Q All right. And where did you go?
A We [Detective Phillips, Detective Fuhrman, Sergeant Rossi, and Sergeant Coon] went to the driveway, showed them the door that was ajar and the jeep, the change and the blood on the driveway. I was showing Detective Fuhrman the blood that was on the gate.
Q The rear gate?
A That's correct. And Sergeant Rossi and Detective Phillips walked down the walkway probably halfway.[6]

Riske didn't simply say that he saw blood on the gate, he was very specific about what he saw:

Q Can you tell us if you see where you saw blood drops on the rear gate on the night of June the 12th?
A There was blood at the bottom, there was blood on this latch, there was blood at the top and my partner directed my attention to blood on the outside on the grating.[7]

While the defense waged their heavy attacks on Fuhrman, they failed to explain why it was that *he* wasn't the man to 'discover' the blood on the back gate. Riske testified that he showed it to Fuhrman:

Q So you stayed outside the rear gate with Detective Fuhrman?
A That's correct.
Q And what did you do there?
A I showed him the blood on the rear gate and, like I said, the blood in the driveway.[8]

In cross-examination, Cochran never challenged Riske about whether or not he was making up the observation of blood, or if there was any possibility of confusing it with berries or rust. He never attacked the strength of Riske's flashlight. These points left conceded, Cochran concentrated on when the photographs of that blood were taken, seemingly accepting Riske's claim of seeing this blood:

Q In fact you also described for us that at some point you saw some blood on the rear gate of the location there?
A Correct. ...
Q By the way, you never at any time ever saw the photographer taking any pictures of the blood which you claim you saw on that rear gate, did you?
A No, I didn't.[9]

Cochran returned to this back gate blood several times during his cross-examination. He had several occasions to challenge Riske's testimony on what it was he saw, yet he never did make that challenge:

Q Were you aware of whether or not any photographs were ever taken on June 13, 1994, of this blood that was supposedly on that rear gate on that date?
A No, sir.[10]

On his third trip to the back gate blood issue during cross-examination, Cochran again questioned when photos were taken, but still didn't challenge Riske's testimony, his memory of the blood, or suggest any reason why Riske would testify to seeing blood when the defense says it simply wasn't there at the time Riske claims to have seen it. Cochran pounds on the date of photography:

Q The photographs Miss Clark showed you to your left with regard to the exhibits and the supposed blood on the rear gate at Bundy, those were not taken when you were there on June 13, were they? ...
A No, sir.[11]

Evidence of more widespread knowledge of this back gate blood during the early morning hours of June 13th came during Cochran's cross-examination of Riske. In reply to defense questioning, Riske explained that it was he and his partner, Officer Terrazas, who discovered the blood, and he gave Cochran a chance to ask challenging questions about his flashlight, but Cochran failed to do so:

Q Now, this blood that you described toward the rear gate, the rear gate of that property, could you see that with the naked eye or did you see that with the use of a flashlight?
A Flashlight.

Q And did you and your partner both see it or did you see it first?

A I saw the blood on the interior. He saw the blood on the exterior.

Q And did you tell the Detectives Lange and Vannatter about this?

A I showed it to Fuhrman and Phillips. I don't know if they told them or not.

Q You showed it to Fuhrman and Phillips?

A That's correct.

Q You did not show it to Lange and Vannatter?

A No.[12]

Cochran tried to suggest that if it were important surely Riske would have shown the lead detectives. But we can see from Riske's testimony that he and Terrazas saw it first and that Riske showed it to at least three other officers: Rossi, Phillips, and Fuhrman. Moving up the chain of command, it was Phillips who showed Vannatter and Lange this blood.

Sergeant David Rossi

On direct examination, Sergeant David Rossi told Marcia Clark that he saw blood on the back gate at Bundy during the early morning hours of June 13th:

Q First of all, the locations shown in these photographs, this last series you have been shown, is that the rear gate you have described?

A That appears to be the rear gate, yes.

Q And do you recall seeing blood on the gate, the lower rung where it was shown in these photographs?

A Yes, I do.[13]

When it came time for cross-examination, F. Lee Bailey had no questions regarding the blood on the back gate. Bailey chose to spend an extended amount of time questioning Rossi about the timing of coroner notification, even though Marcia Clark later established that it wasn't even Rossi's responsibility to contact the coroner. This is very peculiar behavior for Bailey. After all, he went into great detail about Fuhrman's flashlight when cross-examining Fuhrman. Why did he fail to ask Rossi any questions whatever about the lighting conditions when Rossi saw this important blood evidence which the defense contends was not there? He was not afraid to challenge Fuhrman regarding evidence which the defense claims only existed illegitimately, so why did he fail to challenge Rossi's identification of this blood?

Detective Ron Phillips

On direct examination, Detective Ron Phillips said that he saw the blood on the back gate during the early morning hours of June 13th:

Q Now, before you entered through the rear gate, sir, was anything pointed out to you to be careful of?

A Well, I was pointed out some blood that was on the top rung of the rear gate and also on the bottom rung of the rear gate and then also at a latch on the rear gate.[14]

Phillips testified that he showed this back gate blood to Vannatter. He was with Detective Fuhrman at the time. So another police officer testified that it wasn't Fuhrman who pointed out this blood, it was Phillips:

Q And when you got to the rear gate area after you finished—after you walked to the end of the walkway, did you point anything out at that location?

A Yes. I pointed out [to Detective Vannatter] the three areas on the gate that had been pointed out to me where blood was.[15]

Johnnie Cochran did not ask Phillips a single question about his observation of the blood on the back gate. Not once did he challenge Phillips or suggest that Phillips was lying about this extremely incriminating evidence against O.J. Simpson. Not once did he mention berries, rust, or discolorations on the gate or elicit any testimony about inadequate flashlights. Detective Phillips's identification of blood on the back gate at Bundy just hours after the murders remained completely unchallenged.

Detective Tom Lange

Detective Tom Lange also testified to seeing the blood on the back gate, when he was questioned by Marcia Clark:

Q When you got to the rear gate, did Detective Phillips point anything out to you? ...

A Pointed out what appeared to be a blood transfer or smear on the upper rung of the gate and what appeared to be two droplets of blood on the lower rung, lower inside rung of the bottom of the rear gate.[16]

Lange testified that he asked Fung to collect the blood on the back gate:

Q Did you make certain requests of him [Dennis Fung] in terms of what to collect?
A Yes.
Q Did you point out the rear gate area to him?
A Yes.
Q And ask him to collect blood from that area?
A Yes.[17]

Lange actually testified more than once that he had pointed out this blood to Fung. But the blood wasn't collected on June 13th. Lange testified that when he returned to the crime scene on July 3rd he saw the same blood on the back gate which he had seen on June 13th:

Q Tell us what date was it that you returned?
A July 3rd, 1994.
Q And what observation did you make?
A I observed the same thing that I observed back on June 13.
Q Which was?
A The blood smear transfer on the upper rung, the blood on the lower rung and this particular item [another blood stain] on the outside of the gate.[18]

In his cross-examination of Lange, Cochran concentrated on the poor procedure followed by the LAPD in collecting the back gate blood. But he did not challenge Lange's testimony that the blood was actually there, he did not ask the witness if the stain could be anything other than blood, and he did not question the adequacy of the lighting the night Lange first saw the blood:

Q Well, let me ask you this: You said in your testimony you saw some blood spots on the back—on the rear gate there at Bundy, on June 13, 1994; is that correct?
A Yes.
Q Those spots had been pointed out to you by Detective Phillips?
A That's correct.
Q You in turn pointed them out to Mr. Fung?
A That's correct.
Q Did you direct Mr. Fung to collect those particular blood spots?
A I directed him to do that and I believe I mentioned to check the entire gate.
Q All right. And you expected that to be done; isn't that correct?
A Yes.

Q   Now, it was not done on June 13th, was it?
A   No.
Q   In fact, it wasn't done on June 14th, was it?
A   That's correct.
Q   And neither the 15th?
A   That's correct.
Mr. Cochran: I won't go any further.
Q   In fact, it was not done until July 3rd, three weeks later; is that right?
A   That's correct.[19]

Cochran brought out the fact that lookie-loos haunted the crime scene, but what difference does this make to establishing a planting scenario? It certainly is very bad practice not to have collected the blood on the 13th. But if the defense theory is that the police at their leisure put Simpson's blood on the gate, then the only relevance of lookie-loos would arise if the defense could find one who didn't see blood between the time the crime scene was broken down and the time the blood on the back gate was collected—unless Cochran had a back-up theory that one of these ordinary folks out for a gruesome look-see just happened to have some of O.J.'s blood in a vial hidden in her sock.

Q   You are aware that after the crime scene perimeter was taken down by Officer Jones and Perridine, p-e-r-r-d-i-n-e [sic], they had a number of lookie-loos and other tourists from the world who came in and around that location; isn't that correct?
A   Yes.
Q   You are aware of that, aren't you?
A   Yes.
Q   You also know that some people placed flowers on the walkway at various places around the Bundy location? You are aware of that also, aren't you?
A   Yes.
Q   By the way, when did you first learn that no blood was allegedly taken from the back gate? When did you first learn that?
A   On that date, July 3rd.[20]

Cochran himself helped the witness provide an explanation for why it took so long to collect the blood on the back gate. When Lange said that before July 3rd he hadn't read the reports of Fung or Mazzola, Cochran did not query the veracity or challenge the reasonableness of this explanation:

Q … How did you determine that there had—that there had been no blood samples collected near the rear gate area of Bundy after June 13th, 1994? How did you make that determination?

A The determination was made as I approached the rear gate and entered on that date. I hadn't been to the rear gate prior to that to examine it. I really felt I didn't have any reason to. As I walked through the gate, myself and others observed what appeared to be the blood smear that was observed earlier on the 13th.

Q So you saw it on July 3rd. Is that what you're saying?

A That's correct.

Q And had you met with the criminalists at any time between June 13th and July 3rd?

A I don't believe so.

Q So you hadn't met with either Fung or Mazzola to discuss their work?

A To discuss their work, no.

Q Had you read any reports from Fung or Mazzola between the dates of June 13th and July 3rd?

A No.[21]

He let Lange repeat his explanation again, without any challenge:

Q And before that time, did you ever read the property report to determine whether or not these stains allegedly from the rear gate had been booked?

A I don't recall seeing the property report prior to that.[22]

Cochran again and again referred to the back gate blood, but never inserted any queries to Lange challenging his observation of it on the night of the murders. Cochran continued to concentrate on the late collection. While this is clearly disturbing to anyone who values an efficient system of evidence collection, it does not rebut the testimony of all the various officers who saw blood there on the night of the murders.

Cochran's only attempt at challenging the presence of the back gate blood during the early morning hours of June 13th was to elicit from Lange the fact that he didn't record seeing this blood in his notes:

Q Now, you shared with us your notes that were written chronologically at the scene on that particular date, June 13th, 1994.

   With regard to the alleged blood spots that were on the rear gate, did you ever write down or log that the blood spots were—that there were blood spots on that rear gate in your notes?

A   I don't believe I did.

Q   And that—wouldn't that have been an important circumstance?

A   Not necessarily. That would fall under the purview of the criminalists collecting them.

Q   I see. So a review of your notes indicate you didn't write that down, right?

A   I don't believe I did.

Q   And that evidence, if it was there, was not collected until approximately three weeks later on July 3rd; is that right?

A   That's correct.[23]

But on re-direct examination, Lange pointed out that he didn't notate *any* of the blood at the crime scene in his notes. This of course includes blood that the defense never claimed was phantom:

Q   You indicated that you did not diagram any of the blood on the rear gate at Bundy?

A   That's correct.

Q   Okay. You did create—did you create diagrams of the Bundy location, sir?

A   Yes.

Q   And that is part of your crime scene notes?

A   Yes.

Q   Did you diagram on those notes anywhere any of the blood that was found at the scene at 875 South Bundy?

A   No.[24]

Cochran finally addressed the condition of the gate during his cross-examination:

Q   ... do you recall that there was some berries or some kind of plant material on that back gate as you walked out the walkway there?

A   Quite a bit of debris, yes.

Q   Was there a tree above that?

A   There are bushes and trees off to the right of the photograph, yes.[25]

Aha, we've struck berries at last! But what does this testimony establish? Lange testified that he saw blood on the back gate and he testified that he saw berries on the back gate. The clear implication, since he saw both, is that *he can tell the difference* between them. Cochran asked no further questions about these berries which became so important in closing argument.

While Cochran had concentrated on the lateness of the collection of the blood, Clark concentrated on establishing that the blood collected on July 3rd was the same blood which Lange observed when he first viewed the crime scene on June 13th:

Q ... on the first time you returned to the rear gate area after June the 13th, which was, as you have indicated, July the 3rd, what did you see?

A I observed a smear of blood—the first thing I observed is a smear of blood on the upper rung of the rear gate that I had observed on June 13th. Additionally, there appeared to be the same two droplets of blood on the lower rung of that gate.

Q The same two—

Mr. Cochran: Leading and suggestive.

A They appeared to be the same two.

Q Could you explain that, sir? You said the same two blood drops?

A It appeared to be the same two droplets that I had observed earlier on June 13th on the inner lower rung of that rear gate.[26]

Lange claimed that the blood stains he saw on June 13th appeared to be the same blood stains collected on July 3rd, and Cochran never challenged him once about this observation. Instead, he repeated himself concerning the late collection, gaining no further ground than he had during his original cross-examination:

Q And we also know that, according to your testimony, there was some alleged blood spots on the rear gate of this premises; is that correct?

A That's correct.

Q And no photographs were taken of those blood spots on June 13th; isn't that correct?

A That's correct.

Q And nobody even bothered to come back and you didn't go back and even check until July 3rd, some three weeks later; isn't that right?

A The rear gate area, that's correct.[27]

And nobody for the defense even bothered to come back to Lange's identification of the blood on June 13th and July 3rd as being the same.

In his last confrontation with Lange over the blood on the gate, Cochran almost conceded that the blood was there while pursuing his refrain of late collection. Cochran's questions included a reference to mistakes, but he never asked if Lange could have been mistaken about his identification of blood on that gate when he first visited the Bundy crime scene:

Q When you told us under oath that you had seen these blood spots on the rear gate at Bundy, yet no photographs were taken of those blood spots on June 13th, 1994, would you consider that a mistake?

A That again was probably a problem with communications. At a crime scene, the criminalist, the print people, the photographers, the other detectives are all given assignments.

The detective in charge, while responsible for their overall performance, can't follow each technician around and make sure that they do every little thing that they ask of them. So you assign out jobs; and that particular assignment came under the purview of the criminalist. Unfortunately, it was not done.

Q Now to get back to my question, was that a mistake that wasn't done? That was the question.

A Was that the mistake of mine?

Q I didn't ask whose mistake. I said, was that a mistake, Detective Lange?

A I would call that a mistake, problem with the communications.[28]

Detective Mark Fuhrman

Detective Mark Fuhrman corroborated Officer Riske and described how he first saw the blood on the back gate:

Officer Riske pointed out some blood on the gate, some smudging on the upper rail of the gate. I noticed some blood dropping on the center of the gate, the mesh part of the gate. ...There appeared to be evidence of blood on the bottom rung of the gate. I noticed a blood smudge around the door turn knob lock on the interior or the east side of the gate.[29]

Fuhrman told Clark that he saw what might have been a partial fingerprint on the back gate, and that Detective Phillips saw it, too. He gave a detailed description of the blood he saw on the back gate.[30]

One of the first things F. Lee Bailey established in cross-examination was that many of Detective Fuhrman's observations at Bundy were made with the aid of Officer Riske's flashlight (which was powerful):

Q ... you made the observations you described for us on direct examination about Mr. Goldman, the other evidence that was lying around?

A Officer Riske was pointing them out with his flashlight.

Q Okay. These are things he had discovered and he was showing them to you. These were not things that you were discovering as a detective, right?

A I was listening and he was pointing them out, yes, sir, that's correct.[31]

The first few times Bailey elicited answers about the back gate, he didn't even acknowledge that Fuhrman was testifying to finding damning blood evidence:

Q Now, after you arrived at the back gate, what time would you say it was then as you arrived?

A I don't know what the time line would be at that point. It would probably take us a couple more minutes to walk back and make the observations on the gate. ...

Q What did you next do?

A Walked out onto the driveway. Officer Riske pointed out blood drops and some change.[32]

Bailey elicited testimony about the blood on the back gate and the possible fingerprint there but did not challenge Fuhrman's observations nor did he challenge the fact that Fuhrman claimed these notes were made contemporaneously with the observations:

Q Now, up to this point, and apart from what Detective—I'm sorry—Officer Riske told you, that you had discovered before you arrived, had you detected anything?

A No.

Q No. All you had done was to observe things that had already been discovered by others and were pointed out to you, correct?

A Excuse me. I would like to correct that.

Q Okay.

A I saw a partial fingerprint on the back gate and I saw two additional blood drops on the gate.

Q Okay. So those are things that you saw presumably for the first time among yourself and your colleagues?

A Yes, sir.

Q All right. And you made due note of those, did you not?

A Yes, I did.[33]

In fact, rather than challenging Fuhrman's claim that he made notes shortly after observing the back gate blood, Bailey approvingly repeated Fuhrman's own testimony, when his question was "And you made due note of those, did you not?"

Perhaps in an attempt to cover all possible bases, Bailey engaged in questioning which suggested someone other than Fuhrman or the police may have planted evidence against Simpson:

Q ... would you agree that when there is delay in a homicide investigation, number one, the perpetrators or perpetrator, as the case may be, have a chance to get further and further away from the scene, correct?

A Well, I think that would be common sense, yes.

Q They have the opportunity perhaps to plant evidence, to mislead the detectives as time goes by?

A I couldn't answer that, sir.

Q They have time—this is no part of your training I take it?

A Planting evidence? No, it isn't.

Q And they have time to structure false alibis all during this period that they are not being apprehended?

A I would probably agree with that.

Q And they are free to kill again, true?

A If that's the circumstance.

Q Well, if they're not apprehended, presumably they have the same freedom that permitted them to accomplish the grisly scene that you had just viewed, true? ...

A I couldn't speculate on a criminal's intent whether he killed once or a hundred.[34]

Lieutenant Frank Spangler

Lieutenant Spangler was not asked about blood on the back gate at Bundy. The prosecution used him primarily to show that Fuhrman had no opportunity to find and abscond with the hypothetical second glove at Bundy. But Marcia Clark did elicit testimony from him about the use of flashlights at crime scenes:

Q Lieutenant Spangler, is it common for police officers to carry flashlights at crime scenes?

A Especially at night, yes, ma'am.

Q And is it—what is the purpose of having a flashlight at a crime scene?

A To aid your vision, to allow you to identify and see potential items of evidence.[35]

While F. Lee Bailey had gone on and on about Fuhrman's little bitty flashlight, he did not challenge Spangler or the equipment his men had at Bundy that night.

Detective Philip Vannatter

Detective Vannatter testified that he saw blood on the gate on June 13th:

Q Now, as you walked down the walkway at Bundy and exited the rear gate, did you notice anything on the rear gate at all?
A Yes, I did.
Q What did you notice?
A I noticed what appeared to be blood wipings along the upper rail of the gate and what appeared to be blood drops on the bottom rail of the gate.
Q And were these blood wipings and blood drops pointed out to you by Detective Phillips?
A They were.[36]

Detective Vannatter was carrying a large flashlight that night, in order to see important evidence like the blood on the back gate:

Q Now, as you approached the crime scene from the front, were you carrying a flashlight?
A Yes.
Q What kind of flashlight?
A A four-cell D battery flashlight, a long flashlight like that. I don't know the brand of it.
Q Okay. How long is that flashlight? How many inches?
A Oh, it is probably I guess 14 inches maybe.
Q Okay. And was Detective Phillips also carrying a flashlight?
A As I recall, yes.[37]

When the defense had an opportunity to challenge these claims by Vannatter, no attack transpired. Robert Shapiro didn't ask a single question about the blood on the back gate. He did not ask questions about berries or rust or discoloration.

Shapiro did however acknowledge that Vannatter was equipped with a powerful flashlight:

Q ... you had a more powerful flashlight [than Detective Fuhrman]?
A Yes.[38]

So Who Was in on It?

One important aspect of all this testimony is seen when put in context. Concerning the blood inside the Bronco, the defense challenged witnesses boldly. Bailey asked Fuhrman directly if he had wiped the glove inside the Bronco, thereby planting incriminating blood evidence. Scheck suggested that Fung was purposely lying about seeing the blood on the bottom of the Bronco door so that his observations would comport with Fuhrman's testimony and thus help the prosecution. And yet the Bundy back gate blood is observed by many police officers and *those observations are not challenged in any way.* By closing, the defense had decided to limit their police conspiracy indictments to the so-called Twins of Deception, Vannatter and Fuhrman.

If a conspiracy at all, rather than a conspiracy of silence this seems to have been a conspiracy of great volume. Witness after witness testified to the blood, typically multiple times and in great detail. The silent part of this conspiracy seems to have been the defense, who never challenged any officer's identification of the blood long before that first police trip to Rockingham or Simpson's voluntary blood offering at Parker Center.

By the time of closing arguments, even Lange had been rehabilitated in the eyes of the defense, so that Cochran told the jury on September 27th:

> ... Lange is different than these other detectives and things. ... Lange is different. He made mistakes. He has misstatements as you're going to see, but he was different.
>
> ... No matter how you asked this man a question or what anybody would want him to say, he seemed to try to answer the best he could. Now, we don't always agree with everything he did, but it was refreshing to have somebody like that who wouldn't be told by these prosecutors or anybody else what to say or what to do even when he's criticized in the paper. That was Lange.[39]

About Riske and his testimony about his academy training, Cochran said "his candor was refreshing".[40] About Detective Phillips, Cochran said, "he's a nice man".[41] Concerning the police in general, he concluded:

> It's not about being anti-police. You saw the police you could believe and you now know the ones you can't believe.[42]

Barry Scheck argued similarly before the jury that just two cops could have framed Simpson:

> They have to prove that this wasn't tampered with beyond a reasonable doubt. When people tamper with evidence they try to do [th]is with some stealth, they try to cover their tracks, and as Mr. Cochran

pointed out, *it wouldn't take more than two bad police officers to do this* and a lot of people would look the other way.[43] [Emphasis added.]

Why did the defense do this? An article in the October 30th 1995 issue of *Newsweek* provided an explanation, centering on defense jury consultant Jo-Ellan Dimitrius:

> Dimitrius noticed that certain parts of the defense case didn't play too well. "Everybody knew that Mark Fuhrman had some significant problems and that Phil Vannatter was close behind," Dimitrius says. But the grandiose indictment of the LAPD is where people said, 'Nah, you've gone a little too far on that'." After a little "gentle tuning," as Dimitrius calls it, the defense lawyers hammered the two detectives for their "big lies" and dropped the notion of a widespread LAPD conspiracy.[44]

And yet, as I have shown above, the Bundy back gate evidence against Simpson simply *cannot* be attributed only to Fuhrman and Vannatter. The conspiracy *must* include those who were willing to perjure themselves about discovering it, pointing it out to others, or simply observing it. If Lange wouldn't be told by others what to say, can we conclude that his observation of blood on the back gate during the early morning hours of the 13th is an honest one? If Riske testified with candor, can we question the fact that he discovered the back gate blood with his powerful flashlight long before Fuhrman or Vannatter even knew double murder had been committed at 875 South Bundy? Does a "nice man" like Detective Phillips commit perjury in homicide cases?

Is the sort of perjury by these officers, required for the defense theory to be correct, so easily countenanced by the lawyers for O.J. Simpson? Is perjury only villainous if you lie about racial utterances made seven or eight years ago, as Mark Fuhrman may have done?

Inefficient Planting Scheme

There are various ways one might go about arranging for officers to testify about seeing blood that wasn't there. One possibility is simple and less risky; another possibility is rather complex and more risky.

In the first case, each testifying officer would be told simply to say that blood was pointed out to him by one person, presumably Vannatter or Fuhrman—these twin devils of deception could flip a coin to see who gets the credit of discovery. This is less risky for an officer like Riske (although pronounced 'risky', his name doesn't mean that he actually likes to take chances). He doesn't have to take responsibility for finding it or remembering who he supposedly showed it to and when he supposedly did this. Moreover, if he later gets cold feet he can either say "well, it looked like blood, but I wasn't sure" or even "I don't actually remember Fuhrman showing it to me". This latter option gives these cooperating officers an 'out' without causing the entire pyramid of testimony to crash. This simple case would also include finding a single spot of blood on the gate, rather than the complicated multiple blood stains which the various officers repeatedly testified to seeing.

In the second case, elaborate testimony has to be created. Riske and Terrazas find the blood and then are the first to show it to various officers who in turn are the first to show it to other officers. This situation also entails more risk, because once agreeing to be part of deception, it's hard to get out of it. Why would someone like Riske—whose only role in the conspiracy is presumably this perjury in acknowledging he saw the blood—actually agree to *finding* it? And each time he claims to have shown it to someone else, isn't that an additional act of perjury? Why would he assume that additional risk when he could insist that Fuhrman take responsibility for the discovery and then for the distribution of this information of a false find?

A Transfusion at the Gate

Let us now consider a different theory: there was blood on the back gate at Bundy, that this blood was left by the 'real killer', and was later replaced with Simpson's blood. This of course isn't what the defense argued—they insisted that the blood was never there until it was planted. The transfusion theory has its own problems:

- Why would the police want to waste time planting and then collecting such evidence when they already had preliminary DNA results which showed it was Simpson who had left the trail of blood drops moving away from the bodies? Why increase their risk? Why even bother?

- Wouldn't there be a danger in removing the original blood? If it is removed insufficiently, the DNA of the real killer could show up in testing. If the gate was washed extensively before the planting, that would be apparent in photos, and to the criminalist, and to defense experts who visited the area between June 13th and the day Dennis Fung collected the back gate stain, July 3rd.

- Why didn't they add a fingerprint? (New York state troopers have recently been convicted for doing just this.) Fingerprints are persuasive to juries, who find them easy to understand. This would have added another completely different form of evidence, enhancing the power of the case.

- How could the planter be sure the neighbors across the alley weren't watching?

CHAPTER 9

DNA on Trial

*Noise proves nothing. Often a hen who has merely laid an egg
cackles as if she had laid an asteroid.*

—Mark Twain

There is a Sherlock Holmes story—one of the best, "The
Norwood Builder"—in which a man fakes his own death, in
part by planting the blood of a couple of rabbits. At the
time that story was written, blood was blood if it looked like
blood. It was not possible for detectives to distinguish human
blood from animal blood, much less to identify different kinds of
human blood.

By 1901, great advances had been made, but human blood
was still human blood, with no distinction possible. Blood transfusions had been tried for centuries, but in many cases they were
fatal, and nobody understood why. In that year, however, the
Austrian scientist, Karl Landsteiner, proved that people were
divided into groups with different types of blood.

Landsteiner discovered that blood contains substances—
antigens and antibodies—which lead to dangerous clumping of
red cells whenever red cells of one type are added to red cells of
another type. Landsteiner named these 'blood groups' A, B, and
O. The following year, the AB group was discovered.

Since then, more than a dozen other ways of identifying and
classifying human blood have been found, the best known being
the division into Rh positive and Rh negative—also discovered by
Landsteiner, along with an associate, in 1940. The main practical
application of these classifications is that blood for transfusions

must come from persons who have blood types compatible with those of the recipients; otherwise, the transfusions will be harmful and probably deadly.

Tests for these blood types have now become commonplace and their results are usually undisputed. But such tests can never identify an individual human being with certainty. These tests—called *serological tests* because they are done on the part of the blood called 'serum'—can often show that a sample of blood could only have come from one in several hundred of the population, but never that the blood must have come from M.L. Rantala to the exclusion of all other individuals.

But now this situation has been revolutionized by the development of DNA testing.

The DNA Revolution

When you were conceived as a fertilized egg inside your mother's body, you were a single cell. That cell divided into two, which divided into four, eight, sixteen, and so forth. At this rate, it's not long before we get into the millions. Your body now consists of about a thousand billion cells.

During the twentieth century, scientists have made one of the most momentous discoveries of all time: almost every one of those thousand billion cells in your body contains a complete recipe for making you. Every time a cell divides to become two cells, each of the two has a complete copy of all the inscriptions for making the unique organism that is you. This 'recipe' specifies whether you will need glasses and at what age. It lays down whether you will have blue eyes or brown, whether you will be right- or left-handed, whether you can curl your tongue, or whether you will suffer from pattern baldness.

This 'complete recipe' is recorded on little pieces of a chemical substance called DNA. (The DNA is organized in strips called chromosomes; a teeny bit of a chromosome is called a gene.) The DNA, for instance, in your earlobe determines the individual shape of your earlobe, but it also contains the information specifying the relative sizes of your various organs, whether twinkies go straight to your thighs, whether your hair curls naturally, whether you are susceptible to kidney stones, whether you are able to taste phenylthiocarbamide, and a million other things about you.

The DNA in every cell of your body is identical to the DNA in every other cell of your body—and different to the DNA in every other person's body, unless they are your clone or identical twin.

The DNA in your body is a tiny amount, but it is made up of very long, thin strands packed with information. If the DNA in just one cell were to be unraveled and straightened out as a single long thread, it would be well over six feet long. If the DNA in all the cells of your body were laid end to end, it would extend to the Sun and back again.

The DNA 'recipe' specifies your facial appearance: in theory, from one of your cells, we could read off what your face looks like (subject to other influences like diet, scars, or the tendency of your language to modify the shape of your jaw).

At present, scientists are a long way from being able to read off a picture of your face from a single cell of your body, but that day will undoubtedly come. For the moment, the code in which the recipe for making you is written is far too complicated, and it will be decades at least before it is completely decoded. But for many purposes, this does not matter.

Cracking the Code

Consider the book you are now holding in your hands. It has a barcode on the back cover. This barcode is unique to this book. No other book, cereal box, or hand calculator has a barcode exactly like this one. To know that this barcode is the barcode of *O.J. Unmasked,* you do not have to know anything about the words on the pages. You don't even have to know the principles by which such barcodes are constructed.

Now, just suppose that the barcode was a complete instruction set for printing copies of *O.J. Unmasked*. This would mean that the barcode would consist of hundreds or thousands of lines, instead of a few dozen. And just suppose, also, that by looking under a microscope at any letter on any page of this book, you could read off the book's barcode. Then, by looking at just one letter, for example the last 'e' on the bottom line of page 57, you would be able to determine that this letter came from a copy of *O.J. Unmasked*. Notice that you would then not have to know anything about the *content* of *O.J. Unmasked* in order to make this identification. You wouldn't have to know what the barcode 'meant' in terms of words, sentences, and ideas. It would be enough to identify the barcode.

This is, roughly, the situation with DNA testing, except that forensic techniques are not yet good enough to work with a single cell, and it is not feasible to inspect every 'line' on the 'barcode'.

A few tell-tale 'markers' are usually enough. But given a few cells, such as white blood cells, from the same person, we know that each one of them contains the whole recipe, or instruction manual, for making just that person and no one else (except that person's clone or identical twin).

The Simpson Blood Evidence

In the wake of the June 12th murders, much evidence was collected on June 13th and June 14th. Additional evidence was collected later: the blood on the back gate was collected on July 3rd; blood on the socks found in Simpson's bedroom was observed on August 4th and collected even later; and a second collection of blood was made from the Bronco on August 26th.

The defense did little to dispute the identification of the blood evidence collected later, relying instead on the theory that it was planted by the police.

This leaves the evidence collected in the hours after the discovery of the bodies. Much of this incriminates Simpson, and includes blood from:

- The trail of blood drops to the left of the bloody shoeprints, this trail was identified by DNA tests to be the blood of Simpson.

- The Rockingham glove, which DNA tests showed to contain the blood of Nicole, Ron, and Simpson.

- The center console of the Bronco which was a combination of the blood of both Ron and Simpson.

- The bloody impression in the Bronco carpet, which was identified as Nicole's.

In response to this evidence, the defense accepted the DNA identification of Simpson. They did not dispute that the blood identified as O.J. Simpson's was indeed O.J. Simpson's blood, but they claimed that this blood got into the evidence samples through contamination. Evidence swatches containing the blood of the 'real killer' were so mishandled, they claimed, that the perpetrator's blood had completely degraded. Later, these swatches, according to the defense theory, were contaminated with Simpson's own blood, thus explaining why the DNA tests revealed a match with Orenthal James Simpson.

In support of this theory, the defense called Dr. John Gerdes as an expert witness. Gerdes has a Ph.D. in microbial genetics and microbiology and is the clinical director of a Denver laboratory which conducts medical diagnostic tests as well as paternity tests. Gerdes testified that he had no forensic experience. He has never collected a forensic sample, never tested a forensic sample, never attended a meeting of forensic scientists, and has never published a paper on any aspect of forensics.[1] Yet one of his professional specialties is to testify in criminal trials that the DQ-alpha PCR test is unreliable.

DNA Tests

Gerdes's testimony was almost exclusively concerned with only one of the several DNA testing procedures introduced by the prosecution. Tests of two major kinds were introduced: RFLP and PCR. RFLP tests use much more DNA than PCR tests and are generally far more discriminating. PCR tests are used on samples too small to subject to RFLP. Gerdes not only questioned the skill of PCR analysts at the LAPD but questioned the validity of the test itself.

The test in question is the DQ-alpha test, the oldest PCR test used in forensics.[2] Every time Gerdes has appeared as an expert witness in criminal cases, he has testified to the unreliability of the DQ-alpha test. He has not testified against the reliability of the RFLP tests. Eleven different stains in the Simpson case were tested using RFLP, including two stains from the Bundy murder scene—one of the stains on the back gate and the blood found on Ron's boot. An outline of the DQ-alpha PCR process and other DNA testing procedures is included in appendix 2.

Contamination

Early in his direct examination Gerdes testified to contamination at the LAPD lab:

Q   Have you an opinion, within a degree of scientific certainty, about contamination at the LAPD laboratory? ...
A   I found that the LAPD laboratory has [a] substantial contamination problem that is persistent and substantial.[3]

The media treatment of this conclusion was sadly typical of their superficial coverage of the Simpson case. Gerdes's conclusion was replayed on television again and again, without any serious attempt to evaluate or challenge it. Some programs which discussed the Simpson case regularly completely ignored the testimony of Gerdes. *Larry King Live* had only one program on the

Simpson case during the four days Gerdes was on the stand and that program dealt primarily with Detective Fuhrman.

Yet Gerdes's conclusion about contamination, generally accepted by people covering the trial, was based on speculation, vague, unsubstantiated possibilities, and misrepresentations of scientific issues. In fact, none of his explanations can account for the DNA results implicating Simpson in the murders, and tests he did not scrutinize actually disprove his theory.

The Korean Database: Contamination or a Dotty Theory?

The first thing Gerdes did to establish his theory that the LAPD lab was severely contaminated was to examine a series of DNA tests performed before the lab began typing DNA in criminal cases. Criminalists were given known samples of blood from a Korean database and asked to type them. The criminalists used the DQ-alpha DNA test, a PCR test which examines a tiny part of a blood gene.

Gerdes examined the Korean database DQ-alpha strips produced by LAPD analysts. Typing results are based on very dark dots which appear on the strip. These dots must be darker than the C dot (the control dot) to be considered a legitimate allele. In addition to these dark dots, Gerdes found several faint dots— every one of them fainter than the C dot. Some dots were so faint that it took considerable time for the man operating the overhead projector in the courtroom to place an arrow at the correct site. Gerdes concluded that almost every faint dot represented human DNA contamination. There are several points to be made about this conclusion:

- Gerdes conceded that things other than human DNA contamination could have caused these faint dots, but failed to acknowledge numerous other causes completely unrelated to contamination in his analysis.

- Gerdes *claimed* they were contamination, but never proved it. His testimony did not provide any arguments to contradict the scientific literature providing numerous noncontamination explanations. His testimony did not refer to any experiments which have established that such faint dots can only be contamination (there are no such experiments). Gerdes pooh-poohed the scientific research which has investigated the possibilities of contamination. This research literature has generally concluded that DNA typing is possible even with contamination, and moreover that contamination is quite rare.

- Even if the faint dots do represent contamination, in every single instance identified by Gerdes, *no typing error was ever made*. If contamination was present it was present in absolutely minute amounts. The so-called contamination was *always* of a degree so small that it did not produce a typeable result—the sample being tested always provided the correct, typeable results.

Other Explanations

Gerdes admitted that one particular artifact could cause faint dots to appear and that in the presence of this artifact, called DX, one could not conclude that a faint dot proved contamination.[4] Even here Gerdes undercounted the DX artifact and thereby overcounted what he claimed was contamination.

More importantly, there are numerous other explanations for these faint dots—explanations which do not include contamination of any kind. Several of the causes of faint dots are listed in the *AmpliType User Guide*, the PCR manual produced by the makers of the DQ-alpha test.[5] Other causes of faint dots are discussed in technical science literature.[6]

Some of these faint dots may be caused by subtypes of the 4 allele. The DQ-alpha strip contains a probe for the main 4 allele but none for its subtypes. Some of the 4 allele subtypes are sufficiently similar to other alleles that they may cross-hybridize causing faint dots.[7]

A much more common source of faint dots is procedural error. The temperature at which the hybridization takes place is critical. An error of just one degree is enough to cause faint dots to appear on the typing strip.[8] The wrong concentration of salt in either the hybridization solution or the wash solution can similarly cause faint dots to appear. Other causes of faint dots include a stringent wash time which is too short or the use of too much DNA in the amplification.[9]

The *AmpliType User Guide* warns that faint dots should be "interpreted with caution".[10] Gerdes threw all caution to the wind, however, as he bravely marched on finding 'contamination' in everything he saw. Caution demands that one find stronger evidence for a hypothesis than just "a wispy little thing", as Kary Mullis, the Nobel Prize–winning inventor of PCR, once described a possible contaminant.[11]

Lack of Proof

Given the numerous other possible causes for the faint dots, it is important to note that Gerdes never proved even a single instance of contamination in the typing of the Korean database samples.[12]

Moreover, when asked about the scientific literature concerned with this issue, he was at times derisive of the people who did research in a field where he has not performed even a single experiment.[13]

Prosecutor George Clarke asked Gerdes if he had read a particular paper by two FBI scientists, Catherine Theisen Comey and Bruce Budowle.[14] Gerdes replied:

> Again it is a demonstration paper. What they dealt with in that paper in terms of contamination is one experiment where five tubes were opened on a bench top. They scratched their head over the tubes, closed them up and showed there was no contamination.
>
> That is a demonstration. Demonstrates that under those limited number of samples they did not get contamination. From that they conclude that contamination is not an issue. That I disagree with.[15]

Gerdes routinely dismissed scientific literature with the term, "demonstration paper", a term unknown to science, to insinuate that such papers reporting scientific findings were somehow inferior. It is interesting to note just what this Comey and Budowle paper, which reports on numerous experiments, does demonstrate:

- Dried bloodstains left in sunlight still gave correct test results after three weeks.

- Dried bloodstains typed correctly even after being left twenty weeks in a greenhouse, some stains left in complete darkness and others subjected to day-night light cycles.

- Blood was placed on swatches saturated with various bacteria, including *E. coli*, left to sit for five days at room temperature, and the correct typing result was still obtained.

- Blood was placed on swatches containing numerous chemical contaminants, including gasoline, motor oil, lye, and bleach, left to sit for five days, and the correct typing result was still obtained.

- Dried blood on a swatch was coughed on for a minute and this did not affect the accuracy of the typing results.

- Thirty-four different substrates—surfaces on which a sample has been deposited—were each tested with five different DNA isolation protocols, only three failed to provide any result at all, and no incorrect typing result was observed.

- A worker scratched her head for thirty seconds over open test tubes containing dried blood swatches and this did not affect the typeable results (this appears to be the only part of the Comey and Budowle paper which Gerdes is talking about—there were five test tubes used in this experiment).

Far more than one experiment with five test tubes, this article is a cornucopia of contamination investigation in forensic circumstances. The paper additionally provides results on still more contamination experiments, as well as artifacts, faint dots, procedural errors, and issues related to mixed samples.

Not only do FBI scientists Comey and Budowle conduct each experiment several times, they use negative controls to provide support for each conclusion, and they also quantify precisely all the variables that it is possible to quantify, making independent replication of their work possible. This mere "demonstration paper" demonstrates exemplary scientific technique.

On the other hand, Gerdes proved nothing.

Database Results Correct and Unaffected

Even if we accept that all or just some of the faint dots identified by Gerdes represent contamination, each and every example identified by Gerdes was very faint. Not one of these faint dots caused the analyst to make an incorrect typing result. As the scientists say, these barely perceptible dots "did not confound the data". The true information was clear and typeable, the possible contamination was weak, untypeable, and never compromised a single result.

From Contamination to Error

After testifying about the contamination he saw in the Korean database typing strips, Gerdes then proceeded to claim that analysts at the LAPD crime lab had made errors when they were tested and that these errors were caused by contamination. Worse, he said, these errors were not acknowledged by anyone in the lab as errors. On direct examination he described in serious tones five errors made by LAPD laboratory analysts.

But a different picture emerged on cross-examination. Prosecutor George Clarke went through each of the strips where Gerdes claimed LAPD analysts had made a mistake.

Error Number One

In the first instance of what Gerdes called an error due to contamination, prosecutor Clarke pointed out that the controls failed. Gerdes agreed with Clarke that because of the failed controls the results should not be reported, nor were they reported:

Q   As far as that control is concerned, if that is not negative, the result shouldn't be reported, correct?
A   That's correct.
Q   And in fact the 1.3, 4 shouldn't be reported because of that activity?
A   That's correct.
Q   Was this result ever reported in a report somewhere?
A   No.[16]

Gerdes then admitted that the analyst did the test again, which was the scientifically appropriate action.[17]

Error Number Two, Déjà Vu

Gerdes's second example of mistyping due to contamination was the *same sample* as the first mistake. The analyst repeated the procedure. On this second try the controls failed again. This, too, was considered a mistake by Gerdes, even though the analyst knew the strip could not be considered typeable due to the failure of the controls.

Q   *Is it your testimony that from this document Erin Riley conclusively established, for purposes of reporting results, that that was a 1.3, 4?*
A   *No. My testimony is that that result was recorded as a type that was an incorrect type as a result of the contamination that was to found in the lab.*
Q   Wasn't Erin Riley—let me rephrase. Didn't she rerun this sample again because of that activity in the negative control?
A   Yes.
Q   Wasn't that the right thing to do scientifically?
A   Yes.[18] [Emphasis added.]

Although Gerdes listed these two cases as mistakes, he was not asked during direct examination whether the sample was tested one more time. It was. This time the controls worked and

Gerdes admitted that the analyst got the correct results. Clarke stressed that by the very nature of the procedures followed by the LAPD analyst, the sample was re-tested until all the controls showed that the protocol had been performed properly:

Q   *She got a correct answer when the controls operated properly, correct?*
A   *Correct.*
Q   *That correct answer is not noted in your chart, is it?*
A   *My chart only records additional alleles. No, it is not. ...*
Q   *Incidentally, if such an incident occurred in your laboratory with activity showing in the negative controls, would you want your analyst to rerun that sample?*
A   *Yes.*
Q   *So Erin Riley did just what you would want her to do with these samples or this sample if she were working in your laboratory?*
A   *That's correct.*[19]

It is not just odd for Gerdes to call these two cases typing mistakes due to contamination, it is scientifically inappropriate. It may be correct to say that in the process of preparing the sample the first two times contamination could have occurred, *but no mistyping result occurred.* The controls alerted the analyst to the problem—that is why controls are employed. These cases clearly illustrate that far from making typing mistakes due to contamination, LAPD technicians recognized when a problem had occurred and took the appropriate steps. When a result consistent with contamination was observed, the test was re-conducted until the test worked properly and no contamination was present. In the end they got the correct result. At no time was there any danger that an incorrect typing result would be reported. A defense which abhors a rush to judgment should value a laboratory that repeats experiments until they perform properly.

For Gerdes to call these 'mistakes' is very misleading. What would we think of a householder who complained bitterly about the dreadful botch committed by the decorator in fitting carpeting, even though all the carpeting fit perfectly, because the decorator made some of the measurements more than once (without billing the householder any more or taking any longer than stipulated to finish the job)? We would no doubt view such a householder as eccentric.

Error Number Three

Gerdes's third example of error came from a rape sample. In

rape samples, a scientist needs to separate the woman's epithelial cells from the man's sperm cells. This is done through a process called differential extraction. In the case Gerdes discussed, both the epithelial fraction (the woman's portion) and the sperm fraction (the man's portion), when tested, resulted in the same genotype being observed—that of the woman. The male's genotype did not appear on the strip. Prosecutor George Clarke suggested through his questioning that this phenomenon is common in DNA rape tests, but Gerdes would not budge; he continued to maintain the test was an example of a mistake:

Q   Dr. Gerdes, with respect to a rapist, isn't it the case that in some cases they don't leave enough DNA?

A   That is true, but in the case of a differential extraction the analyst is supposed to look at the specimen and observe sperm before they go ahead with the differential extraction, and if there is sperm there you should find the allele from the sperm and in this case that didn't happen.

Q   Well, is it your testimony that a trained forensic DNA analyst would look at those results and conclude that the 1.2, 4, came from somebody other than the victim?

A   They would most likely conclude that it came from the victim, the 1.2, 4. ...

Q   *Dr. Gerdes, a trained analyst would look at those results and they wouldn't exclude a 1.2, 1.3 as being a donor of sperm in that sample, would they?*

A   *No, they wouldn't,* and this person is a 1.2, 1.3. That is an error.[20] [Emphasis added.]

Gerdes's answers are instructive. When pressed, he sometimes reverted to attacking *the test*, rather than sticking with his attacks on the LAPD analysts. But even if the DQ-alpha test is flawed for rape samples, that is a special circumstance irrelevant to the Simpson case. Moreover, Gerdes was just plain wrong when he claimed that sperm which can be viewed microscopically must necessarily type on a DQ-alpha test. In fact, in low enough amounts, such visible sperm will not produce a typeable result.[21] At the end of this line of questioning, Gerdes still maintained that it was an error because the proper genotype didn't occur, while admitting that *the results would not lead a trained analyst to make an error which would exclude the actual rapist.*

Error Number Four, *Déjà Vu All Over Again*

The fourth typing 'error' due to contamination identified by Gerdes was the same sample as in error number three. After examining the results on number three, the analysts chose to do it again. On this occasion, there again was not enough sperm in the sample to provide a typeable male genotype. Gerdes called this another 'error' and again maintained that if sperm were observed microscopically, then the sperm should be typeable using DQ-alpha.

'Errors' number three and four are interesting because, of course, they have nothing to do with contamination. Gerdes's testimony is relevant to the Simpson defense only insofar as it shows the possibility of contamination. But these two so-called errors do nothing to advance that argument.

Error Number Five

The fifth and last typing 'error' identified by Gerdes was a sample consisting of human hairs. The DQ-alpha type of the hair root was correctly identified by the analyst. But a different genotype was observed on the hair shaft. Because the genotype was different on the hair shaft, Gerdes declared this a contamination error.

It is the hair root which contains the DNA. Hair shafts consist of dead cells and are not in general a source of DNA. So Clarke asked Gerdes if this DNA could have come from the person who plucked the hair:

Q If somebody else plucked a hair out, had trouble plucking it out or whatever, had to deal with the hair manually, if enough of that went on, couldn't you detect the DNA of the person who pulled the hair?
A It certainly is possible that in the manipulation of—of that item in the LAPD by the way they manipulated it, they introduced foreign DNA there.[22]

Gerdes admitted that the root typed correctly. He acknowledged that you sometimes find foreign DNA on a hair shaft. Nonetheless he not only calls this an error but insists that it is contamination.

Gerdes's position should be contrasted with that of Simpson defense consultant Edward Blake, who was never called by the defense to sit in the blue chair and testify. Blake has done extensive research on DQ-alpha typing of hairs. In some cases he has found information on the hair shaft to be quite important.[23]

What the So-Called 'Errors' Tell Us

Examining the errors which Gerdes claimed occurred in the LAPD lab, several things become clear:

- The number of 'errors', using his generous and idiosyncratic definition, is very small indeed, only five.

- Since 'errors' one and two were the same sample, and errors three and four were the same sample, Gerdes found only three different samples with contamination.

- Two 'errors' concern differential extraction in rape cases, and problems of this sort simply are not contamination. Specifically, these problems are the result of the inherent difficulty in completely separating sperm from epithelial tissue. Moreover, the specific problems encountered in rape samples have no bearing on the Simpson case.

- In the two cases where no one disputed that contamination was present ('errors' one and two), the LAPD analysts detected the contamination via the controls. They followed the correct procedure and retested until the protocol was completed properly—contamination did not result in any mistyping.

How to Testify with Statistics

Gerdes conducted a nearly unprecedented, comprehensive examination of virtually all the LAPD DQ-alpha strips run by analysts at the LAPD lab. The number of strips was over a thousand. This included the Korean database strips and the testing strips already discussed. He presented to the jury several charts. One was entitled "Runs: Percent with Contamination by Month, May, 1993, through August of 1994". It looked approximately like the graph shown in Figure 1.

In figure 1, the x-axis (the bottom of the chart) lists each month in chronological order. The y-axis (the left-hand side of the chart) represents the percentage of PCR runs which had one or more contaminated strips. A 'run' was defined by Gerdes as all PCR tests done on a single day.

The essential point in constructing this graph was that any single faint dot on a given day meant that the entire run was considered contaminated. So whether there was one faint dot out of a hundred strips on a given day or two faint dots on the only two strips done in a day, both of these days would be measured as a run with contamination.

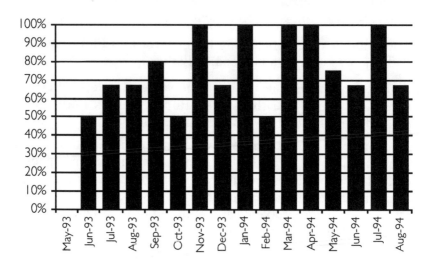

Figure 1. Percentage of contaminated runs per month

Similarly, if in the course of an entire month PCR tests were only done on one day, and only one strip was identified as containing contamination, this would mean that the percent with contamination for that month would be computed as 100 percent.

In the first month, May 1993, forty-five strips were run using PCR and Gerdes did not identify any contamination.

In June 1993, the LAPD did four runs on four different days. Gerdes determined by viewing each of these runs "in the context of one another" that two of these runs were contaminated.

What he said was that a possible contamination on a single strip renders the entire run contaminated. But in some cases, he declared contamination even when a single strip could not be determined by him to contain any contamination. This is an instance where Gerdes undercounts the DX artifact, the phenomenon which causes certain faint dots which Gerdes himself admits is not contamination.[24] By undercounting the DX artifact, he ensures that the number of contaminated strips will be larger.

Flaws in Gerdes's Contamination Theory

Some of the problems with this graph, and the conclusions drawn from it, can be easily summarized:

- No contamination is actually established, as is discussed in the previous section.

- A single instance of possible contamination renders an entire run contaminated by Gerdes's definition. This use of a single instance to characterize an entire group of strips as contaminated masks the large number of strips which show no problems whatever.

- Gerdes measures the percentage of contamination when the truly relevant statistic would be the *degree* of contamination on any strip. For example, if 50 percent of the strips were contaminated so lightly that no typing error occurred, this would not be a particular problem. But if only 5 percent of the strips were contaminated and they all resulted in typing errors, that would be serious.

- In previous cases, Gerdes had never examined all the strips from any other lab, yet on the basis of limited knowledge about other labs, he was prepared to draw a strong conclusion about contamination at LAPD. This conclusion was not based on comparable data from other labs.[25]

- Presenting the information in this form could result in the paradox that the number of contaminated strips could be declining over time but the percentage of contaminated runs could be increasing. One way this could happen would be if the number of strips per run were increasing and the number of contaminated strips remained constant.

- Some months have a very small number of runs, others have a large number of runs. It may not be appropriate to evaluate the data by month.

Gerdes maintained that his chart showed a build-up of contamination. However, analysis of the data itself doesn't support such a conclusion. Moreover, even if there was a 'build-up', Gerdes only established that there are more faint dots over time. *He never established that the contamination in any case was so significant as to affect the typing results.*

To show how easy it is to prepare a chart which supports any given conclusion, Gerdes's information could just as well be presented as in figure 2, which contains all of his information, and is presented not by month but by quarter.[26]

Looking at the data presented in this manner, one could conclude that contamination was going down at the LAPD laboratory during the time the first evidence in the Simpson case was handled by the LAPD scientists. This chart is based on exactly the same data as the chart Gerdes prepared for the jury, but this new chart supports a conclusion opposite to that of Gerdes: the frequency of contamination is falling in the LAPD lab. Of course, this presentation of the data is just as misleading as Gerdes's chart.[27]

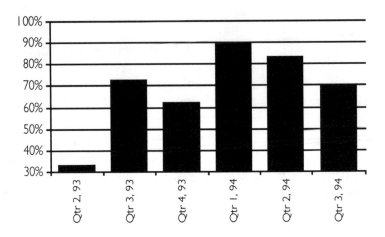

Figure 2. Percentage of contaminated runs per quarter

Causes of the Contamination

The contamination Gerdes maintained was present in the LAPD lab could come from three different sources:

- PCR carryover contamination (amplicon contamination)
- Extraction procedures and chemicals
- Mishandling (including both at the crime scene and the lab)

Let's look at each of these in turn.

Amplicon Contamination

The PCR technique creates millions of copies of DNA molecules even from a very small starting sample. The PCR product is new DNA created by the DNA synthesis in each cycle of the PCR process. Because each end of the PCR product is complementary to the primers used in the PCR reaction, each PCR product is capable by itself of giving rise to another PCR product.[28]

One of the problems with PCR is the unique nature of PCR product contamination. An amplicon is a single molecule of PCR product. Inadvertent placement of a minute number of amplicons in a reaction where they don't belong can cause trouble. This is because the PCR product is only 242 base pairs of DNA whereas the human genome is three billion base pairs. So an individual PCR product weighs less than an individual genome. Therefore equal amounts, by weight, will have vastly more copies of the amplicons than copies of the human genome. Thus the amplicons will swamp out the other sample in the PCR reaction because there are so many more copies of amplicons than human DNA.

Gerdes considered amplicon contamination to be a potential problem at the LAPD. He addressed in particular the way PCR products moved from one part of the lab to another.

PCR Work Flow at LAPD and DOJ

Gerdes testified that it was important to have a one-way work flow when performing PCR because this reduces the risk of cross-over contamination. Scheck guided Gerdes through a description of the LAPD PCR facilities, which Gerdes had visited in preparation for his testimony. Extraction takes place in the serology lab at the Piper Tech building. PCR sample preparation, amplification, and hybridization are done at Parker Center. Samples are then taken back to Piper Tech.

Q Is bringing the amplicons or the PCR product back into Piper Tech consistent with the process of having a one-way work flow?

A No, because, you see, you've gone from low DNA and right at this step, you've created high DNA by amplifying it, and this is at a different location, totally different building. But now they turn around and they go back to this building. *So they're carrying back high levels of DNA into the area where there should be only low levels of DNA.*

Q Are you familiar with the setup at the Department of Justice in terms of the flow of work?

A Yes.

Q Do you recall the testimony of Gary Sims with respect to stating that after amplification, that PCR product never leaves the amplification room in that laboratory?

A Yes.

Q Is that true here at LAPD?

A No.

Q Is this a good and sound laboratory practice?

A No.[29]

On cross-examination, Gerdes was confronted with photographs of the LAPD PCR facilities, facilities which he himself had visited. He had to admit that the distance between the evidence handling area and the PCR products area *was the same at both LAPD and the Department of Justice* because PCR products brought back to Piper Tech are taken to a room far away from the extraction site. The one-way flow is just the same at these two labs, and Gerdes ought to have known it because he had visited LAPD on two separate occasions:

Q   You testified yesterday that following amplification of DNA, amplified DNA, that is, was brought back to the Los Angeles Police Department in the same area, correct?

Mr. Scheck: Objection, again. Misstates the testimony.

The Court: Overruled.

The Witness: I stated that it was brought back to that same location. It is not specifically the same room, but it is the same location.

Q   Okay. So it is not brought back to the same room; isn't that correct?

A   That's correct.

Q   You have been to the Department of Justice?

A   Yes.

Q   When they are done amplifying DNA, where do they take it?

A   It remains in the amplification room.

Q   Where is the amplification room in relationship to the extraction room?

A   I believe the extraction room is in a—is down a hall and in a large room near the entrance of the building and the amplification room would be a different room. You know, basically in the same building, though.

Q   Okay. What are they separated by? How many feet, approximately, Department of Justice?

A   If I recall correctly, the hall would be fifty to a hundred feet perhaps.

Q   ... In your opinion is that [the Piper Tech product gel electrophoresis room] the same area as DNA extraction is conducted at Piper Tech as reflected in the top three photographs?

A   It is in the same building. It is not the exact same room.

Q   What separates those two areas?

A   There is a hallway of—I don't know how long. I don't recall. Fifty feet perhaps.

Q   There is more than a hallway, isn't there?

A   Well, there are doors into each of these labs as well.

Q   Aren't they separate secured rooms?

A   I believe they are separate rooms, yes.

Q In your opinion is that the same area, that is the product gel electrophoresis area, as the extraction area?

A It is—

Mr. Scheck: Objection, asked and answered.

The Court: Overruled.

The Witness: It is not the same area. ...

Q Yesterday you described these materials as being brought back to the
same area at Piper Tech, correct?

A Yes.

Q Today you have conceded that in fact those areas, that is, the extraction room and the product gel electrophoresis room, are not the
same area, correct?

A They are not the same room.

Q Well, they are not the same area, are they?

A I guess not.[30]

One must be troubled by Gerdes's original claim on direct
that "they're carrying back high levels of DNA into the area where
there should be only low levels of DNA". It is hard to see how the
defense could not be deliberately attempting to mislead on this
issue, since they had tried to raise this very point months earlier
in the trial. Cross-examining Dr. Robin Cotton, director of Cellmark Diagnostics which did some of the DNA tests in the case,
Peter Neufeld asked about separation of DNA products at LAPD:

Q And by the way, in your laboratory [Cellmark], to avoid the possibility
of getting that amplified product back to the original location, I believe
you said that you have a series of different rooms that the item of
evidence moves through and it's a one-way street; is that correct?

A Yes.

Q Do you have any knowledge, Dr. Cotton, as to whether or not the
Los Angeles Police Department laboratory—

The Court: Sustained.[31]

A judge who was very permissive throughout the trial could
instantly see that this line of questioning was inappropriate for
that witness, even without an objection from the prosecution.

Frequent Flying Amplicons

For amplicons to have been the source of all DNA test
matches to O.J. Simpson, these amplicons would have had to be,
in the words of Marcia Clark, co-conspirators. This is because had
the amplicons landed on any of the swatches attributed to the

victims, a clear and strong signal on tests of those swatches would have been identified as Simpson's, too. (This might cause a lazy thinker to imagine that the evidence showed that the perpetrator had just walked away from his own murder.)

In addition, two amplicons for each locus tested would have to deposit themselves specifically on the swatches attributed to the murderer (because we have two alleles at each locus: one from our mother and one from our father). Taken together, the Bundy blood drops were subjected to thirty-four PCR tests. So for amplicon contamination to explain the results at all of the labs, thirty-four pairs of amplicons had to drop on the 'real murderer's' swatches, and not just in any random combination. The *right* seven pairs had to fall on each of the Bundy blood drop swatches tested with the seven different PCR tests and the *right* six pairs had to fall on the Bundy blood drop swatches tested with six PCR tests. The odds are nothing short of outlandish that of all the amplicons in the laboratory the only ones which caused mis-typing were those which paired themselves up to match O.J.'s genotypes for all the PCR tests used and these pairs chose to settle themselves only on swatches which could be attributed to the killer.

Even Gerdes admitted under cross-examination that if multiple genes are tested, then the likelihood that the typing result is due to amplicon carry-over contamination is low:

Q   ... As far as contamination is concerned, isn't it true that if you use a second gene, a third gene and a fourth gene, that the likelihood of all of them being contaminated is pretty low?

A   Again, it depends on the source of contamination. If the contamination is due to cross-contamination, that is the transfer that we talked about early on when samples are handled, that is going to be repeatedly typed, no matter how many genes you look at, as the same DNA.

Q   Let's talk about carry-over contamination. Is what I just said to you correct?

A   In terms—in the sense of carry-over, yes.[32]

But this amplicon theory to explain DNA matches with Simpson isn't just highly unlikely, it is out of the question. The evidence was typed using tests at other laboratories. Cellmark used the Polymarker PCR test and the California Department of Justice used the D1S80 PCR test.

The gaping hole in the amplicon contamination theory is that the LAPD does not conduct any D1S80 PCR tests. The significance of this is that the LAPD *has no D1S80 amplicons*. The LAPD simply had no way, even if they had tried, to place D1S80 amplicons in O.J.'s DNA on those swatches.

Extraction Procedures and Chemicals

Gerdes also considered the PCR extraction protocols at the LAPD to be suspect. Extraction is the first part of the PCR typing procedure. This is where the DNA is purified and separated from the bloodstain and the swatch.

The Stir over Chelex

Special chemicals are used to perform these DNA extraction protocols. Gerdes took particular interest in the extraction chemicals of LAPD analyst Collin Yamauchi, who performed DQ-alpha testing on some of the evidence items.

Gerdes made a fuss over the failure of the LAPD crime lab to aliquot their Chelex solution. An aliquot is a small volume removed from a larger volume, and taken away for further use. Gerdes proclaimed that Yamauchi's large bottle of Chelex, which appeared to have been in the lab for months, created unacceptable risks of contamination. However, Gerdes must have known that it is a technically difficult proposition to aliquot a solution of Chelex. Not only that, the *AmpliType User Guide* specifically resists advocating such a procedure. Instead, the recommended protocol is to remove an aliquot from the master bottle (the bottle which got Gerdes so upset) when needed, place it in a clean beaker, and remove the amounts needed for each DNA extraction from the beaker.[33] In this way, an analyst never places lab tools inside the Chelex bottle itself, which is how Gerdes imagines potential contamination would occur.

Thus, the aliquots are made just prior to the time of use. Gerdes's frustrations over the large bottle of Chelex he observed is similar to crying over spilled milk. A generous amount of Chelex is meant to be placed in the beaker at the time of use with the unused portion simply thrown away.

Extraction Distraction

Gerdes testified on direct examination that the handling of samples on June 13th and 14th by Collin Yamauchi during the extraction phase of PCR was in violation of various forensic protocols:

Q   Now, are there rules or practices, to your knowledge, in the various protocols for handling samples in forensic labs in other DNA laboratories with respect to handling a reference sample in the same location and in the same period as evidence samples?

Mr. Clarke: Objection, no foundation.

The Court: Overruled.

The Witness: Yes, there are definite protocols for that.

Q   And what are those protocols and what is your understanding of those practices? What are the rules?

A   The rules are that you never handle a reference sample at the same time as any evidence.

Q   Now, when you say "at the same time," what are we talking about? Are we talking about—could you please describe that.

A   … Well, "same time" means in the same setting I guess is the way I would describe it, and that doesn't mean that it is in a sequence of events. It means that you don't have—you have a separation in time by a matter of a span of at least, you know, twenty minutes or a half an hour.

There is no really exact time period, *but the way it is described in these protocols*, is that you handle the reference sample, you put it away, *you bleach down, you totally clean up*, you allow a period of time and then you can handle evidence.[34] [Emphasis added.]

During cross-examination, Clarke showed how correct he was to object to Scheck's question. Gerdes's reply demonstrated his answer was not based on his knowledge of forensic protocols, but on his own peculiar view of what ought to be done:

Q   Do you recall also describing that after a reference sample has had DNA extracted from it, that there should be a clean-up with bleach of that area where that is taking place and then evidence samples can be extracted? Do you recall that testimony?

Mr. Scheck: Objection, misstates the testimony in terms of the specifics.

The Court: Overruled.

The Witness: I recall that testimony.

Q   What forensic protocol says that?

A   That all—all—the TWGDAM guidelines and a variety of protocols from individual labs that I have read specifically state that reference samples should be handled at a separate time and place than the evidence items.

Q   But as far as this procedure of reference samples, cleaning the area with bleach and then extracting DNA from evidence samples, what forensic protocol requires that?

A   Well, it is amazing. None of them say it that specifically. Those are
     pretty common sense things, though, if you are a microbiologist.[35]

Prosecutor George Clarke asked Gerdes again if he could cite
any protocol at all which calls for the Gerdes treatment:

Q   Dr. Gerdes, what forensic protocol says to do those things?
A   There is no forensic protocol that specifically says to do those things.[36]

Not only was Gerdes misleading on direct examination about
the existence of such forensic protocols, but he was simply wrong
in suggesting that diluted bleach can do anything to avoid the
problem of cross-contamination of human DNA. Bleach kills
bacteria but it does not destroy human DNA. An FBI study subjected forensic-type samples to various environmental insults. In
one part of the study, swatches with equal amounts of full-
strength bleach and human blood were left for five days. Even
after five days the human DNA was still correctly typeable using
the DQ-alpha test.[37] Concerned as he is with cross-contamination
and given his claim that he is well acquainted with the forensic
literature, Gerdes should have known this.

Failed Extraction Theory

Gerdes may well have been correct about some general problems of extraction contamination. But these problems simply
don't advance the defense argument that LAPD handling resulted
in contamination which affected the results of the other two
laboratories testing the evidence.

Any extraction-based contamination at LAPD would only
have affected those swatches tested at the LAPD. Gerdes himself
conceded this:

Q   Dr. Gerdes, isn't it true that what you described yesterday, actually day
     before yesterday, about what might have happened to those samples
     that went to Cellmark and DOJ as far as DNA extraction cross-
     contamination could not have happened?
A   I wouldn't state it—if you restrict it to only the extraction stage, that is
     true.
Q   You have described the extraction stage as one of those stages that
     cross-contamination can occur, correct?
A   That's correct.
Q   It could not have happened with the Cellmark and DOJ samples,
     correct?
A   Not at the extraction stage.[38]

Contamination from Handling

By closing argument the defense came to rely on contamination during evidence handling as the explanation for why so much DNA evidence yielded multiple, significant matches to O.J. Simpson. Barry Scheck's mantra in his argument to the jury was "garbage in, garbage out." A primary source of support for this was the testimony of Gerdes.

The defense claimed that the handling of evidence on June 13th and June 14th by Dennis Fung, Andrea Mazzola, and Collin Yamauchi caused the evidence swatches which contained the highly degraded blood of the real killer to be cross-contaminated with fresh, high-concentration blood from Simpson's reference sample or from the Rockingham blood trail (also composed of Simpson's blood).

Gerdes testified that the effect of cross-contamination might be aided by a 'carrier'. By carrier, Gerdes meant additional DNA that won't be detected by PCR because it is nonhuman, but by virtue of its abundance makes the small contaminant easier to isolate. In the case of the Bundy blood drops, under the assumption that they were completely degraded, the swatches would be full of bacterial DNA. Gerdes said this could serve as a carrier.

The significance of this to Gerdes is that bacterial DNA might be present in much larger amounts than the original human DNA which it has so completely eaten, according to the defense degradation theory. Hence, if later, such as in the lab, a tiny amount of human blood should find itself on the same sample, then at each stage of the extraction procedure where a little bit of DNA could be lost, it would be more likely that the bacterial DNA would be lost since it is present in such excess. So he had no trouble convincing himself that the Bundy blood swatches could have been contaminated with Simpson's blood even though the substrate controls (which would not be rife with bacterial DNA) showed no such contamination.

How did handling contamination happen? The defense maintained it occurred in the room where Collin Yamauchi worked. On June 14th, before handling the Bundy blood drop swatches, he opened Simpson's reference vial. When doing this some blood spilled and also some may have been dispersed in the air as an aerosol. According to the defense, this aerosol contaminated the Bundy blood drop swatches as well as the Rockingham glove.

The next day, the defense suggested that the near simultaneous handling of the reference samples from Nicole and Ron, the evidence from Rockingham, and the samples from the Bronco resulted in cross-contamination. In this case, Gerdes said he saw evidence that the reference samples of Nicole and Ron had been contaminated with Simpson's blood from one of the Rockingham swatches.

High–Low or Low–High?

These cross-contamination theories of the defense have several problems. The first is that the cross-contamination seems to operate in two opposite directions, depending upon the result the defense wishes to suggest.

The mode of transfer which resulted in Simpson's reference blood being on the Bundy blood trail swatches was a 'high to low' transfer. This means that a source high in DNA (the reference vial) contaminated a source low in DNA (the Bundy blood swatches). When tested, the low source drops out and only the high source is measured. This, the defense said, explains all the DNA matches to Simpson on every one of the Bundy blood drops, no matter which lab tested them.

But the very next day, the contamination proceeded in the opposite direction. Now the defense said that a lower volume DNA swatch—one of the Rockingham blood drops containing Simpson's blood—contaminated the high-volume DNA swatches containing Nicole's and Ron's fresh reference blood. The nature of the cross-contamination, moving from high to low one day and low to high another day, is clearly not only contradictory but *ad hoc*.

Contamination Takes a Rest

The second problem with the defense cross-contamination theory is that it has a dramatic effect on DNA typing results only when the swatches of the perpetrator are involved. The real killer benefits from the contamination, Simpson is inculpated, but nothing else is affected.

This can be seen from an examination of Item 42. Item 42 is a sample of blood taken from the large pool of blood around Nicole's body. When Yamauchi used PCR on this blood, he observed dots identifying Nicole. But the C dot was so faint that he and others in the lab declared the result inconclusive. This is highly suggestive of two things:

- It is very unlikely that the Bundy blood drops were completely or nearly completely degraded. Being single drops, they would have dried quite rapidly after they fell on the walkway. Nicole's pool of blood, being so large in volume, stayed wet far longer. Bacteria need moisture to grow, so bacterial degradation in the pool of Nicole's blood would have been significantly greater than bacterial degradation in the Bundy blood drops. Yet the sample from the blood pool was just *slightly* too degraded to provide a typeable result. The actual DNA results on the Bundy blood drops are consistent with samples experiencing less degradation than the blood in the pool around Nicole.

- Where's the contamination of Item 42? Since this blood came from around Nicole's body, which had bled profusely, it would be fantastic to imagine that this was someone else's blood which just happened to be contaminated with Nicole's blood. So the dots on the DQ-alpha strip which represented Nicole's genotype could not be due to contamination. Yet here we have Gerdes's perfect carrier swatch: a piece of cotton cloth full of degraded DNA just waiting for some DNA of greater volume to fall upon it. The greater volume DNA declined the invitation.

No Contamination Signature

The idea that there was contamination on such a massive scale as to affect so much evidence without the contamination causing any peculiar results makes no sense. Had Item 42 typed as O.J. Simpson, for instance, that surely would have been a clear signal that something was wrong. But there is nothing strange or remarkable about the test results. As it happens, one of Simpson's lawyers, William Thompson, pointed out in a paper accepted for publication the very month of the murders, that false matches due to sample handling errors should at least in some cases "produce improbable results that signal the possibility of an error."[39] In a case with so much DNA evidence, one would have thought at least one such case would have appeared had contamination really caused the typing results identifying Simpson.

Rather than being improbable, in fact, the test results are remarkably consistent:

> ... if the 4 allele [on the steering wheel of the Bronco] did not come from a 1.3, 4-donor [Goldman], this is the only allele in the more than 400 alleles among the 45 stains that could not have come from the principals. Otherwise all the alleles in every stain are contained in the

DNA profiles of the principals.[40]

A Once-in-a-Lifetime Event

The defense theory of cross-contamination was meant to explain why the Bundy blood drops and other pieces of evidence produced DNA matches with Simpson even though (on the defense theory) it wasn't Simpson's blood at the crime scene.

But for all of Gerdes's testimony of contamination at the LAPD, he never once found an example of mistyping due to contamination! 'Contamination', which was always faint and never affected the results, mushroomed just at the time of the murders of Nicole Brown and Ron Goldman. Suddenly, this contamination caused mistyping of twenty-two different swatches containing the Bundy blood drops, as well as the Rockingham glove.

Not only did Gerdes fail to prove this had ever happened before at the LAPD, but there is no evidence that forensic DNA typing results used in *any trial* have ever been incorrect.

One of forensic DNA's biggest critics recently declared that he now supports the use of DNA in the courtroom. Eric Lander had been vociferous in his attacks on forensic DNA and served once as an expert witness for the defense in a criminal case tried by Simpson lawyers Barry Scheck and Peter Neufeld.[41] But before the Simpson trial began, he joined with Bruce Budowle, previously one of his intellectual foes on this issue, to write an article declaring the "DNA fingerprinting dispute laid to rest".[42] Lander and Budowle concede that there were problems in the early days of forensic DNA, including contaminated samples, but even with these problems, "there is no evidence that these technical failings resulted in any wrongful convictions."[43]

Serology Solves the Case

In addition to the vast amount of DNA evidence introduced at trial, some conventional serological testing was performed. One piece of evidence tested was Item 49, one of the Bundy blood drops. The serological results were all consistent with O.J. Simpson. Prosecutor Clarke asked Gerdes about the serological tests:

Q If conventional serological techniques were used in this case and results were obtained from stains from genetic markers other than the DNA markers, don't those constitute additional cross-checks of results?

A   Yes.
Q   But you didn't look at any of the serological results?
A   No.
Q   Did you believe it was important to know about any such results?
A   No. My function was to look simply at the science involved and the data involved in PCR.[44]

As we have previously shown, Gerdes never actually did any-thing to prove his hypothesis of contamination. So it is hardly surprising that he decided not to consult the serological data, since he must have known that they provided actual, hard evidence against his theory.

Gerdes's failure to consider information relevant to the issue he is investigating is simply bad scientific method. His approach is purposely limited which makes reaching the truth unlikely. Scientific procedure requires painstaking observation of all the pertinent data available.

George Clarke asked Gerdes if he thought the serological techniques could detect cross-contamination:

Q   Is it your testimony that such cross-contamination would necessarily never be detected by serological techniques?
A   I think it is highly unlikely because PCR is the most sensitive method possible and those items would have very little amount of material.[45]

Perhaps because he was pleased with the answer he got the first time, Clarke made sure of Gerdes's position:

Q   With respect to this area of cross-contamination, is it your testimony that contamination wouldn't be picked up by serological techniques?
A   It depends on the specimen, but I think if it is a specimen with very small amounts, the PCR technique is more sensitive than most serological techniques.[46]

What Gerdes is saying is that the contamination he has ob-served is very small. It is too small to be detected by serological tests, and too small to affect the serological results.

The Emperor Has No Clothes

So if the serological tests are consistent with Simpson, this is proof that Gerdes's theory is wrong: the blood wasn't contami-nated with a tiny amount of O.J.'s blood, the blood actually was O.J.'s blood. Why? The contamination which caused the DNA typing results is teeny-tiny. If Gerdes's theory were correct, the serology results from one of the Bundy blood drops should not register Simpson's protein markers.

Serology tests were performed on Item 49, one of the Bundy blood drops, using significantly more blood than the PCR tests.[47] The test results matched Simpson's blood profile. The probability of getting such a match from an innocent person unconnected with the crime is 1 in 200.[48]

Those odds may sound less powerful than the match probabilities associated with the DNA stains. But we should remember that less than a decade ago this was the only sort of match statistic offered to juries. The tremendously impressive figures associated with DNA evidence are new in courtrooms.

Even more important, this serological match not only corroborates the DNA results but actually disproves Gerdes's entire theory. The Gerdes explanation for the Simpson DNA typing results was that they could be attributed entirely to extremely small amounts of cross-contaminated blood. The serological tests, using far more blood than the Gerdes theory can possibly account for, show that Gerdes's hypothesis is just plain wrong.[49]

CHAPTER 10

Shoes and Socks

It is right that each man should measure himself by his own foot.

—Horace, *Epistles*

William Bodziak, a shoe impressions expert from the FBI, testified that the bloody shoe impressions left at Bundy were made by size 12 Bruno Magli shoes containing a sole made by the Italian company Silga. This shoe is so rare that when Bodziak began by consulting the FBI's reference collection of thousands of shoe impressions, he could not identify the imprint.

Upon first examination, Bodziak believed that these shoe impressions might be from a very expensive Italian shoe. He contacted some seventy-five manufacturers and importers of such high-end Italian shoes, showing them a composite sketch of the heel impression as well as photographs from the Bundy crime scene. He sent a similar inquiry to eight international law enforcement agencies. Seven of these agencies did not have the impression in their computer databases.

Bodziak did get two positive results. The National Police Agency in Tokyo had such a heel in their collection and identified it as made in Italy. Bodziak also received a reply from a shoe importer in New Jersey. This led to the identification of the Bundy shoe impressions as from Bruno Magli shoes with a Silga sole.

Bodziak learned that the shoes which left the bloody impressions at Bundy were distributed in the U.S. only in 1991 and

1992 and cost approximately $160. He identified the Bundy shoe impressions as resulting from a size 12 shoe and testified that only slightly over 9 percent of the general public wears a size 12.

Bodziak was asked to compare the Silga sole to the soles of shoes worn by various police officers who were at the Bundy scene during the early morning hours of June 13th:

Q … were you able to include or exclude the officer's [sic] shoeprints as having created any of the prints that you saw at the Bundy location?
A I was able to exclude those officer's [sic] footprints as having made any of the distinguishable, you know, the Silga design that I pointed out previously this morning. That Silga design is *totally different* than any of the designs of these officer's [sic] shoes.
Q And just for the record, the package of six photographs that I sent— just showed you, included Phillips, Fuhrman and Roberts?
A That's correct.[1] [Emphasis added.]

His testimony then went on to exclude various other officers who were at Bundy. On cross-examination, these eliminations were never challenged by F. Lee Bailey or even broached during Bailey's questioning.

Since the bloody shoe impressions did not extend to the end of the alley behind Nicole's condominium, Prosecutor Hank Goldberg asked Bodziak what could account for a bloody shoe impression in the Bronco. Bodziak explained that the blood on the very bottom of the shoes, the part which directly contacts the walking surface, disappears first. But blood in the crevices and grooves of the sole lasts longer. When someone steps into a vehicle a short time after bloodying their shoes the carpet can be pushed up into the grooves pulling out the blood.[2]

The Bronco Shoe Impression

While Bodziak was not unequivocally positive that the impression in the Bronco carpet was created by a Bruno Magli shoe with the Silga sole, he nonetheless found characteristics consistent with that type of shoe:

And I was not able to make—take an overlay and actually reconstruct the exact position of that shoe to the point where I could say it was absolutely the Silga design and even go farther and say it was the same. There just wasn't enough detail and of course it is not representing the normal design of the case, but it is just wherever there happened to be some blood up in the grooves and wherever the carpeting had to go up, it just randomly whipped down …

… I did notice that there was this area here which could possibly have been a border of the shoe, and there also is some little what I call squiggles or little "S" shapes which might represent the curved areas between the design elements, but they weren't clear enough or reliable enough to make any kind of a positive determination. …

…This area here, (indicating), was the area that I referred to that might be the border of the shoe, and this area down here, (indicating), where it changes direction, kind of like an "S" is an example of that possible—the negative area of the shoe. …

… if you follow the grooves between the design elements, they change direction, so there is gentle curves between those design elements, and that would be the area that would be—still might be some blood in it at that point back down the driveway, that far from the actual crime scene.

And these little changes of directions that you can see down here, (indicating), as well as this border, and you really can't see any of them clear enough to make an overlay, *but you can see something that suggests that, but there is just not enough detail to absolutely say that that is representative of the Silga sole.*[3] [Emphasis added]

Goldberg then questioned Bodziak on the envelope found at the murder scene which contained the eyeglasses of Juditha Brown, Nicole's mother. Bodziak identified a partial impression fragment about an inch long which contained two design elements of the Silga sole as well as evidence of the double border of the Silga design.

One important aspect of this testimony that the partial fragment on the envelope is consistent with a Silga sole is that this shows that a shoe impression *off* the walkway was consistent with the shoe impressions *on* the walkway. The defense later tried to suggest that there were shoe imprints on some of the evidence found off the Bundy walkway. But they could not produce any matching walkway imprints. This resulted in a theory which put blood on the shoes of a perpetrator in the area where the murders took place but who somehow left the murder scene without leaving any other shoe impressions.

Bailey's Theories

F. Lee Bailey's cross-examination of Bodziak was notable for several reasons: he never challenged the identification of the shoes as Bruno Magli, he never challenged Bodziak's testimony that Fuhrman's shoes are completely different from the shoes which left the bloody impressions, and he never elicited testimony that the Bronco impression could have come from any shoe other than a Bruno Magli. Bodziak also testified on direct that he examined the Bronco carpet in the presence of two defense representatives. This was not a subject of Bailey's cross-examination either. (Nor was there ever any defense testimony on the Bronco shoe impression.)

Instead of concentrating on these central issues, the defense case limped as Bailey pursued rather peculiar lines of questioning. For example, he asked Bodziak if it were possible that there were two murderers who purposely outfitted themselves with the same size of the rare Bruno Magli shoe. Bodziak rejected this possibility, noting that in his twenty years of studying crime scene shoe impressions he had only a couple of times found perpetrators wearing the same brand of shoe, but these shoes were of common make and not the same size.

> To conjecture with what I know about this, that two people independently bought size 12 Bruno Magli shoes at different points or over different months apart from the same store or at different stores— and they were only sold by 40 stores—and just happened to commit this crime together is impossible for me to believe. ... Just—in my opinion, it wouldn't happen. It's—it's uncanny. I don't believe it happened and I don't believe it happens intentionally or otherwise.[4]

Bailey suggested the idea that the perpetrator didn't actually wear a size 12, but had a much smaller foot and wore the larger shoes to throw off detection. Bodziak again drew his on vast experience and rejected the possibility:

> ... I know of one possible case in over 20 years where this happened, and a person wore his brother's shoes. And I don't think it was to throw anybody off. I think he didn't have any shoes. So it became quite evident what happened because the brother was on a naval I think ship out in the Pacific and they knew it couldn't be him. ...
>
> My experience is that shoes are a personal item of clothing and people generally wear shoes that are their's [sic] except for social economic reasons or hand me downs of brothers and things of that nature. An adult who is affluent enough to purchase their own shoes generally regards their shoes as their own and those are the shoes they wear.

Bailey and Bodziak did agree on some issues. But these were helpful to the prosecution, and didn't seem to support any defense theory at all. Bodziak agreed with Bailey's suggestion that blood on shoes dries rapidly. This testimony further damaged the defense claim that Fuhrman left the bloody impression in the Bronco, since there was a long period of time between Fuhrman's being in the presence of the victim's blood and Fuhrman's being in the vicinity of Simpson's Bronco at Rockingham. Bailey also helped to establish how rare the murder shoes were, drawing this answer from Bodziak:

> I only know for size 12, there were a total of 299 size 12's only that were shipped in—that were distributed throughout the United States.[5]

Dressing up for Murder

Prosecutor Hank Goldberg had relatively little work to do on re-direct since the important aspects of Bodziak's original testimony were not weakened. But Goldberg did take the time to belittle the two-killers-with-identical-shoes theory:

> And, sir, is there anything that you observed in your analysis in addition to what you've already told us in terms of the wear characteristics of the shoes which would be helpful to us in resolving this scenario that you were given in which two individuals purchased two size 12 Bruno Magli shoes in 1991 or '92 and then saved them for a special occasion where they wanted to dress up in their nice Italian loafers for the purpose of committing a murder?[6]

Bodziak agreed once again that Bailey's hypothetical was hardly plausible.

The Socks

A pair of dark dress socks were found on the floor of Simpson's bedroom the day after the murders. Blood found on these socks was identified as being Nicole's and Simpson's. The blood found in the ankle area of one sock was subjected to seven PCR tests and fourteen RFLP tests. These tests identified the blood as Nicole's. The probability of getting a coincidental match from a person unconnected with the murders was computed to be between 1 in 7.7 billion and 1 in 41 billion.

Marcia Clark described these socks in her opening statement as the end of a blood trail which pointed unequivocally to Simpson's guilt:

The mere fact that we find blood where there should be no blood in the defendant's car, in his house, in the driveway and even on the socks in his very bedroom at the foot of his bed, that trail of blood from Bundy through his own Ford Bronco and into his house in Rockingham is devastating proof of his guilt.[7]

The powerful DNA match to Nicole, as well as the DNA tests which identified Simpson, were not challenged by the defense. Instead, Simpson's lawyers claimed that the blood on the socks was planted there to frame their client.

In his closing argument, Barry Scheck advanced many reasons why the jury should believe that the blood was planted. First, he pointed out that Dennis Fung did not observe any blood at the time he collected the socks. Yet, a *defense* blood expert, Herbert MacDonell, testified that under normal lighting conditions it would be difficult to see the small blood stains on these dark socks:

Q Now, your examination [of the socks] on April the 2nd was done with a very high intensity light; is that right?
A Yes. High intensity.
Q And microscope; is that right?
A Correct.
Q And you will agree, will you not, that the observation of blood on those socks was a difficult one in view of the dark color of the fabric, sir?
A Not when you've got good high intensity illumination. It would be difficult in this room, yes.[8]

Barry Scheck asked defense expert Dr. Henry Lee about the socks. Lee examined a photo of the socks as found in Simpson's bedroom. Scheck asked him if he could see any blood on the socks:

Q Now, you were shown a picture that's 596 on cross-examination of the socks in Mr. Simpson's bedroom. Do you recall that?
A Yes, sir.
Q And you indicated that that was the best quality photograph you had been able to see prior to this occasion.
A Yes. That's an excellent photo.
Q See any blood on those socks, Dr. Lee?
Mr. Goldberg: Objection.
The Court: Overruled.

Mr. Goldberg: Calls for speculation.
The Court: Overruled.
The Witness: I can not determine any bloodstain on there or not.
Mr. Goldberg: I didn't hear the last part of the answer.
The Court: He said he cannot determine any bloodstain on there or not.[9]

This is interesting testimony, because no blood was visible on the socks in that photograph. When asked if he saw blood, Dr. Lee could have said, quite reasonably, "I don't see any blood". But instead he specifically said that *he couldn't tell*, clearly implying that under some circumstances blood on dark socks is difficult to see. Lee obviously gratified prosecutor Hank Goldberg, who wanted to make sure the jury heard the answer.

Scheck went further in his closing argument. About the socks and the police failure to observe blood before August 4th, in his staccato, bulldog style he claimed, "Most important piece of evidence. Examining it for purposes of court."[10] He tried to make it sound sinister: this most important piece of evidence was examined with a trial in mind and still no blood was observed early on. But of course in the early days of the police investigation the socks *weren't* a "most important piece of evidence". They were taken from Simpson's bedroom on the day following the murders. On that day, Fung saw a trail of blood drops moving away from two dead bodies. He saw a trail of shoe impressions in blood at the crime scene. He saw a glove at the crime scene and one which appeared to match it—covered in blood—at Rockingham. He saw blood inside and outside the Bronco. He saw blood on Simpson's driveway, in Simpson's foyer, and in Simpson's private bathroom. With all that obvious blood, it's hardly surprising that Fung and the other investigators didn't consider the socks a "most important piece of evidence" as Scheck claimed.

The Little Red Balls

To support the defense theory that the blood was planted on the socks, the defense called two experts in the analysis of bloodstains and blood spatter. Both these experts examined the socks. Their analysis revealed that with respect to one particular stain, there were three related parts:

- Blood on the outside of the sock, on the ankle area. This was called surface 1.

- This blood went through to the inside of the sock. This was called surface 2.

- Little red balls and flakes were found on the inside of the sock across from surface 2. This was called surface 3. (Imagine that you are wearing a sock. Surface 2 is one side of the sock which touches your ankle. Surface 3 is the other side of the sock, touching the other side of your ankle).

The significance of the balls and flakes, according to the defense witnesses, is that a transfer of blood from surface 2 to surface 3 could only be done under two concurrent conditions: first, no foot could be in the sock because a foot and ankle keep these two surfaces from touching each other; and second, transfer of blood from surface 2 to surface 3 requires that the blood be wet at the time of transfer. From this, the defense argued that the blood was planted—the socks were put on a flat surface, blood smeared on the ankle area, and this act of smearing blood on the outside caused the blood to seep through to surface 2 and then to surface 3.

The prosecution offered several explanations for how the wet transfer could have occurred. By closing argument, Scheck had dismissed all of these:

> Now, during the course of cross-examination of Dr. Lee and Professor MacDonell, the prosecution sent up some hypothetical explanations for this that I'll view with you and each one of them was rejected by Dr. Lee, Professor MacDonell, but Dr. Lee in particular, as I recall, I think they gave him all of them, as highly improbable.
>
> Lots of things are possible, but he said these explanations were highly improbable.[11]

Like the claims that Henry Lee's pronouncement that there was "something wrong" with one of the Bundy blood bindles meant that there was tampering, Scheck's report of Lee's testimony concerning the socks is similarly misleading. In fact, Lee never adopted any particular theory for how the wet transfer of blood occurred. And he *never* said that he believed the blood was planted. In fact, Lee testified that he couldn't tell how it had happened:

> Q   And the mode of transfer would be the exact mechanism, in other words, was it a hand, was it a gloved hand, was it an object, what is it exactly that caused that blood transfer; is that correct?

A   That's correct.

Q   Now, with respect to that issue, the mode of transfer, were you able to render any opinion regarding the mode of transfer onto the socks?

A   There are numerous possibilities. I cannot tell you which one is definitively one method.

Q   So would it be fair to say that on that this is an area where you were unable to render an opinion on that question, mode of transfer?

A   Yes, sir.[12]

The prosecution put forward a number of innocent explanations for the wet transfer. I will consider only two of the several possibilities which were advanced.

Nicole Made the Smear

The prosecutors suggested that the blood was transferred to Simpson's socks at the crime scene, perhaps by Nicole's own hand. The wet transfer might have occurred when Simpson returned home, took off the socks, and pinched surface two next to surface three with his hands. Or perhaps when the socks were dropped on the floor, surface two was left in direct contact with surface three. Scheck addressed this in his closing argument:

> ... at the time of the killings there could have been a touch with the finger from the victim of Miss Nicole Brown Simpson on the leg and that it wasn't dry when Mr. Simpson somehow got into that Bronco, came back to Rockingham ... Got into the house, took off the socks, left them there and then it is still wet. So if it is still wet when he takes off the socks, you get the transfer to surface 3.
>
> Well, there is a big problem with that. Then you should have seen something on the carpet if that is what happened. It doesn't make sense. It doesn't fit.[13]

Scheck's argument here is mistaken. Nothing about a transfer from one surface of the sock to another requires that the carpet also be stained. One surface of the sock touches another, and the blood is transferred—there is nothing in this mechanism which makes the carpet a required recipient of blood transfer.

In fact, the evidence presented by the defense makes even the possibility of the carpet being stained unlikely. The amount of blood involved in the transfer from surface 2 to surface 3 is not even visible with the naked eye, it is such a small amount. So why should any of this tiny amount additionally be transferred to the carpet? The amount is so small, it wouldn't spatter or drip.

Moreover, even if blood had somehow transferred to the carpet according to the defense's own expert it would not have been visible without a microscope.

The defense argued that the wet transfer could not have taken place in Simpson's bedroom because the blood would have dried on the sock between the time of the murders and the time Simpson took off his socks. The prosecution countered that if Simpson had sweated during the commission of the murders, that would have kept the blood from drying on his socks. Scheck addressed this, too, in his closing:

> Next explanation is going to be sweat. Well, there was a stain from the crime scene, but sweating in the sock and then the sock is taken off and then somehow by process of sweat it transfers to surface 3. Dr. Lee and Dr. MacDonell said ridiculous, highly improbable you would see that same diffusion as with the pheno test and we don't see it.[14]

Note how Scheck pretends not to understand the prosecution argument by saying "somehow by process of sweat it transfers to surface 3". It is not the sweat which is the suggested *cause* of transfer, it is the act of taking off the socks. After they are off the foot, they are held in the hands and various surfaces which had previously been kept apart by the foot and leg may now be touching. The only role sweat plays in this innocent explanation is that sweat is the reason why blood would not dry between the time it was applied to the sock at Bundy and the time it was removed at Rockingham.

In maintaining that Lee and MacDonell had characterized this explanation as "ridiculous, highly improbable", Scheck was being less than entirely truthful. In his questioning of Herbert MacDonell, Peter Neufeld specifically asked about very large amounts of sweat:

Q In addition to experiments, sir, can somebody who is trained make an assessment on whether or not those socks were *soaked in perspiration* at about the time that the blood was put on them?

Ms. Clark: Objection. That calls for speculation.

The Court: Overruled.

Ms. Clark: Beyond the scope of his expertise, your honor.

The Witness: Yes.

The Court: Overruled.

Q And did you do that, sir?

A   I examined the photograph again which showed very clear staining and no evidence of dilution or diffusion.

Ms. Clark: Objection. That is speculation again, beyond his expertise.

The Court: Overruled. Overruled.

Q   And had there been *extensive perspiration*, would there be evidence of diffusion?

Ms. Clark: Objection. Speculation, your honor.

The Court: Overruled.

Ms. Clark: No foundation.

The Court: Overruled.

The Witness: I would expect to see it, yes.[15] [Emphasis added.]

Similarly, when Scheck questioned Henry Lee, the answer also depended upon an inordinate profusion of perspiration:

The bloodstain on the surface still in an intact shape, if a bloodstain dissolves, say, the socks *with a lot of sweat* should become a diffused pattern. But again, I can not rule out any possibility. May be possible, but unlikely.[16] [Emphasis added.]

Not only did neither of these defense experts call the sweating scenario ridiculous, but both of them were envisaging a situation where the socks were sopping in sweat. This is hardly required for the prosecution theory, and it is not even very likely for the part of the sock which contained the stain in question, which is the ankle. If socks do become drenched in perspiration while worn, it is of course the part inside the shoe which generally gets this wet.

Surely this is an instance where we can appeal to common-sense reflection upon matters of common experience. A man undergoes the intense physical exertion and emotional excitement of slashing two human beings to death, flees the scene in confusion with his adrenaline pumping, gets to his house within a few minutes, and removes his socks. Does anyone seriously doubt that perspiration might keep his socks damp enough, for those few minutes, to prevent a wet bloodstain from completely drying out?

The prosecution theory only requires enough perspiration to keep the blood from drying and this amount of sweat not only wouldn't drench the socks but is an entirely reasonable assumption corroborated by limo driver Allan Park's observation that Simpson claimed to be hot that night even although Park didn't physically observe Simpson dripping in sweat.

Pheno Testing Caused the Transfer

Another innocent explanation offered by the prosecution was that in the course of conducting a phenolphthalein test, a presumptive blood test, the blood on the sock was rewetted with a cotton swab and the manipulation of the swab over the sock might have caused the transfer of small amounts of blood to surface three. Scheck addressed this in his closing argument, saying:

> ... Dr. Lee and Dr. MacDonell said that that doesn't make sense when you look at the stains because if that brushing had occurred you would see a diffusion and you don't see that kind of diffusion and that is not the way you do the test anyhow.
>
> Just touching it couldn't cause that kind of transfer through to surface 3. Highly improbable said the leading forensic scientists in America.[17]

Scheck asked Lee if a swab used for phenolphthalein testing could have been the mechanism of transfer. Lee, even under Scheck's friendly prodding, did not describe this possibility as "highly improbable". Lee suggested that there would be variability from one criminalist to another, and thought it was relevant to point out that he himself did not do the swabbing:

A   If a phenolphthalein test, the technique used properly, in other words, not soaking the swab wet to wet, usually just moist the swab, it's not sufficient liquid to redissolve because the contact of the swab to surface should be brief. Shouldn't have that, but I can not rule out all the possibilities. As a scientist, I only can tell you some may be consistent with, some may be high unlikely.

Q   Is this one unlikely?

Mr. Goldberg: Calls for speculation.

The Court: Overruled.

The Witness: This *probably unlikely*, but I can not rule out. *I'm not the one did the swabbing.*[18] [Emphasis added.]

Defense expert Herbert MacDonell admitted under cross-examination that the little balls on surface 3 corresponded *with the area where the pheno test was conducted.* Further, he admitted that he did not know the specific conditions of the testing:

Q   You do not know how much pressure was applied by the person swabbing the sock with that Q-tip, correct?

A   That's correct.

Q   You do not know how much water was used in swabbing the sock with that Q-tip, correct?

A   I don't know how much they used. I know how much they should have use [sic].

Q   Okay. But you don't know how much they did use, do you?

A   That's correct.

Q   You don't know how large an area was swabbed, do you?

A   No, I don't. ...

Q   ... in the swabbing process with a wet Q-tip using an amount of pressure you are not aware of, it is your opinion, based on what you saw, that the periphery was not sampled in that manner, that the center of the scene was sampled in that manner, correct?

Mr. Neufeld: Objection as to the form of that question.

The Court: Overruled.

The Witness: Yes, that's correct, if it was very wet, the Q-tip.

Q   And it is your opinion, sir, that the little balls on surface 3 came from that center part of the stain where you opine the swabbing was done?

A   It was done through the cut-out, which is basically the center.

Q   Which is where you opine the swabbing was done?

A   That's correct.[19]

Little Red Balls Establish Very Little

Both of the defense experts admitted that they didn't even know for sure if the little red balls on surface 3 were related to the bloodstain on surfaces 1 and 2. *If* the little red balls were related to surfaces 1 and 2, then a wet transfer was the mechanism, they testified. Both of the experts admitted that they didn't even know for sure if the little red balls were blood—they did not test them. Neither of these experts made any attempt to quantify the specific number of little red balls and the associated flakes, which might have helped to discriminate between a tampering theory and the pheno theory. *And neither of the defense experts ever testified that their wet transfer theory meant that the blood was planted.*

CHAPTER 11

EDTA:
Evidence Does Tell All

Blood will tell.
— L.C. Blochman, *See You at the Morgue*

How can you tell if blood was planted or was actually deposited during the commission of a crime or shortly thereafter? This became a major issue in the Simpson trial. Blood found on the back gate at Bundy was identified by DNA tests as O.J. Simpson's. Blood found on the socks at the foot of O.J.'s bed was identified as his own and Nicole's. The defense did not challenge the DNA test results providing these identifications. Instead, the Simpson defense team argued that the blood was planted there by police, who used Simpson's reference blood sample as a source of this incriminating evidence.

The prosecution tried to address the question of whether blood was planted or not by sending it to the FBI for state-of-the-art toxicological tests.

When Simpson voluntarily gave police a sample of his blood the day after the murders it was placed in a purple-top test tube which contained an anti-coagulant called EDTA.[1] The prosecution sent samples of the gate and sock stains to the FBI so that they could be tested for the presence of EDTA. The prosecution reported that the FBI tests showed that the gate and sock blood did *not* contain this anti-coagulant and thus these stains were not created with blood pilfered from Simpson's reference vial. The defense hired their own expert who scrutinized the FBI tests, and this expert said there was EDTA in the gate and sock blood.

Perhaps weary of the time-consuming cross-examination of all their witnesses, or just the general length of the trial, the prosecution did not introduce the FBI tests during their case in chief. But the defense wanted to argue the EDTA issue in front of the jury. Since their own witness did not perform any EDTA tests, in order to use their expert they had to introduce the tests of FBI Special Agent Roger Martz. So Martz was called as a witness by the defense.

Martz used the same procedure on all the blood he tested. From all of the materials to be tested, both evidence and controls, he created cloth cuttings about two millimeters square. He soaked the samples in water to extract the blood and EDTA, if any. He then used a system called LC–MS which stands for liquid chromatography and mass spectrometry. In this procedure a portion of the sample is pushed through a short liquid chromatography column and then fed into the mass spectrometer. The procedure involves complex principles and the results require a considerable amount of scientific knowledge to interpret, but in the end the mass spectrometer is capable of positively identifying EDTA to the probable exclusion of all other non-related compounds. This procedure can also yield estimates of the amount of EDTA present in the sample.

The question Martz addressed was not whether there was any EDTA in the evidence bloodstains, but rather was there EDTA in amounts consistent with blood from purple-top tubes which the defense suggested was ultimately their origin. To put it another way, Martz wanted to know if the EDTA signature of the evidence matched the EDTA signatures of the various reference vials. This distinction is important because the defense argued *any* suggestion of EDTA in the evidence was indicative of foul play. But since the amount, *if any*, of EDTA in a normal, healthy person isn't actually known (but is believed to be quite small), 'hints' of EDTA simply aren't enough to prove the defense's theory.

Martz's Results

Martz tested the evidence samples using three different techniques. No matter which technique he used, the results were the same: there was no EDTA-preserved blood on the sock or gate stains, but clearly observable EDTA in the reference samples of O.J. Simpson and Nicole Brown Simpson.[2] Agent Martz observed that EDTA-preserved blood has an EDTA concentration of about 2,000 parts per million.

Noise versus Substance

Frederic Rieders, a toxicologist called as an expert witness by the defense, claimed that his analysis of Martz's data revealed the presence of EDTA in the sock and gate samples.

The LC–MS provided information on the different ions which resulted from putting the samples into the machine. Both Martz and Rieders agreed that the data showed signals consistent with the presence of a 293 ion and a 160 ion. (An ion is an atom or molecule which has either gained or lost one or more electrons or protons, giving it an electrical charge. It is only when atoms or molecules are charged that a mass spectrometer can detect them.) The 293 ion and the 160 ion are two of three ions needed to identify EDTA.

Martz and Rieders disagreed on whether a 132 ion was present. This 132 ion is the third ion required to positively identify EDTA. Martz testified it was not present. Rieders said that it was. There are three important things to note about Rieders's identification of the 132 ion:

- In his original report, prepared for the defense, he did not say that he had found the 132 ion. The first time he made this claim was on the witness stand.

- When Rieders showed Marcia Clark what he said was the 132 ion (represented by a peak on a graph), it was no different from adjacent signals identified as 'noise'. Martz testified that for a peak to be significant it had to be three times larger than the noise. This is the generally accepted minimum ratio employed in mass spectrometry and chromatography of all sorts. The peak Rieders identified was at the level of the background noise, noise inherent in the machine. What Rieders identified as a peak is no more a peak than the background buzz coming from a stereo speaker is music.

- In addition to the presence of the three ions, Martz testified that these ions must be present in a specific ratio to be identified as EDTA. Rieders never demonstrated this ratio.

Far and away the most important part of Rieders's testimony was his claim that the third ion was present. But it was not. This alone establishes that EDTA was not identified in the gate and sock stains. Everything else in Rieders's testimony is unimportant compared to this, because without the third ion, his other claims are irrelevant.

Is It EDTA?

Martz admitted under questioning by defense attorney Robert Blasier that the 293 and the 160 ions were present, and that they were consistent with EDTA. However, he pointed out that the 293 and the 160 ions alone could be consistent with other compounds as well, for example a steroid-type chemical. In addition, Martz did a search of a chemical database called the *Merck Index* and told the jury:

> Well, in the Merck Index, I believe molecular weight 292 and 293, there were probably approximately about 50 compounds that would give those molecular weights. But what you have to consider is, there's probably multi thousand compounds that have a higher molecular weight that you would also have to consider as giving the same results.[3]

So without being able to positively identify the 132 ion, or observe the specific ratio of the three ions required for EDTA, one cannot eliminate any of these other possibilities. Agent Martz limited himself to the conclusion that the two observed ions, 293 and 160, *could be consistent* with EDTA.

There is a great deal of confusion over the significance of this aspect of the testimony. It has been argued that Martz varied between saying there was no EDTA present and perhaps there was EDTA present. This is inaccurate. Martz consistently testified that neither the gate nor the sock stains contained EDTA in a concentration consistent with preserved blood. Such an enormously high level of EDTA was trivially easy for him to detect when present. In the gate, the sock, and his own unpreserved blood, he conceded the presence of two of the three required ions for EDTA. He considered this to be completely insignificant since the third ion was not identifiable (and this ion is easily identifiable in the case of EDTA-preserved blood), the specific ratio of the three ions could not be observed (and this ratio is easily observable in the case of EDTA-preserved blood), and the level observed, *if it was EDTA at all*, was between one hundred and one thousand times less than that of EDTA-preserved blood.

Martz's concession that the two ions were consistent with EDTA has been interpreted in a seriously misleading way. It is like putting a baker under oath and asking him if sugar and eggs are consistent with a chocolate cake, even after the baker has already testified that he could not find either flour or chocolate, which are required to identify a chocolate cake. All three ions have to be present to make an identification of EDTA. All three were *not* present.

Mountain out of a Molehill

Rieders, on the other hand, maintained that he definitely saw EDTA in the test results. In describing just how much EDTA he saw, he asserted to Marcia Clark:

Q So the amount of EDTA found in the evidence stains on the gate and the sock were in parts per million; is that right?

A Yes. Because you cannot detect anything that is less than parts per million in any of the samples that he prepared or tested. His [Martz's] detection limit is in the parts per million.[4]

By stating that he detected EDTA at the detection limit of the machine, Rieders was admitting that if he did see EDTA, he saw it in only parts per million—single digit parts per million. *But EDTA from a purple-top tube is in two thousand parts per million, two thousand times higher than the level Rieders saw.* So Rieders not only failed to find the required third ion, he also failed to detect EDTA in quantities anywhere near the level of preserved blood.

Sample Size

The defense suggested that Martz's claim that there was no EDTA-preserved blood in the gate or sock samples could not be trusted, because he did not accurately quantify the amount of blood he used in each of his tests on the evidence samples. Since he didn't measure exactly how much blood from the gate or sock he used, it is conceivable that he tested far too little of the evidence to provide accurate EDTA readings. It's also conceivable, on the defense view, that he may have used far too much of the reference EDTA blood from Simpson, so that the high EDTA reading for that blood was not due to a difference in EDTA concentration between it and the evidence samples, but due simply to the fact that he may have used much, much more of the reference blood. In other words, if the evidence sample was much smaller than the blood tested from the EDTA tube, of course you will get very different test results. The results in such a case would not reflect differences in EDTA concentration, but would reflect merely different-sized samples.

However, Agent Martz had already realized that it was important to determine the minimum detectable amount of EDTA-preserved blood. He found that the minimum quantity of preserved blood required for his equipment to detect EDTA was half a microliter. This is an amount of blood about the size of the tip of a sharpened pencil.

Martz further concluded that the issue of sample size was simply not relevant to any possible error. When asked about the effect of discrepancies in the amount of EDTA extracted from an evidence stain versus a reference sample from a purple-top tube, Martz explained:

> In my opinion, it would have no effect whatsoever. We're dealing with chemicals that are placed in blood at 2,000 parts per million. That is a very, very, very large quantity of any substance in the blood. It's very easy to distinguish 2,000 parts per million from what could possibly be one part per million.
>
> If you notice, I said "possibly." I'm not even convinced that what was found in my blood and in the sock and in the gate was EDTA. I was not able to prove that. If it is, it's still in the parts per million at the most. And to distinguish between parts per million, one or two parts per million and 2,000 parts per million in chemistry with analytical instruments is very easy to do.[5]

Thus, for sampling size error to explain Martz's results in favor of the defense, one of the following would have to be true:

- Martz used a half microliter of blood or less every single time he tested a gate stain or sock stain or his own unpreserved blood, in spite of his twenty years' experience estimating sample sizes.

- Martz miscalculated the size of the known EDTA blood samples and this miscalculation was one hundred to one thousand times off *every time*.[6]

The Bottom Line

The simple fact of the matter is that Rieders had no valid argument to support a claim of the presence of EDTA in either the gate or the sock stains. The necessary 132 ion peak he claimed was present could not be scientifically distinguished from noise. Any errors in quantification by Martz could not possibly be large enough to explain the massively different readings for the reference blood and the evidence samples.

The blood found on the back gate and on the socks did not come from an EDTA purple-top tube. The only reasonable supposition is that this blood was somehow conveyed onto these objects a very short time after it had been flowing in the veins of O.J. Simpson and Nicole Brown Simpson.

CHAPTER 12

The Four Faces of Fung

Lawyers earn their bread in the sweat of their browbeating.

—James Huneker, *Painted Veils*

D ennis Fung, LAPD criminalist, was on the witness stand for nine days, most of that time answering defense questions under cross-examination. What is most widely remembered about his testimony is that the defense established that he made many errors and was far from perfect at his job. But the defense did more than this. They attempted to show many faces of Fung, forming a completely contradictory picture when taken all together. Fung was portrayed by the defense in at least four ways:

- Inefficient, perhaps incompetent.
- A man good at his job, so that if he failed to notice something—like blood on the gate—it must not have been there.
- A man afraid of the police, who kept his mouth shut; a passive participant in a criminal conspiracy.
- A willing conspirator who would not only testify in ways that would help the prosecution and cover for Mark Fuhrman, but also had actively participated in a criminal conspiracy to frame an innocent man.

The First Face of Fung

The bulk of Barry Scheck's cross-examination went to establishing the first face of Fung: a man who couldn't perform his job properly. Not even the smallest error was overlooked by Scheck, whose questioning, peppered liberally with sneering and stage disgust, brought to mind George Orwell's observation in a book review, "if he were killing a mouse he would know how to make it seem like a dragon."

Scheck established that Fung repeatedly failed to record specific information in his records, for example, the forms for evidence collection lacked times for many pieces of evidence. Fung and Andrea Mazzola failed to collect every piece of evidence, including a piece of paper which was near the bodies. Fung was not proficient in state-of-the-art collection procedures, in particular he admitted that his use of plastic bags to store swatches with blood on them contributed to DNA degradation. He observed others doing things which were inappropriate, like using a blanket from the condo to cover the body of Nicole, and did not object. He failed to wear gloves at all times during evidence collection. Under Scheck's questioning, Fung admitted that the reason a second collection of blood had to be made from the Bronco was because he had not collected very much the first time he swabbed for blood. It was Fung who on June 28th was sent to 360 North Rockingham pursuant to a search warrant to look for a knife. He didn't find one. The so-called mystery envelope the defense tried to introduce at the preliminary hearing contained a knife which the defense maintained was at the house when Fung searched, and he failed to find it.

The Two-Faced Fung

The defense was not content with questioning Fung's competence. Barry Scheck accused Fung of possessing a convenient memory, of shading his testimony to favor the prosecution, of prevaricating, dissembling, and even outright lying.

Scheck suggested that Fung testified in ways beneficial to the prosecution:

Q Are you saying you don't recall, sir, because you think that that's going to be of some assistance to the prosecution's case here?
Mr. Goldberg: Your honor, that's argumentative.
The Court: Sustained.[1]

Scheck implied that Fung had a selective memory, which always operated to the detriment of O.J. Simpson:

Q Is there any reason, Mr. Fung, that you don't want to remember

Detective Lange being in the evidence processing room with the sneakers when you walked in there?

Mr. Goldberg: Argumentative.

The Court: Sustained.[2]

Scheck accused Fung of tailoring his testimony to accord with photographic evidence:

Q   Wasn't your intention, when you were doing this search of the Bronco on June 14th, to collect every red stain you could find in that vehicle?

Mr. Goldberg: Your Honor, it is asked and answered. Argumentative.

The Court: Overruled.

The Witness: I tried to collect a representative sample of the red stains that were in that vehicle.

Q   Mr. Fung, are you saying that you are trying to—you tried to collect a representative sample because you have seen subsequent pictures of the Bronco and there is in some places just as many red stains three months later as when you conducted your search?

Mr. Goldberg: Assumes facts not in evidence.

The Court: Sustained.[3]

He accused Fung of knowing that bloodstains in the Bronco 'reappeared':

Q   Umm, at some point, before you came to testify in this case, did you have discussions with anybody at the SID laboratory about the fact that stains that you identified on June 14th seemed—on the console, seemed to reappear in August of 1994?

Mr. Goldberg: Your Honor, it is argumentative and assumes a fact not in evidence.

The Court: Sustained.[4]

He accused Fung of knowing that blood he collected from the Bronco in August was not there in June:

Q   And you are saying that is what may have happened because if 305 [a bloodstain on the Bronco console] weren't there on June 14th, but it were there on August 26th, that wouldn't be very good, would it?

Mr. Goldberg: Argumentative, your honor.

The Court: Sustained.[5]

Judge Ito permitted none of these questions to be answered. He agreed each time with prosecutor Hank Goldberg's objections. But Scheck was clearly able to communicate many of his outlandish theories to the jury, simply by uttering queries even without receiving an answer. One of the disappointing aspects of the coverage of this trial was the long stream of commentary about how useful this technique is, with almost no commentary about how wrong it is for the jury to consider utterly unsubstantiated lines of questioning as relevant to their verdict.

In another approach, Scheck was again faced with numerous sustained objections. But he continued to hammer Fung about his receipt of Simpson's reference vial from Detective Vannatter, suggesting that while Fung was a liar, he wasn't a very good liar:

Q Was that a slip, Mr. Fung, where you were accidentally revealing the truth, that you received the blood vial after you received the sneakers?
Mr. Goldberg: It's argumentative.
The Court: Sustained. ...
Q Mr. Fung, are you having some trouble keeping this story straight about getting the blood vial, blood sample from Detective Vannatter from Rockingham?
The Court: Sustained. Sustained. Counsel, that's not a proper question. ...
Q And when you saw these series of [video]tapes, Mr. Fung, you realized that you had been caught in a lie, didn't you?
A No.[6]

Scheck went further than asking Fung if he lied. Scheck even accused Fung himself of stealing some of the blood from O.J. Simpson's reference sample:

Q And at some point that morning, before you left to go search the Bronco at the print shed, you poured off some blood from Mr. Simpson's blood vial?
A No.
Q Well, did you participate in pouring off some blood from Mr. Simpson's blood vial with Mr. Yamauchi?
A No.[7]

In a lengthy series of sometimes very nasty questions, Scheck also accused Fung of lying about seeing four red stains on the doorsill of O.J. Simpson's white Ford Bronco the day after the murders:

Q Let me put it directly to you, sir. On June 14th, when you examined the Bronco, did you see four red stains on the door sill of the Bronco?
Mr. Goldberg: Your honor, I object to counsel's tone of voice. I also object because this does not refer to the area that was related to the testimony by Fuhrman.

Mr. Scheck: I object to that objection.

The Court: Overruled.

Mr. Scheck: It's a speaking objection.

The Court: It is a speaking objection. Proceed.

Q   My question to you, sir, on June 14th, did you see four red stains any-where on the exterior of the Bronco door?

A   There were stains present, but I did not collect them. ...

Q   Now, did you report to anyone seeing a red stain on the exterior door of the Bronco on the morning of June 14th?

A   No.

Q   Did you make any notation of it?

A   No. ...

Q   So it's your testimony or is it your testimony that on July 6th, you went to Viertel's at the request of Miss Clark and you looked for bloodstains on the exterior of the Bronco door?

A   The exterior of the Bronco door by the door sill, yes.[8]

Scheck continued this line of questioning by suggesting that if Fung had seen such stains, he would have reported them to Marcia Clark:

Q   And are you saying that after looking at those dark spots, testing them for the presence of blood at Miss Clark's request, that you did not im-mediately return and report to her what you had seen and what you had done?

A   I don't recall if I did or not.

Q   Are you saying you don't recall, sir, because you think that that's going to be of some assistance to the prosecution's case here?

Mr. Goldberg: Your Honor, that's argumentative.

The Court: Sustained. ...

Q   Can you think of any possible reason that you would not tell Miss Clark on July 6th or 7th what you'd seen on the bottom of that Bronco door if you'd seen it?

Mr. Goldberg: Assumes facts not in evidence and it's argumentative.

The Court: Overruled.

The Witness: This was a minor thing in my mind. I didn't—I didn't—in my mind, I didn't place a lot of significance on it. It was a request she made of me and I performed the phenolphthalein test, and at a later time I said I've done it and that's all I thought about it.

Q   A minor thing.

The Court: Is that a question?

Q   You thought it was a minor thing?

A   I didn't—I didn't think it was—needed a report written at the time I did it.[9]

Scheck then concentrated on Fung's failure to fill out paper-work related to these bloodstains on the Bronco doorsill:

Q Well, you didn't fill out a report about doing this until October?
A That's correct. ...
Q Well, isn't that your general practice; that when you perform a pre-sumptive test on an item of evidence in the case, you make a report about it?
Mr. Goldberg: Your Honor, it's irrelevant. He did make a report.
The Court: Overruled.
The Witness: In certain instances, yes.
Q You would make a report about it if it really happened, if you really went out there and saw those dark spots and did a presumptive test, right?
The Court: I am going to sustain the court's own objection to that question. ...
Q Mr. Fung, isn't it true that you never saw any red stains on the bottom of that Bronco door on July 6th?
A No. I did see a stain that gave a positive for the presence of blood at the bottom of the door sill there.
Q Isn't it true, Mr. Fung, that you never removed anything from the bottom of that Bronco door on July 6th for purposes of performing a presumptive test?
A I did perform a presumptive test on a dark stain at the door sill of the driver door. ...
Q And is your testimony, sir, with respect to red stains in the Bronco that you've given to this jury in any way motivated by a desire to cover for Detective Fuhrman?
A No.[10]

The defense's theory was that Fuhrman never saw these bloodstains on the Bronco on June 13th because they weren't there. Fung never saw them later or tested them later, because they weren't there. If the blood was ever there, according to the defense, it was planted long after the fact. Scheck's bullying and derisive cross-examination was designed to signal that something was amiss with these bloodstains.

Since there is no June 13th photograph of these stains, one must rely on the testimony of Detective Fuhrman to conclude that they were present then. That much is supported by the trial record.

But Scheck goes off in a wild direction, suggesting that there was no blood on the Bronco door for days or even weeks. This makes no sense and contradicts the rest of the defense theory regarding blood in the Bronco. The glove found at Rockingham was covered with blood. The defense maintained that Fuhrman picked up this glove from the murder scene at Bundy, took it to Simpson's home and used this glove to plant evidence in the Bronco. They argued that Ron and Nicole's blood was on the console of the Bronco because Fuhrman rubbed the glove there before he planted it behind Kato's room. They argued that the bloody impression on the carpet was made by Fuhrman when he stepped into the Bronco to plant the console blood. Yet Scheck's theory on this Bronco doorsill blood is that Fuhrman reported seeing it without having planted it. Why would he do that? He supposedly had this rich source of plantable blood and yet he *didn't* plant blood on the sill contemporaneously with the console and carpet blood—that makes no sense.

One possibility is that Fuhrman planted blood in the Bronco, then dropped the glove behind Kato's room and only later realized that blood on the sill would be important evidence. This still leaves much unexplained. Why is this Bronco doorsill evidence, in addition to everything he had already planted, necessary? The defense argued that the blood on the Bundy back gate was planted. This blood was collected on July 3rd. So by the defense's own theory, the conspirators are already adding evidence to the pot by July 3rd. So why hadn't they added the Bronco doorsill blood evidence? There seems to have been very little rush to plant accompanying the rush to judgment.

Just a Passive Conspirator?

Why would Fung lie on the witness stand? Scheck suggested it was because Fung was afraid of the detectives:

Q Mr. Fung, are you fearful of these detectives, Vannatter and Lange?
A I'm not fearful of them, no.
Q Are you aware—who—Michele Kestler is the head of the laboratory?
A Yes, she is.
Q Are you aware that her husband works as a detective in Robbery/Homicide with Detectives Lange and Vannatter?
Mr. Goldberg: Assumes facts not in evidence and it is also irrelevant.
The Court: Overruled.
The Witness: Yes, I am.

Q Are you fearful, sir, that in a dispute between yourself and either Detective Lange or Vannatter that you could not count on the support of Michele Kestler?

Mr. Goldberg: This is—I will withdraw the objection.

The Witness: No.[11]

Did the defense really believe that Dennis Fung was a liar and a blood thief? Or even just a passive conspirator, afraid of his superiors? It seems most unlikely. At the conclusion of Dennis Fung's testimony he had brief contact with many of the people from the defense table. Photos and video showed some of the defense lawyers and Simpson himself shaking Fung's hand, putting a hand on his shoulder, or patting him on the back. Dan Abrams of Court TV reported that as Fung was about to step behind the bar, he was called over to the defense table, where these friendly greetings took place. This transpired at a time when the jury was not in the box, but some of the jurors were still in the courtroom, waiting to file out. It is one thing for a defense lawyer to try and convince the jury that there is some doubt about a witness's testimony. Following a harsh cross-examination, such a lawyer may wish to indicate 'no hard feelings' to the witness. But if a lawyer actually thought that the witness was a willing participant in a dastardly conspiracy to convict his client of a double-homicide he didn't commit, does warm hand-shaking and amiable back-slapping seem very likely? Detective Fuhrman was not so treated.

By the time of closing argument, the defense had abandoned their lying Fung hypothesis, relying instead on duplicity by Fuhrman and Vannatter. But of course Scheck's own questioning shows that *if Fung is telling the truth, then at least some of what Fuhrman and Vannatter are of accused of doing couldn't be true.* For example, if Fung is telling the truth, then there *was* blood on the Bronco doorsill. If Fung is telling the truth, then the additional blood he collected from the Bronco in August was in fact present immediately after the murders.

The Efficient Mr. Fung?

The defense pointedly chose to never challenge any of the many police officers who testified that they saw blood on the back gate at Bundy during the early morning hours of June 13th. That testimony remained unopposed during the entire evidentiary portion of the trial, even while DNA tests revealed that the blood on the gate, like blood drops leading away from the bodies, was the blood of O.J. Simpson. Instead, the defense used an inconsistency in an attempt to argue that this devastating evidence against Simpson had been fabricated by a police conspiracy.

The defense employed the argument that since there was no clear picture of two of the three gate stains (Items 116 and 117) on June 13th, this meant there was no blood on the gate on June 13th. Not only is this argument not the most reasonable interpretation of the evidence, but it is also illogical.

The defense proceeded as if the lack of June 13th photos of all the bloodstains on the gate was the only peculiarity in the photographic evidence. But in fact the photography was not conducted even close to exhaustively. None of the Bundy blood drops was photographed with a ruler by them and only one of the Rockingham blood drops was photographed with a ruler. There was no photo log showing the time or sequence of the crime scene photos. The defense themselves established that many things at the crime scene were not photographed, including:

- The burning candles on the first floor and the candles in the bathroom
- The ice cream cup
- Nicole's phone with the speed dialer (the defense later obtained their own photo of this)
- The door of Nicole's Jeep which was slightly ajar
- The bottom of Nicole's feet at the crime scene (some photos showed her feet but no "direct-on shot", to use Cochran's term, was taken)

There is no reason that conspirators would have wanted to avoid any such photographs. The police could not possibly have known on June 13th that any such photos could have exculpated Simpson. Or inculpated him for that matter. Yet in the case of one particular photo—the back gate—the defense insisted that its absence proved the blood on the gate was planted.

What is most peculiar about this argument is that it relies on Dennis Fung. Since Fung didn't see the blood on the back gate, the defense argued that was evidence it wasn't there. They suggested that because there were no photos of stains 116 and 117 (two of the three bloodstains on the back gate), that was corroboration of the lack of blood. But in the absence of Detective

Lange, who was in charge at the Bundy crime scene, Dennis Fung was the one who directed the police photographer. Lange was called away from the Bundy crime scene at 12:15. He left to join his partner, Detective Vannatter. So the failure of Fung to get good pictures of the back gate isn't independent evidence of lack of blood.

This reliance on Fung to prove that no blood was on the back gate on June 13th contradicts both the other defense positions on Fung. If Fung were a liar, afraid of detectives and willing to testify as they required, why didn't he say he saw the blood but forgot to collect it? Why didn't he say he thought Criminalist Mazzola collected it, and he never checked to see that she had? Why didn't he say that in the confusion of all the events of the day he simply forgot?

If Fung doesn't do his job well, that itself explains why he didn't collect the blood. The defense established there was other evidence he didn't collect. When it helped the defense prove that the blood evidence may have been degraded, they were happy to rely on Fung being bad at his job. But when he failed to collect the back gate blood or get the back gate photographed, suddenly this became evidence of conspiracy rather than the typical Fung inefficiency so well-established by the defense. The anomaly of the missing back gate photographs is just that: an anomaly consistent with the many other small errors made at the crime scene by Dennis Fung and others.

That this is an anomaly is supported by the fact that one of the three bloodstains on the gate *is* visible in a photograph of the gate taken June 13th. Mr. Scheck's famous bulldog question "Where is it, Mr. Fung?" referred only to one back gate stain, Item 116:

Q Didn't you tell us on direct examination that you, looking at this picture, saw a mark here on the gate which you thought could correspond to a blood drop that you saw on July 3rd?
A Yes. ...
Q By Mr. Scheck: You see what is marked as 116?
A Yes.
Q As a blood drop on the rear gate?
A Yes.
Q That's what you saw on July 3rd?
A Yes.
Q Let's look back at the picture of the gate on June 13th. Where is it,

Mr. Fung?

A   I can't see it in the pic—photograph.[12]

Bundy back gate stain 115 *was* visible in this photograph. How can this be explained? If this wasn't really blood, what was it? If the conspirators were clever enough to plant blood on some rust or berries that might have looked like blood in a photo, then why would they add blood to parts of the gate which didn't already look like blood? After all, one stain on the gate makes the point, so why would they plant three? And why plant on the gate at all? By July 3rd, the first test results of the Bundy blood drops were already completed and these tests identified Simpson as the person who left that blood. Why is any additional blood from Simpson required at the crime scene?

The Credibility Card Mysteriously Not Played

There is another reason why using Dennis Fung to establish lack of blood on the back gate is so strange. Defense experts Michael Baden and Barbara Wolf visited the crime scene twice before Dennis Fung collected the gate stains on July 3rd. Defense expert Henry Lee visited the scene once during this time. Rather than relying on some of the most credible witnesses of the trial, like Baden or Lee, the defense used a man whom they again and again established did not do his job very well. Even before they testified, it was known that defense witnesses had visited the Bundy scene and had looked at the gate. Carl Douglas told Judge Ito on May 22nd that these experts had in fact *observed the back gate:*

Doctors Baden and Wolf were present at the Bundy crime scene, Your Honor, on June 24th and they were allowed into the crime scene on that occasion by Mr. Lewis Brown who was also present. ...

At no time on that occasion, Your Honor, did they touch, handle or remove any stains related to the rear gate or Items 115, 116 or 117. The following day, Your Honor, on June the 25th, they returned to the—to the same location with Dr. Lee and again on that day they did not touch, handle or remove anything related to any stains related to the rear gate.

They noted at that time that that rear gate had all kinds of powder from fingerprinting and they did not handle it.

They object, Your Honor, to any suggestions that they caused the removal of any stains from that gate and they played no role in doing anything like that.[13]

The defense experts were right there at the gate before the LAPD collected those bloodstains! Why weren't any of them asked to testify about what they had seen?

Can there be any doubt that the claim of no blood on the back gate would have been far more credible had it come directly from the lips of Michael Baden or Henry Lee rather than from the sometimes confused Dennis Fung? Why didn't the defense employ one of these highly respected witnesses who were at the crime scene before this blood was collected? The defense repeatedly referred to the "credibility card" when arguing about Mark Fuhrman, but the credibility of their own case is undermined by their failure to question Baden or Lee about the back gate stains.

The defense never said *when* they thought the back gate blood was planted. One might conclude in light of the defense expert's visit that the blood was planted before Baden, Wolf, and Lee arrived at the crime scene. Such a conclusion would be wrong, for the defense argued that the fact that the blood on the gate wasn't degraded was part of the proof of its planting.

According to the defense's own theory the blood could not have been there since before June 24th (the date of the first visit by defense experts) until it was collected on July 3rd and not have degraded. Moreover, why would the cops plant blood and leave it for at least ten days before asking Dennis Fung to collect it? The crime scene wasn't protected during this time—how could they know that Nicole's family, neighbors, the real estate agent charged with selling the condo, potential purchasers, or lookie-loos wouldn't obliterate the evidence? Why fabricate evidence and then fail to collect it? Would the cops rush to plant and then crawl to collect?

CHAPTER 13

Fuhrman on Tape

I know you lawyers can, with ease,
Twist words and meanings as you please

—John Gay, *Fables*, 1727

The Fuhrman tapes were one of those things which could get almost anybody's blood boiling, but for different reasons. Some were delighted at the prospect of the jury being regaled with Fuhrman's crude banter. Others were appalled that the trial should be derailed when the defense had failed to show any proof of Fuhrman's misconduct.

The Fuhrman tapes were made over the course of ten years by an aspiring screenwriter named Laura Hart McKinny.[1] She wanted to write a story about a strong female police officer who had to contend with sexist colleagues on the force. Detective Mark Fuhrman served as an advisor to her, helping her with realistic dialogue, proper police procedures, and a gritty story. McKinny agreed to pay Fuhrman $10,000 upon the sale of the screenplay. She taped her conversations with Fuhrman, and then later transcribed them.

The defense found out that the tapes and transcripts existed, and that they recorded Fuhrman repeatedly using the word 'nigger' as well as telling stories, often in the first person, of police brutality and misconduct.[2] The defense traveled across the country and fought in two courtrooms before they won the right to ask Ito to let them play Mark Fuhrman's own words to the jury. A North Carolina judge refused to release the tapes to Simpson's attorneys, on the ground that they were obviously preparatory material for a work of fiction (and therefore immaterial to the Simpson case), until compelled to do so by an appeals court. A simple, salient fact about the tapes is that the only thing Fuhrman said directly relevant to the Simpson case was that *he did not plant the glove.*

But the defense persisted and cut out several dozen of the choicest nuggets. Tapes and legal arguments were delivered to Judge Ito. No doubt many people supposed that Ito would draft one of those legal rulings most noted for its excessive use of the passive voice and its liberal sprinklings of legal case references.

Shocking the World

But Judge Ito's actual response was both highly unusual and a remarkable gift to the defense. He told the defense that he didn't *need* to hear all of the tape excerpts the defense wanted played, along with their legal argument for admitting them before the jury. Ito had already listened carefully to all the tapes and had scrutinized the transcripts. But he permitted the excerpts to be played in open court (outside the presence of the jury) because, he said, the public wanted to know.

If it was just a matter of the public's right to know, then Ito could have simply unsealed the defense's paperwork which included the text of all the material the defense cited. And Ito did, in fact, do that. But also, he put the jury on ice so that the general public could hear the Fuhrman tapes played in open court.

On top of all that, Ito also felt the need to talk to the jury about the Fuhrman tape delay, without of course telling them that it was the Fuhrman tape delay they were experiencing. He seemed to be doing all he could to make the delay irresistibly interesting to them, in effect baiting them to worm a word or two out of their spouses. NBC reporter John Gibson even suggested that the Fuhrman tapes debate might have been the 'conjugal visit card'. The prosecution ought to have been, and no doubt was, perturbed by Ito's remarks to the jury. On the other hand, when Ito compared their length of sequestration to the Manson jury, the defense ought to have been perturbed—Manson is one of the most hated convicted murderers in America and Simpson was entitled to his presumption of innocence. In general, Ito ought to have indulged all the lawyers less, including himself. Less lawyer's talk, more testimony—a simple idea. By the end of the trial, I half expected that one of the jurors would hire her own attorney to argue in front of the judge in favor of less arguing in front of the judge (and more testimony in front of the jury).

Are the Tapes Relevant?

It's hard to see what could possibly make the tape excerpts where Fuhrman told tales of police misconduct relevant to the Simpson trial. It was never disputed that the purpose of the meetings between Fuhrman and McKinny was so that McKinny could write a screenplay. On the face of it, the tapes were an imaginative exercise for preparing a work of fiction. McKinny wasn't preparing a documentary, so she never made any attempt to discover whether any of the stories Fuhrman told her were true. Fuhrman wasn't under any duty or reasonable expectation to tell the truth in this context. And even supposing Fuhrman's stories to have been offered as factual, ex-cop turned cop-story-novelist Joseph Wambaugh reports that cops routinely puff themselves up under these sorts of circumstances.

There are three possibilities about the content of the Fuhrman tapes:

- Everything Fuhrman says is true.

- Everything Fuhrman says is untrue.

- Some things are true and some things are untrue.

If everything Fuhrman says is true, then there was no need to play any of the tapes to the jury, because among all the other things he said while the tape recorder was running, he maintained that he did *not* plant the glove he found behind Kato's room.

If everything Fuhrman says is untrue, then what's the point? Lying, bragging, or simply concocting racy stories for a screenwriter can't possibly be relevant to Simpson's guilt or innocence.

If some of the things Fuhrman says are true and some are untrue, then surely the judge has to have some basis for deciding which is which. If Ito knew some of the stuff was fantasy, then he couldn't possibly put it before the jury. How could Ito decide fact from fiction simply by listening to the tapes?

Commentators fell over each other to show the greatest indignation over the tapes. But being indignant about imaginative constructions is neither here nor there. It is, of course, entirely possible that a man engaged in preparation of a work of fiction might happen to include incidents which would betray his own real-life misdeeds. But this would have to be *shown*.

And if these tapes represented only the musings of a perverse Walter Mitty, why should they even be considered as relevant to the facts surrounding the murders of Nicole Brown Simpson and Ronald Goldman?

After the Ruling

After Ito had ruled that the only portions of the Fuhrman tapes which would be disclosed to the jury were two instances of Fuhrman uttering the word 'nigger', commentator temperatures went up.

Numerous analysts waxed indignant that more of the tapes were not to be played to the jury. Lawyer-commentator Victoria Toensing pointed out that the misconduct statements were hearsay, pure and simple. How do you admit that into evidence? Her question was unaddressed by the commentary corps, which purported to be anguished by Fuhrman's words.

The day the ruling was announced, at least one commentator, holding a copy of the ruling in his hand, said on television that he was too upset to read it. If he had, he might have shared with viewers some of the following conclusions from Ito's ruling: Fuhrman is a "significant although not essential witness against the defendant".[3]

Regarding the idea that Fuhrman planted the glove, Ito wrote:

> ... there must be some evidence in the record from which counsel might argue, however reasonably or unreasonably, that Fuhrman moved a glove from the Bundy crime scene to the defendant's Rockingham residence for the purpose of placing blame for two brutal and savage murders upon the defendant. ... This assertion [that Fuhrman planted the glove] is not supported by the record. The underlying assumption requires a leap in both law and logic that is too broad to be made based upon the evidence before the jury. It is a theory without factual support.[4]

How many reporters covering the case noted that Ito wrote in this ruling that there wasn't even evidence to argue unreasonably (let alone argue with reason) that Fuhrman planted the glove?

In reviewing the very first instance presented by the defense of Fuhrman's so-called abuse of his power, where Fuhrman talked about arresting someone who calls a police officer a foul name, Ito wrote (without additional detail): "This is clearly an instance of suggesting a scenario for the screenplay. As such, it has no relevance."[5]

The second instance of abuse by Fuhrman presented by the defense was a case where Fuhrman talked about ripping up a suspect's driver's license. The defense quoted Fuhrman as saying on the tape:

> Well, I'm sure he will have, because if he's got that attitude, he's probably gotten several tickets from policemen, and he hasn't taken care of them. He's going to go to the station, because he won't have any identification because when he gives me his driver's license, I'll just rip the fucker up.[6]

What is not in the defense's "Offer of Proof" is what Ito said came next on the tape: "McKinny then asks Fuhrman if he has ever falsified a police report, Fuhrman replies, 'Never.'"[7]

Concerning the third instance of abuse by Fuhrman presented by the defense, where Fuhrman talked about picking a scab to produce a fresh wound as evidence, Ito wrote, "No factual basis has been offered in support."[8]

Again and again, Ito pointed out in his ruling that there is no factual support for the stories told by Fuhrman.

Two of the instances quoted by the defense included talk of beating suspects (excepts 9 and 14). Ito, who listened to the entirety of the tapes (with the exception of those portions mentioning his wife, now LAPD Captain Margaret York) concluded, in his ruling on excerpt 14:

> This incident appears to be the same as Incident 9, with the addition that one of the suspects died as a result. That addition increases the likelihood the account is fictional. No factual basis has been offered to prove the existence of an incident involving Fuhrman where a suspect was beaten to death.[9]

In other words, these two incidents appear to be the same story told twice, with some details different on each telling. If this is so, then at least one of the tales is not factually correct. And, manifestly, the fact that Fuhrman felt free to extemporize variations like this has some relevance for whether *any* of the stories were ever intended as factual reports.

What is most troubling about media commentary on the Fuhrman tapes, is how easily Ito's conclusions were rejected by people who had only heard the portions which the defense selected. The same commentators had for months told Simpson case followers that one of the most important aspects of cross-examination was that it bought out issues which the side offering the witness may not have wanted the jury to hear. In the case of the Fuhrman tapes, we had a judge—who is not an advocate for either side—point out important facts not disclosed by the defense and his considered views, based on the tapes in full context, were discarded as practically irrelevant.

Millions of viewers and readers were repeatedly presented with discussions of the tapes which treated them simply as Fuhrman's candid, factual recollections. Even a journalist who had done no more than glance over Judge Ito's ruling on the tapes would have been aware that this was terribly misleading.

This lack of commentator context is also revealed in their discussion of the prosecutors' suggestion that they would ask Ito to recuse himself. When the issue of Ito's forced recusal was being hotly debated only days before the Fuhrman tapes ruling, most commentators couldn't explain the prosecutors' actions. Why would they, so late in the trial, suggest that they would even consider taking steps to have Ito removed from the case? One law professor pointed out that Marcia Clark and Christopher Darden put the defense in the position of publicly expressing their trust and respect for Ito. This would then put the defense in a less tenable position come post-conviction appeal, when their arguments claiming Ito had been unfair and his rulings illegal would seem insincere, and perhaps even too late. But one of the qualifications, it seems, for being a television commentator is that you mustn't remember the past. And so there was no detailed commentary on how incongruous Cochran's fulminations over the Fuhrman tape ruling seemed ("the cover-up continues" he said in a press conference) in light of his adulation of Judge Ito only days earlier.

Several commentators—defense lawyers, of course—were upset because Ito only allowed two instances of the 'nigger' utterances to be put before the jury. Why? Because it would be more powerful to hear all forty-one. But they seemed to want those things admitted for precisely the reason the *California Evidence Code* says they shouldn't: because they would be more prejudicial than probative. The defense was able to tell the jury there were forty-one utterances. That clearly impeached Fuhrman, who had testified under oath that the word had not passed his lips in the past decade.

Revisiting the Rockingham Search

The defense hoped to use the Fuhrman tapes as new evidence in support of a motion to suppress evidence found at Rockingham. The defense had already argued this issue twice before, first at the preliminary hearing in front of Judge Kathleen Kennedy Powell and second before Judge Ito earlier in the trial. Both times their motion was denied. Ito denied the motion again. In light of his arguments mentioned above, it is hardly surprising.

The sort of things contained in the Fuhrman tapes which might have supported a ruling in favor of the defense were tenuous at best.

- All of the incidents of so-called misconduct discussed in the tapes were directed at the poor and black. The defense wanted this material to be read as simply black. Fuhrman might despise blacks of all incomes, but there was no showing of any willingness, even in the context of discussing fiction, to fabricate evidence against black celebrities or rich blacks.

- Fuhrman specifically said on the tapes that you have to do things differently in affluent neighborhoods than in the poor sections of town:

  You have to be a switch hitter. You have to be able to look at your area and at how you talk to people. Look at how [you] deal with things and what you can and can't do even with a criminal. You can go out in Bel Air, and somebody gives you a hard time in broad daylight, and slap them. Damn it, I want to know what's going on! You just don't do that. I mean, it's obvious. But when you're down south end, Watts, the metropolitan area, when you're on skid row, you use your stick more than your mouth. You don't care. Don't try to tell people to go here, go there. You just use your stick, they'll move. They see no problem with that. They're where they are not supposed to be.[10]

- While Fuhrman did relate stories of cops covering up for each other (and any evidence that these stories are factual accounts of what he did personally is so far still lacking), he made these statements with reference to certain specific partners and to the 77th Division, where he no longer worked at the time of the murders. He didn't mention Detective Phillips, his partner the night of the murders. Neither Lange nor Vannatter knew Fuhrman before the early morning hours of June 13th, 1994. It is quite a leap to suggest that Fuhrman's few statements regarding a 'code of silence' apply to *all* cops, including Phillips, Lange, and Vannatter; or to all the other officers who showed up at Bundy or Rockingham, including Donald Thompson, the black officer who had been at both crime scenes and was the policeman who handcuffed Simpson on June 13th.

The defense spent considerable time and effort on the McKinny tapes. They nosed around the entire country, looking for information on Fuhrman, truffling long and hard. And yet they could not produce one single documented case of abuse by Fuhrman.

Nor, at the time of going to press, has any such case been turned up subsequently. For all we know, such proof of misconduct may never be forthcoming. After the trial, the *Los Angeles Times* interviewed several police officers who worked with Fuhrman during the period when he made the first nine tapes—1985 to 1987. Those interviewed included blacks, Hispanics, and women. None of them could recall a single episode where Fuhrman engaged in anything improper. While representatives of the union representing black officers of the LAPD took issue with these officers, they have yet to produce any actual evidence of Fuhrman misconduct.

One could reasonably say that police officers, even those of a race or sex that Fuhrman is purported to hate, have an interest in supporting the LAPD. But public defenders do not. On his CNBC prime time cable program *Rivera Live*, Geraldo Rivera reported a few months after the verdict that an investigation had been conducted by the Los Angeles Public Defender's Office. They examined cases concerning Mark Fuhrman going back several years and could not find any evidence of police misconduct.

It is, of course, possible that at any moment evidence may appear establishing that Fuhrman did engage in acts of police misconduct, but that still wouldn't show that he did something wrong in the Simpson case.

Does Motive Matter?

The defense tried to avoid the issue of showing any proof of Fuhrman's planting by saying that the Fuhrman tapes were a 'credibility card' and not a 'race card'. But the defense theory of the case specifically required more than Fuhrman lying about what evidence he found: it required that he planted it. Evidence to specifically support planting was never offered by the defense. Motive alone—Fuhrman's alleged racial hatred—was offered in the defense closing argument.

People who accepted this argument were often the same ones who rejected the motive evidence against O.J. Simpson. Yet the difference in the motive evidence against Simpson and Fuhrman is striking:

- Simpson was shown to have beaten his wife, and to have threatened her. Fuhrman was never shown to have done anything wrong against any suspect or defendant, let alone O.J. Simpson.

- Physical evidence at Bundy and Rockingham supported the claim that Simpson murdered his wife and her friend. No physical evidence supported a claim of planting or any other misconduct by Fuhrman.

By suggesting that Fuhrman planted the glove at Rockingham, the defense was able to turn the scrutiny away from Simpson and toward the police. And yet, had the Rockingham glove not been found behind Kato's room but had instead disappeared along with the knife and other murder clothes, *Simpson would still have been linked to the murders by the Bundy glove alone*. This fact was practically lost from sight because of the attention paid to the planting theory.

Fuhrman's Victim Wasn't O.J.

Few people seem to have noticed that, if we accept some of the defense reasoning, the Fuhrman tapes suggest that Fuhrman did *not* plant evidence against Simpson. In offering the Fuhrman tapes as potential evidence, the defense wrote:

> Statements made by Detective Fuhrman at approximately the same times as the alleged Kathleen Bell incident about his willingness to lie, to plant evidence, to frame innocent persons and to cover up police misconduct would be directly relevant to his credibility.[11]

Kathleen Bell was a defense witness who testified that in either 1985 or 1986 she heard Mark Fuhrman say, "If I had my way I would gather—all the niggers would be gathered together and burned."[12] All forty-one utterances of the epithet 'nigger' on the Fuhrman tapes were in 1985, 1986, and 1987. There are no later recordings of him saying this word. One possible conclusion is that Fuhrman was at his worst during this period. And yet we know that Fuhrman was called to 360 North Rockingham in 1985 because of a domestic dispute. He found Simpson and Nicole in the driveway. A car windshield had been smashed, Simpson was standing near a baseball bat, and Nicole was covering her face, sobbing. Simpson admitted that he had smashed the windshield of the Mercedes. And yet Fuhrman, this cop who the defense contended loathed interracial couples, a cop who would do anything it takes to arrest and even frame an innocent black man, this cop did nothing whatever to O.J. Simpson that day. Like the other cops who had been called to intervene in these 'domestic disputes' over the years, Fuhrman walked away.

Marcia Clark brought out on direct examination numerous things a malevolent cop might do in Fuhrman's situation, when called to Rockingham in 1985:

Q Now, back in 1985, we were talking about you responded to the defendant's home on—at 360 Rockingham pursuant to a call where you saw a woman crying, leaning up against a Mercedes Benz. Do you recall that testimony, sir?

A Yes, ma'am.

Q Did you ever fill out a report that described that event?

A No, I didn't.

Q Now, you saw that the woman involved with Mr. Simpson was a white woman, didn't you?

A Yes.

Q Did you take any steps to further investigate that incident?

A No.

Q Did you make any effort to encourage that the defendant be prosecuted for it?

A No.

Q Did you attempt to persuade Miss— Let me back up for a second. The woman that you saw there crying up against the Mercedes Benz, did you—have you since determined who that was?

A Well, since it was told to me who it was, yes.

Q And that person is?

A Nicole Brown Simpson.

Q Did you attempt to persuade her to seek prosecution for the incident?

A No.

Q Could you have done so?

A Yes.

Q Did you notify any news media about that incident?

A No, I didn't.
Q Did you call the *National Enquirer?*
A No.
Q Could you have padded [sic] the defendant down after that incident?
A I believe, considering the call, yes, I could have.
Q Did you?
A No.
Q Could you have asked for his identification as a result of that incident at that time?
A Absolutely.
Q Did you?
A No. ...
Q Could you have called your supervisor to come and further investigate the incident?
A Yes.
Q Did you?
A No, I didn't.
The Court: Mr. Bailey, can you hear?
Mr. Bailey: Yes, Your Honor, thank you.
Q Could you have interviewed Mr. Simpson concerning these incident— that incident?
A Yes.
Q And did you?
A No.
Q Could you have interviewed Nicole Brown concerning the incident?
A Yes.
Q Did you?
A No.
Q Could you have insisted on some further follow-up of that incident?
A I could have, yes.
Q Did you?
A No.[13]

F. Lee Bailey addressed this issue in cross-examination:

Q When you were at the scene, did you have any power to pat down anybody there? Would that have been appropriate police conduct?
A Which scene is this, sir?
Q '85, the Mercedes.
A Oh, I believe I could have, yes.
Q Well, Mr. Simpson didn't have anything on him or in his hands resembling a weapon, did he?
A No.

Q   No. What would be the basis that you would walk on a person's land and pat them down? Do you have a legal right to do that?
A   At some point you do.
Q   And did you have any legal right to arrest him?
A   Oh, no, I didn't.[14]

Bailey seemed to be making the point that Fuhrman didn't do particular things because he didn't have a legal right to do them. But the defense theory is that Fuhrman did all sorts of things which were illegal simply because of his racial views. The 1985 incident involving Simpson, Nicole, and Fuhrman was an occasion where Fuhrman might easily, and perfectly legally, have done all sorts of things to cause Simpson trouble—*and would have done these things if indeed he generally acted the way the defense claimed*—but Fuhrman did none of these things.

In the end, we know of just one person who could conceivably be called a victim of Mark Fuhrman's 'misconduct': Nicole Brown Simpson. Like so many other policemen before and after him, Fuhrman let the 1985 incident slide.

CHAPTER 14

The Fates Conspire

We wrestle in our present state
With bonds ourselves have forged—and call it Fate.
                              —Bhartrihari, *Nîti Sataka*

Almost from the moment O.J. Simpson was charged with the murders of Nicole Brown Simpson and Ronald Goldman the pundits began to speak of the importance of reasonable doubt. Hardly ever brought into the discussion was just what reasonable doubt *is*.

In the Simpson case, many people seemed to take it for granted that acceptance of a police tampering theory—or even acceptance of the *possibility* of police tampering—constituted reasonable doubt. But surely to be reasonable, any doubt must have a rational basis and be able to suggest at least the bare outlines of some explanation other than the one offered by the prosecution.

The police tampering theory fails this test for at least three major reasons. First, as I have shown throughout this book, the individual theories of planting are untenable. Second, even if we assume that the individual theories are sensible, when stitched together, the alleged tampering incidents make little sense. Third, even if we assume that the overall conspiracy is believable, the tampering theory alone is incomplete.

The Peculiar Tampering Mosaic

It is always possible, for any crime, to postulate a conspiracy sufficiently powerful to explain the apparent evidence against any defendant. Throughout this book, I have questioned conspiracy theories specific to individual pieces of evidence and shown why they should be rejected. But one can also look at the entire conspiracy, assume for the moment its power and efficacy, and ask "why would the conspirators set about to do things as the defense contends?"

To aid in such analysis, it is useful to look at the numerous separate instances of tampering which are alleged against the police:

Defense Tampering Theory

Date	Nature of Tampering	Blood Planted	Amount Planted
June 13th, early morning	Fuhrman rubs glove in Bronco	Ron's	Very, very minute
June 13th, early morning	Fuhrman makes bloody footprint	Nicole's	Moderate
June 13th, early morning	Fuhrman drops glove at Rockingham	Ron's, Nicole's	Glove is covered in blood
June 13th, late night	Blood planted on Bundy swatches	O.J.'s	Small amounts, degraded
June 13th, late night	Blood planted on Rockingham glove	O.J.'s	Very small
On or before July 3rd	Bundy back gate	O.J.'s	Generous
On or before August 4th	Simpson's socks	Nicole's	Generous
On or before August 4th	Simpson's socks	O.J.'s	Generous
On or before August 26th	Bronco Console	Ron's	Very, very minute
On or before August 26th	Bronco Console	Nicole's	Very, very minute

Taken all together, this conspiracy seems quite ridiculous:

- We have a conspiracy powerful enough to plant blood on numerous pieces of evidence at numerous different times without leaving any sign of such tampering, yet days and even weeks pass from the time of the murders before much of the evidence is even found. How can these conspirators be powerful enough to plant the evidence but so ineffective in getting criminalists to find it or even look for it?

* Since the defense contended the sock blood contained EDTA, presumably Nicole's planted blood came from the autopsy EDTA vial. There was a similar vial for Ron. So why does the conspirator in charge of pilfering take so much more of Nicole's blood than Ron's? All of the so-called planted blood of Ron Goldman is in extremely small amounts (except the blood on the Rockingham glove). This suggests that the conspirators had access to Ron's blood after the murders but for some reason chose only to abscond with trace amounts at the same time deciding to snatch much larger amounts of Nicole's blood. Why does such a powerful conspiracy make such a limiting decision, particularly when Ron's blood—since Simpson didn't know him—cannot possibly be explained as an innocent coincidence?

* Why is Simpson's planted blood degraded on the Bundy blood drop swatches, but not on the back gate or Simpson's socks, blood which was planted later?

* Why do both the amounts and the quality of blood planted see-saw over time? For example, a generous quantity is placed on the sock, but later a minuscule amount is planted in the Bronco.

* Vannatter obtained the blood vial containing Simpson's reference sample at about 2:30 P.M. on June 13th. The Bundy crime scene had not yet been broken down. Why didn't he insist the crime scene be left intact until he had a chance to plant the blood on the back gate so it could be collected immediately?

* The amounts planted on the Bronco console were extremely small, so small that the defense mocked the prosecution for even describing the Bronco as full of blood. Why would Fuhrman plant such a minuscule amount of blood in the Bronco if his intent was to viciously frame an innocent man? After the conspirators learned just how small the samples taken from the Bronco right after the murders were, the defense theory is that they re-entered the Bronco and applied more blood to the console. Why did they *again* plant such puny amounts?

- Why plant on the console a second time when someone would have to explain the reason for not collecting this blood the first time? Why not plant the blood in a location like the glove box, where it could be more easily argued that it was easy to miss the first time? The defense conspiracy theory maintains that the police engaged in almost ineffective planting in the Bronco, when there is no possible reason to do it this way. They could have made one, large, useful plant there. Instead, the conspirators, by the defense account, made three separate, new plants in the Bronco, introduced into evidence as Items 303, 304, and 305. Even after this supposed second plant, prosecution witness Gary Sims described Ron Goldman's component in stain 305 as weak. Similarly, he described Nicole's component in stains 303 and 304 as weak. The only person whose alleles were present in strong, clear form on the DQ-alpha and D1S80 tests on all three of these stains was O.J. Simpson. He was the one person the conspirators did not have to establish had left blood in the Bronco, since that had already been proven by earlier tests and was not even disputed by the defense. So why would they plant more blood of the victims, but in such ridiculously minute amounts?

The Conspiracy of Fate

Another major problem with the police tampering theory is that it is a very limited explanation. It attempts to explain *some* of the evidence against Simpson, but fails to shed any light on numerous other pieces of evidence, which no one ever argued was planted.

So to accept the police conspiracy theory as grounds for reasonable doubt, one would also have to accept that all of the following evidence against Simpson was due to a vast concatenation of coincidences: the shoeprints in his size at the murder scene, the Bundy glove matching gloves he wore at football games, the fiber evidence linking the socks in his bedroom to the shirt on Ron's murdered body, the hair found at the crime scene consistent with Simpson, Nicole's blood found on the Bronco steering wheel, the thumps made behind Kato's room (where the second glove was found) just minutes before Simpson approached his own front door, Simpson's failure to answer the limo driver's buzzes for twenty minutes, Simpson's multiple cuts and abrasions on his left hand, Simpson's lack of an alibi, Simpson's flight in Al

Cowlings's Bronco on June 17th, and so on.

For the police conspiracy theory to explain the evidence against Simpson it must be coupled with an implacable conspiracy of fate. Somehow the unpredictable forces of the world cooperated in this astonishing set of coincidences that ended up implicating Simpson, quite independently—but corroboratively—of anything which could have been done by crooked police officers.

Even the defense's theory that Fuhrman was a rogue cop out to frame Simpson requires a certain intervention of fate to work. If the cop conspiracy theory is true, it could still only have been luck which caused a bloody impression made by Fuhrman's shoe in the Bronco to be identified as consistent with the bloody shoe impressions at Bundy, impressions identified as coming from a very rare shoe.

Many people who accept the police tampering theory belittle the indubitably unplanted evidence. One approach is to address only a single narrow aspect of a single piece of evidence. For example, the fact that the murder shoes were a size 12 and Simpson wears a size 12 is rejected as inconclusive because many people wear this size. (In fact, less than 10 percent of the population wears size 12.) Among the details overlooked is such an argument are: that the particular size 12 shoes in this case are very rare; that they were very expensive; and that they were sold by only forty stores in America, including Bloomingdales—a store where Simpson had more than once purchased size 12 shoes.

Furthermore, the shoe impressions form only a small portion of all the indubitably unplanted evidence. Much of this evidence is a matter of probabilities—but how would you feel about someone who claimed to have been struck by lightning five times on the same day?

CHAPTER 15

The Jury

A jury consists of twelve persons chosen to decide who has the better lawyer.

—Robert Frost

The process of questioning prospective jurors is called *voir dire*. In the dialect of French spoken long ago by the Norman rulers of England, *voir dire* means "to speak truly". We can only wonder just how much some of the potential Simpson jurors actually forgot rather than purposely chose not to disclose and thereby also wonder just how much truth was, in fact, told. Did Jeannette Harris lie on her juror questionnaire about not being subject to spousal abuse? Or did she actually forget or perhaps believe that what happened in her past wasn't abuse?

Outrageous, Invasive Questions

Perhaps more important in the Simpson case than the answers given by prospective jurors are the questions themselves. There can be little doubt that the questioning required far more scrutiny than Judge Ito provided. While lawyers are permitted to probe into a potential juror's ability to render a fair and impartial verdict, the lawyers for both sides in the Simpson case were interested in learning more. Many of the questions were clearly designed to elicit information from potential jurors irrelevant to their ability to be fair. The venire (the panel of potential jurors from which an actual jury is selected) was asked to complete a questionnaire: a thick sheaf of paper containing around 300 questions. Michael Knox, who sat on the jury until March 1st, recalls the enormous set of queries: "They hit us with a sixty-one-page questionnaire that had 294 questions to be answered. ... Just filling out that questionnaire took about four hours. Like I said, a real drag."[1]

While many questions did probe an individual's possible bias in the case, numerous questions amounted to nothing more than a rummage through each person's life. Many questions were very personal and hard to justify from the standpoint of identifying bias or in light of Ito's wish for an 'anonymous' jury. Jeffrey Toobin, covering the trial for *The New Yorker,* characterized some of the questions as "an absurd and insulting fishing expedition". He concluded, "after reading the questionnaire in its entirety, one longs to yell on behalf of the three hundred and four poor souls who had to fill it out, 'None of your business!'"[2] Here is a sample of some of the questions posed to potential Simpson jurors (the numbers are the actual numbers on the questionnaire):

14. Where were you born?

39. While in school, what was your favorite subject?

40. What was your least favorite subject?

49. Spouse-partner's place of birth?

142. Have you ever had any personal interaction with a celebrity (such as writing a celebrity a letter, receiving a letter or photograph from a celebrity, or getting an autograph from a celebrity)? Yes? No? If yes, please explain:

145. Please name the person for whom you are a great fan and describe why you are a fan of that person?

186. Have you ever dated a person of a different race? Yes? No? If yes, how did you feel about it?

191. When you were growing up, what was the racial and ethnic make-up of your neighborhood?

201. A. Do you have a religious affiliation or preference? Yes? No?

   B. If yes, please describe:

   C. How important would you say religion is in your life?

   D. Would anything about your religious beliefs make it difficult for you to sit in judgment of another person? Yes? No? Possibly?

   E. How often do you attend religious services?

202. What is your political affiliation? (please circle)

   1. Democrat 2. Republican 3. Independent 4. Other (please specify)

203. Are you currently registered to vote? Yes? No?

204. Did you vote in the June, 1994 primary elections? Yes? No?

205. Do you consider yourself politically: Active? Moderately active? Inactive?

211. Have you ever provided a urine sample to be analyzed for any purpose? Yes? No? If yes, did you feel comfortable with the accuracy of the results? Yes? No?

212. Do you believe it is immoral or wrong to do an amniocentesis to determine whether a fetus has a genetic defect? Yes? No? Don't have an opinion?

222. Do you have (please check) Security bars? Alarms? Guard dog? Weapons for self-protection?

230. Have you ever seen a crime being committed (other than where you were the victim)? If yes, how many times and what kind of crime(s)?

244. What type of books do you prefer? (Example: Non-fiction? Historical? Romance? Espionage? Mystery?)

248. Have you ever written a letter to the editor of a newspaper or magazine? Yes? No? If yes, what was the subject matter of your comment:

251. Which television news shows do you enjoy watching on a regular basis?

252. What are your leisure time interests, hobbies and activities?

254. What accomplishments in your life are you most proud of?

255. What groups or organizations do you belong to now or have you belonged to for a significant period of time in the past? (For example, bowling leagues, church groups, AA, Sierra Club, MECLA, National Rifle Association, ACLU, YWCA, PTA, NAACP, etc.)

257. Are there any charities or organizations to which you make donations? Yes? No? If yes, please list the organizations or charities to which you contribute:

270. How many hours per week do you watch sporting activities?

271. Name the last three sporting events you attended.

273. What are your favorite sports? Why?

274. Name the most significant sport figure, sport program, or sporting event scandals you recall.

275. Does playing sports build an individual's character? Yes? No? Please explain your answer whether you answer yes or no:

276. Do you seek out positions of leadership? (Please check answer) Always? Often? Seldom? Never?

277. Please name the three public figures you admire most.

What possible effect on impartiality can one's regularity of church attendance, appearance in a voting booth, or participation in a bowling league have? There is no reason to assume that any of these things would affect a person's ability to be impartial. Whether one seeks out leadership positions may be relevant to who is selected as jury foreman, but why should the lawyers litigating the case need to know?

Common Sense and Privacy

This deep probing into the potential jurors is all the more peculiar when one remembers that one person actually seated on the jury (but removed before opening statements were presented) was an employee of Hertz. While both sides agreed that, given the information before them, he could be fair, one still wonders why Ito didn't exercise his own discretion. After all, O.J. Simpson was closely associated with Hertz for decades and even an honest man might feel unconscious or unstated pressure not to further embarrass his employer by finding its long-time spokesman guilty of double murder. The Simpson case put jury selection in some strange Never-Never Land where a man who worked with the defendant's most visible employer was accepted for jury duty, while numerous others were rejected for unstated reasons which could well have been based on their favorite high school subject, the topic of a letter to a newspaper written a decade earlier, a taste for John Grisham novels, or attendance at a Harlem Globetrotters game.

In addition to Judge Ito's lack of common sense, he may not even have looked at all the questions. This lack of scrutiny is suggested by bizarre question number 48 which asks if the potential juror's spouse is "widowed, divorced, [or] separated". How can a correct answer be "widowed"? While reporters covering *voir dire* observed that some in the venire had a deadpan look, there were no reports of potential jurors who were actually dead.

Presumably, the question was aimed at learning about the previous history of the potential juror's current partner. Nonetheless, written in the present tense, the question is laughable. Given the constant reports of Ito's proclivity for detailed examination of issues, the fact that this error slipped by him may be evidence that he simply let the lawyers ask anything they wanted, without examining the questions thoroughly. Further evidence of this is question 23 which asks "If not currently employed outside the home, please check the category that applies to your employment status: Homemaker? Unemployed—looking for work? Unemployed—not looking for work? Student? Retired? Disabled?" This question fails to list the obvious possibility that a person may be self-employed and working from her home. Additionally, while the questionnaire is usually cited as containing 294 questions, this is incorrect. The last question is numbered 294, but because the numbering was never checked, it is haphazard toward the end: several numbers are repeated twice and there is no question 272. The total number of questions is actually 302. So much for attention to detail.

Surely at some point matters irrelevant to bias should be permitted to remain private. Why should the attorneys and the judge have any right to know where someone's spouse was born or what sort of people they have dated in the past? Unless it was O.J. Simpson, why should a juror have to disclose which celebrities have sent him an autographed photo? Should anyone besides the IRS be allowed to compel information about which charities have received a potential juror's money? As he did throughout the trial, Ito tossed the jurors' rights and dignity out the window in order to accommodate unreasonable requests from the lawyers.

Ito's usual negligent approach to the lawyers meant that each side, armed with 302 bits of personal information, had the opportunity to aim for a jury predisposed to them while at the same time stripping each member of the venire of his right to privacy. This is not something Ito had to permit, and we can only wonder why he didn't put his judicial foot down. In federal courts, the judges conduct the *voir dire*. Ito didn't have to go that far, but neither did he have to veer off in the opposite direction.

Jury Consultants and 'Scientific' Jury Selection

The kind of information sought in the Simpson questionnaire is considered valuable to advocates in both choosing a jury and then arguing before it. Just how valuable is subject to dispute. Jury consultants have recently become more visible, but the effect they have on trials is not clear. While jury consultants vary considerably in their approaches, one fundamental aspect seems to be nearly uniform: based on their study of the issues of the case and study of the general public's views, they recommend to trial lawyers which potential jurors should be stricken from the panel. If such jurors cannot be eliminated "for cause" the attorney can strike them using a peremptory challenge, a mechanism permitting a lawyer to excuse a potential juror without offering any reason.

Jury consultants were used by both sides in the Simpson trial. The defense employed one of the country's most famous consultants, Jo-Ellan Dimitrius. She worked for the defense in both Rodney King trials and, ironically, for the defense in the Reginald Denny trial—a case resulting from the riots following the acquittal of her clients in Simi Valley. She was consultant in the McMartin child abuse case (her client was Peggy Buckey) and in the 'Night Stalker' trial of Richard Ramirez. Her colleagues believe her to be effective, sometimes frighteningly so. In a magazine biography of her, Gay Jervey wrote, "Indeed, when watching the Simi verdicts at Litigation Science's offices, one of her colleagues turned to Dimitrius, recoiling like a snake, and said, 'You're really scary.'"[3]

The prosecution was reported to have made use of jury consultants from Decision Quest Inc. But how much they relied upon Decision Quest is open to question. After the trial it was reported that the prosecution failed to follow many recommendations and that they dropped Decision Quest altogether from fear that use of consultants would be viewed as improper for prosecutors.

Even Simpson himself weighed in publicly on the issue of jury consultants. In his book *I Want to Tell You*, he complained:

> This game aspect [of the justice system] has gotten to the point where the prosecution can go to Arizona, as they did, and present their case against me to a mock jury. They're trying to find out which citizens are better suited for the prosecution. I mean, better suited for a conviction. Now I find myself in a place where I even have to have my own expert, an expert on jurors to tell me which citizens are going to be more suited for me. When you're doing that kind of "scientific" research, you're not after justice anymore, you're after winning. My own lawyers are part of the system.[4]

Two recent books on juries each discuss jury consultants and draw different conclusions. In his book *The Jury*, Stephen Adler, law editor for the *Wall Street Journal*, provides a case study which concentrates on the role of a jury consultant. The case concerned a boy injured while riding his bicycle at dusk without a light. He was struck by a car driven by woman who had been drinking. The problem for the plaintiff was that the driver's insurance and her personal assets severely limited the amount of money they could reasonably expect to receive from her. So they decided to sue the restaurant where she claimed she had been drinking. Since it was part of a national chain, it was a perfect deep-pocket defendant. Even though the lawyers had no evidence that the driver had consumed beer at the restaurant or had actually even been in the restaurant, use of a mock jury before the trial even began helped the plaintiff frame what Adler points out were very weak arguments. The mock jury was actually angry at the idea that the national restaurant chain should even be sued; they took seriously the issue of personal responsibility. So the plaintiff's attorneys decided to change their approach, and argue that the restaurant had the legal responsibility to ensure patrons were not served liquor when they were already intoxicated and that this abrogation of their responsibility was the partial cause of the accident. This pre-trial use of jury consultants to shape the case appeared to have worked: by the time the plaintiff went to trial the case was markedly stronger, peremptory challenges were used to eliminate potential jurors believed to be less inclined to accept the plaintiff's arguments, and the restaurant defendant settled the case in mid-trial.[5]

On the other hand, Brandeis University professor and former prosecutor Jeffrey Abramson concludes that jury consultants have little provable effect on a trial's outcome, notwithstanding the self-serving remarks of jury consultants themselves.[6]

So-called scientific jury selection began with the 1972 trial of the Harrisburg Seven. Father Philip Berrigan, Sister Elizabeth McAlister, and five other defendants were accused of conspiracy to raid draft boards, the destruction of draft records, and a plan to kidnap then National Security Advisor Henry Kissinger. Some liberal academic social scientists agreed to help the lawyers defending Berrigan. They conducted detailed interviews of hundreds of residents of the area where the trial was to be held: Harrisburg, Pennsylvania. Relying on their research, they devised a rating system to evaluate potential jurors based on answers given during *voir dire*. A rating of one was considered the best for the defense and a rating of five the worst. The jury was hung on the major charges (the vote was 10–2 for acquittal) and they found the defendants guilty of only a minor offense (smuggling letters out of prison). The jury consultants declared this a victory for scientific selection, but Abramson points out that the two jurors who held out for a conviction were given a rating of "two" by the jury consultants, and thus were actually judged to be very favorable to the defense. Moreover, because these two jurors became close during the course of the case, they re-inforced each other during deliberations. Such alliances were not even considered as a factor by the jury consultants.[7]

Abramson examines several other trials and concludes that claims of jury consultant efficacy are most pronounced in their own literature and in superficial newspaper accounts. The factual evidence for their effectiveness, he argues, is noticeably lacking.[8]

But it doesn't seem to matter whether one agrees with Adler or Abramson. If Adler's case study is typical of scientific jury selection, then it perverts the process by ensuring bias. If Abramson is correct, then extensive *voir dire* not clearly aimed at bias is a waste of everyone's time, a violation of privacy, and an invitation to use peremptory challenges for bizarre reasons. Laurence Powell, one of the officers twice-tried for beating Rodney King, once pointed out that Dimitrius would draw conclusions about potential jurors even from the shoes they wore.[9] Both Adler and Abramson reach similar conclusions regarding peremptory challenges: they should be greatly curtailed or even eliminated.[10]

In the 1986 Supreme Court case *Batson v. Kentucky*, the Court held that prosecutors could not use peremptory challenges to systematically remove potential black jurors in criminal cases with black defendants. In subsequent cases, the Court has ruled that no lawyer may use peremptory challenges to excuse potential jurors on the basis of race or sex. This set of cases could well lead to the complete judicial elimination of peremptory challenges, as suggested by Thurgood Marshall in his concurring opinion in Batson: "The inherent potential of peremptory challenges to distort the jury process by permitting the exclusion of jurors on racial grounds should ideally lead the Court to ban them entirely from the criminal justice system."[11]

Whether or not custom-designed juries decide cases differently than those assembled without the use of jury consultants, their use may erode general confidence in the jury system and sour the public on jury verdicts:

> ... one obvious consequence is that the jury system loses much of its moral authority. Why should we defer to the decision of a group of individuals who have been selected for their likely partisanship and then persuaded by many of the same techniques that sell soap and

breakfast cereal? When verdicts come to seem more manipulated than majestic, one thinks of *Brave New World* more readily than *12 Angry Men*.[12]

Does Knowledge Equal Bias?

The problem of bias resulting from pre-trial publicity is not new in American trials. One of the most important examples is nearly 200 years old. Aaron Burr served as U.S. Senator from New York from 1791 to 1797. In the presidential election of 1800 he tied with Thomas Jefferson. The U.S. House of Representatives named Jefferson president and Burr vice-president. Burr ran for Governor of New York in 1804 and lost. In 1807 he was charged with treason, accused of gathering armed men on Blenner-hassett's Island in 1806 in order to effect an armed takeover of New Orleans.

Newspaper coverage was extensive. Supreme Court Chief Justice John Marshall presided at his trial, acting as a circuit judge. When Burr claimed that many potential jurors should be excused because they could not render an impartial verdict, Marshall ruled that anyone on the venire who had formed a decisive opinion on any essential element of the charges against Burr must be removed from the panel. But Marshall did not find potential jurors objectionable merely for knowing a lot about the case or even having opinions about the case as long as those opinions did not include ones relevant to the essential elements of the crime. In deciding this issue Marshall wrote:

> It would seem to the court that to say that any man who had formed an opinion on any fact conducive to the final decision of the case would therefore be considered as disqualified from serving on the jury, would exclude intelligent and observing men, whose minds were really in a situation to decide upon the whole case according to the testimony, and would perhaps be applying the letter of the rule requiring an impartial jury with a strictness which is not necessary for the preservation of the rule itself.[13]

The important distinction drawn by Marshall was that having information about a case was not a cause for disqualification, but an inability to be open-minded about the facts to be presented at trial was. According to Abramson:

> ... Marshall was careful to stress that a person did not lose his ability to be an impartial juror simply because he had read the papers. Bias

was not some kind of contagious disease people caught from reading inflammatory articles. ... The focus of the *voir dire* must not be on the nature of the newspaper articles but on the nature of the opinions expressed by the would-be juror prior to trial.[14]

The jury impaneled to decide the Burr case did contain many men who were already well informed about the case. Some held opinions about Burr which were negative. Yet this jury acquitted Burr, probably because Marshall ruled for the defense regarding the inadmissibility of much of the evidence. Based on the proceedings in court, even those who were informed about the case were able to put their prior knowledge aside and decide it on the merits.

Oliver North and Others

Lt. Colonel Oliver North testified before Congress and to a national television audience about his participation in the Iran-contra scandal. He was granted immunity for his congressional testimony. He was tried in 1989; the charges included obstruction of Congress, conspiracy to defraud the federal government, and destroying documents. Because North was granted immunity for his testimony before Congress, the judge presiding at his trial discharged potential jurors who had extensive knowledge of those previous proceedings. Further, the judge excused all potential jurors who indicated on their questionnaire that they had seen or read about any of North's testimony. During the oral questioning, further jurors with prior knowledge of the case were discharged, even those who described themselves as having "rudimentary prior knowledge" or who had listened to the hearings "with one ear". Jurors who passed muster included one who said that North was a "head of soldiers, or something like that" and one who "never read the newspapers except to see the comics and horoscopes". The person who became forewoman said during *voir dire* "I don't like the news. I don't like to watch it. It's depressing."[15]

In 1990 a Cincinnati art museum and the museum's director were tried for obscenity because they exhibited the photographs of Robert Mapplethorpe, some of which were explicitly homo-erotic. The judge dismissed the only potential juror who regularly visited museums and who in fact had seen the Mapplethorpe exhibit, while one person who was actually placed in the jurybox never went to museums. Similar situations arose in the Mitchell–

Stans trial and the Menendez retrial, where ignorance was valued far above fair-mindedness.

Ignorance and Ito

Lance Ito joined this line of judges who valued ignorance over a healthy curiosity about the world around them. Ito removed from consideration for jury service people who said they read a newspaper during the selection process. He also discharged those who watched television, listened to radio, or visited bookstores.

All these cases call into question the integrity of jury verdicts. Why should people trust verdicts in cases where the jurors are admittedly among the least informed people in the community, the people least concerned with *any* of the major issues of the day? The ideal of a jury representative of the community is impossible in such cases.

The Simpson Jury Speaks

Abraham Lincoln once said that it is better to remain silent and be thought a fool than to speak up and remove all doubt. As long as the Simpson case jurors remained silent, defenders possessed of skills commensurate with those of Barry Scheck could continue to maintain that the jury's decision was based on reason, logic, and the evidence.

Three of the jurors decided to publish their views on the case in a book. *Madam Foreman: A Rush to Judgment?* was first printed in November 1995.[16] It can only further fuel claims that the jury completely failed to understand what was happening in the case of *The People of the State of California v. Orenthal James Simpson.*

The Rockingham Glove

One of the clearest indications that these jurors simply didn't understand the evidence presented to them concerns the glove found behind Kato's room at Simpson's Rockingham estate. Juror Carrie Bess never comprehended any of the testimony that some of the blood on that glove was identified as O.J. Simpon's:

> Had the cut [on O.J.'s hand] been as bad as they say it should have been, some of his blood should have been on the Rockingham glove somewhere, but none of his blood was on it. ... I would say if his finger was cut and he was handling these things—if he was wearing them—his blood should be on one of those gloves. And his blood

wasn't on either one of those gloves."[17]

Did Bess fail to hear the testimony that DNA tests on three different portions of this glove yielded a match to Simpson? Wasn't she listening when Scheck vigorously cross-examined analyst Collin Yamauchi, suggesting that Yamauchi's careless handling of the glove near Simpson's reference blood might have been the explanation for Simpson's DNA being on the glove? Did she think it odd for Dr. John Gerdes to testify that cross-contamination might account for Simpson's blood on the Rockingham glove, since she thinks none of Mr. Simpson's blood is on it? Why did she think Barry Scheck spoke so passionately in closing argument, explaining how he thought the defendant's blood might have gotten on the glove well after the murders?

Bess obviously didn't listen to Marcia Clark, either. In closing argument Clark pointed out that Simpson's blood was on that glove, and a lot of other evidence, which perhaps Bess missed as well:

> So what do we find on the Rockingham glove, the one he [Simpson] drops? We find everything. Everything.
>
> We find fibers consistent with Ron Goldman's shirt. We find the hair of Ron. We find the hair of Nicole. We find the blood of Ron Goldman. We find the blood of Nicole Brown. And we find the blood of the defendant. And we find Bronco fiber from the defendant's Bronco. We find blue black cotton fibers just like those found on the shirt of Ron Goldman and on the socks of the defendant in his bedroom.
>
> And on this glove he is tied to every aspect of the murder; to Ron Goldman, to Nicole Brown, to the car, and of course that is why the defense has to say that the glove is planted, because if they don't, everything about this glove convicts the defendant, where it is found, what is found on it, what is found in it, even a black limb hair found inside the glove. Everything about it convicts him.[18]

One of the few things the two sides did not disagree about was the presence of Simpson's blood on the glove. The dispute was over how the blood got there, how little of Simpson's was present, and how the defense thought it was peculiar that Simpson's blood was only near the wrist area. The defense maintained Simpson's blood found its way onto the glove in the testing laboratory at the LAPD, as a result of cross-contamination. The prosecution argued that Simpson spilled his own blood on it either during or after the commission of the two murders.

Yet the vital fact that Simpson's blood was on the Rockingham glove was not known to juror Carrie Bess.

The Mazzola Connection

The jurors repeated many times that they understood the DNA evidence. The jury foreman, Armanda Cooley, wrote:

> ... I did not find DNA too complicated to grasp. ... These spots that you filed, 48, 49, 50, 51, and 52 [sic]. I wanted to see this. ... Going through those autorads and those aliels [sic] and how they talk about degrading and how much blood it takes. I see us not being so naive on those points. ... We reviewed the autorads, and there were no problems in any of that information, we understood it thoroughly. ... We know about aliels [sic], gels, we know all of that. A lot of us felt we could now earn a medical degree.[19]

Perhaps it's a minor issue to point out that the foreman, when discussing the vitally important Bundy blood drop evidence, misnumbered them (they are actually Items 47, 48, 49, 50, and 52). Perhaps none of these jurors or anyone at Dove Books had a dictionary to consult in order that they might spell 'allele' properly.

But when Madam Foreman muses further, the immense level of misunderstanding becomes clear. Cooley asked: "Did you know that Mazzola had the same type of blood, the same aliels [sic], that O.J. had? What about the people who were close to the scene who might have had the same type, too?"[20]

Mazzola and Simpson have the same type of blood? Even the defense did not argue that Mazzola was the source of any of the blood evidence which DNA tests showed matched Simpson.

As it turns out, for the DQ-alpha genetic locus, Mazzola and Simpson do have the same genotype.[21] Cooley was paying attention when that fact was revealed. But her mind must have wandered when it was disclosed that for the D1S80 locus, Simpson and Mazzola share no common alleles. She seems to have missed the fact that the five polymarkers yield a different profile for both Simpson and Mazzola. And what about the RFLP tests, tests more discriminating than PCR? Does this juror imagine that Mazzola and Simpson have the same RFLP profiles for all the loci tested? Evidence to support such a conclusion certainly is nowhere to be found in the trial transcript.

The DNA experts went to great pains to explain that matches

at multiple loci were powerful precisely because at a single locus there will be lots of people with a given genotype. (The two alleles each person has at a given genetic locus is called their genotype for that locus.)

The fundamental notion that the number of loci tested is vital to understanding the power of a DNA match was completely lost on the jury foreman. Did she fail to notice that as the number of DNA tests on any given piece of evidence went up, the match statistics became more powerful?

The Bundy blood drops simply cannot be attributed to Mazzola—all but one of them were subjected to all seven of the PCR tests and all seven tests matched Simpson. The other Bundy blood drop was subjected to six PCR tests, and all six matched Simpson. Taken together, all of these tests excluded Mazzola. To imagine that she might have been the source of the Bundy blood drops, *or any of the blood evidence in the case,* is utter lunacy. Even the defense, always ready to entertain far-fetched hypotheses, didn't argue that. Mazzola's genotypes were only introduced into evidence in order to exclude her as a possible contributor to the stain on the Bronco steering wheel—the only piece of blood evidence which could arguably not have come from the three principals (O.J., Nicole, and Ron) in the case.

The Bundy Blood Trail

At the end of the book, several journalists, lawyers, and journalist-lawyers asked the jurors some questions. Geraldo Rivera asked them, "How can you explain away O.J.'s blood at the murder scene, found hours before his blood sample was taken?"[22]

Madam Foreman, Armanda Cooley, replied, "We can't explain it away. I don't think anybody has really tried to explain it away. Me, personally, I have not tried to explain it away at all. That was not one of the issues and that was definitely not the reasonable doubt we based our decision on."[23]

Can anyone actually take seriously a juror who says that the Bundy blood drops *were not an issue* in rendering a verdict in this case? Was she paying so little attention that she hadn't even taken a position on whether the DNA matches to Simpson were the result of cross-contamination, as fancifully surmised by Gerdes? Are the Bundy blood drops really irrelevant to guilt or innocence? Did she think Judge Ito was excluding the Bundy blood drops when he told the jury just before they began deliberations, "Both the prosecution and the defendant have a right to expect that you will conscientiously consider and weigh all the evidence ..."?[24]

Juror Marsha Rubin-Jackson's answer to Rivera's question was:

> But by them being so degraded they could have been there before. Prior to the murders. He visited that place often. See, the first blood they found was the blood that was on the gate, two, three days later, or two weeks later. Samples 47, 48, 49, 50, 52 were all degraded. It could have been there prior to the murders.[25]

Rubin-Jackson seems to be suggesting that the back gate blood was found first. It is true that every officer asked about the back gate did testify that he saw it on June 13th. But it's also the case that the Bundy blood drops were identified even before the back gate blood was seen. That's a minor discrepancy with the record.

More importantly, this juror seems to have forgotten the testimony that when observed on June 13th the Bundy blood drops appeared fresh. Dennis Fung testified to this on direct examination:

> Q Now, when you looked at these items of blood drops that you described as being the trail, what condition did they appear to be in?
> A They appeared to be fresh blood stains.
> Q Did they appear stepped in?
> A No.[26]

Even the defense never thought it was plausible to argue Simpson might have left the blood before the murders, and there was no evidence introduced during the trial to support such a conclusion.

Juror Carrie Bess answered Rivera's question by saying:

> I didn't have a problem with it being the same type as O.J.'s, but the only thing I had a problem with was that it was so degraded you couldn't read some of it. Most of it you couldn't read. The part that they really read, which I think were samples 50 and 52 coming out the back gate, was the only drops that they really, really could say was O.J.'s and the one that was on the fence that had EDTA in it. And I really can't speak out for that because they never tested to see what the kids' blood drops were. They never compared anybody else's blood.[27]

Just what was Bess *reading*? There was never any problem 'reading' the DNA tests done on the Bundy blood drops. The thirty-four PCR tests done, the five RFLP tests, and the handful of serology tests were perfectly clear: every single one of these tests matched Simpson.

The idea that this blood could have come from either of the children of Nicole and O.J. is sheer fantasy. It is just impossible for this to have been the case. As these jurors were told, we get our DNA from our parents. For each genetic locus we get one allele from our father and one from our mother. One of the genetic loci tested on these blood drops was D1S80. Simpson's genotype for this locus is 24, 25. Nicole's genotype is 18, 18. It is impossible for them to have a child with the alleles 24, 25 like Simpson. The children's genotype would be either 18, 24 or 18, 25. So the D1S80 test *alone*—which identified the genotype of this blood as 24, 25—completely rules out the children as possible contributors of the Bundy blood drops.

Officer Riske

Cooley said that Officer Robert Riske "seemed to be an honest officer".[28] Rubin-Jackson observed that Riske: "was one of the best witnesses they had. ... He wasn't trying to cover up."[29] But neither of these jurors explains how they reconcile this with several aspects of Riske's testimony which sharply contradicts central theories of the defense. Riske told the jury he saw only one glove at Bundy, and he was at the murder scene long before Detective Fuhrman. Riske testified that he saw blood on the back gate during the early morning hours of June 13th, while the defense maintained there was no blood there at that time. Riske said that the photograph of Fuhrman pointing at the glove was taken "when it was just starting to get daylight"[30] after Fuhrman had returned from Rockingham, although the defense maintained the photo was taken before Fuhrman ever went to Rockingham. If Riske was honest, did these jurors think it was pure chance that his memory comported with the prosecution theory? What did he see on the gate, using his high-powered flashlight, if it wasn't blood?

EDTA

At least two of the jurors said it was significant that there was EDTA in the sock and gate blood, but not in the Bundy blood trail.

One obvious conclusion would be that the Bundy blood drops weren't planted—that they represented evidence completely unrelated to a purple-top tube. Not only wasn't this the conclusion drawn, but their statement of the facts are wrong. The Bundy blood drops weren't tested for EDTA and even Barry Scheck had told the jury this in his closing argument:

> Well, admittedly, to be fair to the prosecution, there's probably not enough sample left from the Bundy blood drops to take them out for EDTA testing. But they didn't do it.[31]

Detective Fuhrman

The foreman's remarks on Detective Fuhrman are rather peculiar. First, in discussing the blood on the Bronco, she writes, "It was dark and he [Fuhrman] finds little lines on a vehicle with a penlight. To me that's unusual unless he has superhuman vision or something."[32] So how did Fuhrman see the glove no one else saw?

Perhaps because of the Fuhrman tapes, the foreman was not ashamed to admit that within moments of merely seeing Fuhrman, she had already prejudged him:

> Mark Fuhrman walked to the witness stand. A moment later, my mind told me that he was a snake. I just sort of knew that he was a snake. Matter of fact, I think in my journal I indicated that my first feeling when I saw him, he sort of looked like a Ku Klux Klan or a skinhead with hair, that type of thing.[33]

And yet, in spite of this, she reported that Fuhrman was "not the main reason we came to our decision. ... he never even came up as part of our reasoning. He was not one of the reasonable doubts as far was we're concerned."[34] One is left to guess just how all the evidence against Simpson can be considered doubtful without Fuhrman playing a vital role. If Fuhrman didn't plant the Rockingham glove, what explanation is there which doesn't include Simpson's guilt? If Fuhrman didn't create a shoe impression in Nicole's blood inside the Bronco, aren't we left with only Simpson having done it after walking away from his victims?

CHAPTER 16

Nothing New under the Sun: Other Notorious Trials

The thing that hath been, it is that which shall be; and that which is done is that which shall be done: and there is no new thing under the sun.

—Ecclesiastes 1:9

The O.J. Simpson trial was followed by millions of Americans, many of whom had never been particularly interested in criminal trials before. While other famous trials were occasionally mentioned in the course of O.J. discussions throughout various media, rarely were the similarities probed. This left the Simpson trial, for the most part, out of context.

Many of the problems encountered in investigation and evidence collection in the Simpson case are commonplace. Many of the arguments made by Simpson's lawyers, particularly relating to a government frame-up, were hardly unique; such arguments have been used many times in cases where the evidence against the defendant was particularly strong and no other defense appeared available. The jury selection process and jury reaction in the Simpson case, too, bear similarities to many other trials.

Examining the Simpson case in light of other trials is instructive, other trials providing a useful basis for comparison. This service was rarely performed during the course of the trial, and even then only superficially, in spite of repeated claims by lawyer-commentators that the Simpson trial provided a rich source of material for the layman to learn about the American justice system. To be truly instructive, the Simpson trial must be considered in light of similar cases.

The Imelda Marcos Trial

A defense which argues that overwhelming evidence against the defendant is due to government nastiness and not culpability of the defendant was not pioneered by O.J. Simpson's attorneys. Gerry Spence had recently used this very approach in his 1990 defense of Imelda Marcos. The parallels between the defense in the Imelda Marcos case and the O.J. Simpson case are uncanny. Strangely, such parallels were never reported or commented upon, even though it was the O.J. Simpson trial which elevated Gerry Spence to household name status. His down-home, folksy approach and his trademark fringed buckskin jacket were broadcast to homes around the world night after night, via the offices of Larry King and other talk show hosts. He was sometimes introduced as Mrs. Marcos's lawyer, but his defense in that case was never compared, not even by himself, to the defense used by Simpson's lawyers. If it had been, many of the tactics used by the Simpson defense might have been viewed more critically by the public.

The similarities start right from the beginning of the two cases. Approximately half of those who were summoned for jury duty in the Marcos case asked to be removed from consideration due to hardship. Two-thirds of those were excused immediately. The Simpson trial, too, found dozens upon dozens of potential jurors excused because the lengthy trial would have visited a hardship upon them. Straightaway in both cases, many of the most educated potential jurors were never considered for duty. One analyst of the Marcos trial observed, "Squeezing into the friendly 'hardship' category is an art form practiced by many busy, well-educated people who otherwise would make excellent jurors in cases such as Marcos's."[1]

Imelda Marcos was tried jointly with millionaire Saudi arms dealer Adnan Khashoggi. James Linn, Khashoggi's lawyer, was anxious to seat middle-aged women on the jury because he felt they would be "sympathetic to the defendants, suspicious of the male authorities who had ordered the indictment, and perhaps more readily enticed than men would be by Linn's own charm, gallantry, and good looks."[2] Of the twelve jurors who deliberated in the Simpson case, six were women between the ages of thirty-eight and sixty-one, broadly fitting into Linn's category of women generally favorable to the defense in a case alleging government misdeeds and tried by a suave defense lawyer like James Linn or Johnnie Cochran.

Like the Simpson defense, the Marcos–Khashoggi defense team were desperately anxious to find jurors who knew little or nothing about the case. A chemist who read *Science* magazine, watched little television, knew who Ferdinand Marcos, Imelda Marcos, and Corazon Aquino were, who was intelligent, articulate, and Asian was excluded from the jury by the defense via a peremptory challenge. Other educated, articulate potential jurors were excluded with peremptories, one excused by the prosecution because she was seen as a potentially strong force for the defense. In the Simpson case, it was Judge Ito who booted potential jurors who regularly read newspapers or frequented bookshops. On top of this, it was widely rumored that Simpson's jury consultant, Jo-Ellan Dimitrius, urged the defense to eliminate potential jurors with a background in science or mathematics. Were the Simpson defense lawyers interested in a fair view of the DNA evidence, or a skeptical view predicated on lack of knowledge? In a book written before the Simpson trial, Simpson lawyer F. Lee Bailey noted, "A lawyer who has what he believes is a very weak case may be interested in impaneling twelve people of limited intellectual ability."[3] In both trials, ignorance was valued far more highly than intelligence or even basic competence at understanding complicated testimony. Sadly, as happens too often in high-publicity cases, fair-mindedness was equated with empty-headedness.

Most of the people actually impaneled in the Marcos–Khashoggi trial were ideal for the defense: they were uninformed about public affairs and had no interest in politics. One insisted that she had never even heard of Ferdinand Marcos.

Imelda Marcos was accused of stealing and spending millions of dollars which belonged to the people of the Philippines. Because much of the money was moved to the U.S. and much of her spending was conducted in New York City, she was tried under American law. Khashoggi was charged because some of what Ferdinand and Imelda Marcos purchased was transferred into his name and many of the documents of transfer were backdated to make it appear such transfers were made before the

U.S. government froze the assets of the Marcoses. The actual charges were racketeering, conspiracy, obstruction of justice, and mail fraud.

As in the Simpson case, one of the prosecutors was a woman. The jurors found her dry and tedious; they never liked her and this seemed to matter. In contrast, Gerry Spence "swept like a crazy country wind into the orderly world of the New York courtroom. Alternately whispering and shouting, exhorting and cajoling, Spence began his opening statement by presenting a portrait of a woman who wasn't capable of crime."[4] Because the jury was composed of people who knew nothing about Ferdinand and Imelda Marcos—including the evidence against them concerning election fraud, as well as the popular support of Corazon Aquino—Spence was able to use his opening statement to paint a glowing picture of a kindly Imelda Marcos, completely ignorant of all her husband's dealings, and entirely separate from them. The jurors didn't know any better. The prosecution objected frequently and the judge often instructed Spence to limit himself to relevant facts, rather than kindly remarks about his client. The most important part of Spence's opening statement was his claim that the U.S. government had made up the case against Marcos for political reasons. He told the jury that Mrs. Aquino came to power in a coup supported by the United States. Like Johnnie Cochran, Spence was able to say many things in his opening statement for which there was no evidence or for which the evidence was excluded because it was deemed irrelevant by the judge. After trial, Spence admitted, "The only time the jury could hear about political issues was in the opening statement, because the judge hadn't allowed any evidence of it."[5] Both Spence and Cochran used their opening statements to put forward outrageous theories in an effort to immediately divert the jury from the overwhelming evidence against their clients.

As in the Simpson case, the prosecution evidence against Marcos was remarkably strong. And as in the Simpson case, there were rumors midtrial that a plea bargain was being negotiated. No plea bargain was struck in either case.

In a parallel to the complicated issues of blood evidence collection and DNA typing which apparently confused the Simpson jury, in the Marcos trial the prosecution had complicated evidence of financial dealings which showed how the Marcoses tried to hide their ownership of various financial assets. Like the Simpson jurors who simply didn't understand the issues surrounding the blood evidence and then claimed this incomprehension was reasonable doubt, the Marcos jurors similarly found the financial evidence overwhelming and blamed the prosecution for not proving its case. One Marcos juror complained after the trial "They should have stopped and explained it to us. They're supposed to prove it to us, right?"[6] Rather than take the painstaking time needed to understand the complicated issues, juries in both cases seemed to find it easier to adopt the defense theory of simply rejecting the evidence out of hand and declare that the case was not proven.

The Marcos prosecution compounded their error by putting transaction after transaction into evidence, instead of limiting themselves to a few examples which would have been more clear to the jury and more easily memorable. This can be compared to the Simpson prosecution which tried to dot so many 'i's during their case in chief (primarily anticipating defense attacks) that the signature itself was often lost to the jury.

Longtime trial followers know that it is not particularly difficult to make most defendants seem like nice people. Longtime trial followers also know that nice people sometimes commit very serious crimes. So whether or not the defendant is a nice person is rarely relevant in determining guilt or innocence. But when there is little else for the defendant to argue, the 'nice person' defense often becomes a main aspect of the trial. Spence was so adept at this tactic that even evidence attempting to demonstrate the extremely opulent nature of their lifestyle—that Imelda had given Ferdinand twenty-four one kilogram bricks of gold as an anniversary gift—was not viewed by the jury as remotely damaging. They were more moved by the tears which Imelda shed during the testimony. One is reminded of Jeannette Harris's observation after her removal from the Simpson panel that she was particularly impressed with the way O.J. comported himself "whether or not he did it".

In the Simpson case, the defense used police mistakes to suggest that the evidence could not be trusted. When the police didn't err, the defense suggested this was evidence of a rush to judgment. In the Marcos trial, Gerry Spence was similarly able to deflect attention away from the actual evidence, and instead get the jury to consider the motives of government agents. The jury wasn't as concerned with what customs officials found when they searched the Marcos luggage, but were disturbed by the very fact that the luggage had been searched so carefully. The jury believed

Spence's claim that this was done as part of setting up the Marcoses for prosecution.

Simpson's lawyers argued strenuously that the domestic abuse claims against Simpson were unrelated to the murders. After the trial, juror Brenda Moran showed how successful this defense tactic was when she said that if the prosecution was concerned with such matters, Simpson should have been tried in another court for that offense. Gerry Spence had already successfully used such an approach when he convinced the Marcos jury that Imelda shouldn't be tried in the U.S. at all; if there was any cause of action against her it should properly be pursued in the Philippines.

Even Cochran's closing argument was reminiscent of Spence's tactics. Spence told the jury that they had power, hoping they would use this power against the prosecutors and in favor of the client he had painted as so deserving of their esteem: "When you deliberate, you have the power ... This is a case about our jury system. It is a case the whole world watches. It is a case in which the jury system will emerge victorious."[7] Simpson's defense lawyers used similar arguments. Cochran, too, reminded the jury that the world was watching: "Your verdict goes far beyond these doors of this courtroom. As Mr. Darden said, the whole world is watching and waiting for your decision in this case."[8] He emphasized the jury's power, "You are empowered to do justice. You are empowered to ensure that this great system of ours works. ... And you are the ones who are empowered to determine what is the right thing."[9] Cochran, like Spence, suggested that in reaching a verdict the jury would be part of a great system:

> This is how our system works. This is what makes it so great. We pass the baton to you and we will be glad. ... Because it is twelve citizens good and true coming together from this community from disparate backgrounds, experience not required, citizenship, the only requirement to do justice, to do right, to right some wrongs, to straighten this out. ... that is what makes the system great, your courage, your willingness to stand up for what is right.[10]

Parallels between the Marcos and Simpson case reach even coincidental levels. The initial jury room vote in both cases was ten for acquittal and two for conviction. One of the two for conviction of Imelda Marcos moved fairly quickly to the acquittal camp. The lone holdout for conviction later said he was tired and frustrated and wanted to get out. He eventually voted for acquittal on all counts. While the Simpson jury spent far less time in the jury room, it is widely believed that they, too, were motivated strongly by the prospect of going home and ending the case. One observer of the Marcos jury summed it up:

> But the main trouble with the Marcos jury had been the jurors. The pool from which they'd been picked had been narrowed considerably when many of the more articulate pleaders had won excuses from the jury clerk and had been dismissed. Then peremptory challenges had taken their unfortunate toll. The hope—that in America no one is too humble to judge, no one too exalted to be judged—had given way to the disappointment of a verdict driven by ignorance and misplaced sympathy.[11]

The Charles Manson Trial

The police-related problems highlighted by the defense in the Simpson case were hardly unique. Numerous, similar difficulties existed in the Charles Manson case. The investigation of the seven Tate–LaBianca murders included the following errors, problems, and inconsistencies:[12]

- The police officers who first responded to 10050 Cielo Drive, the site of the murder of Sharon Tate and four other people, were confused as to when they first arrived there: one officer testified that he arrived about 9:05 A.M., which was before he supposedly received the Code 2 call to respond. The officer who arrived next said he got there at between 9:15 and 9:25, while a third officer, who arrived after these first two, testified he was there at 8:40.

- One of the officers at the crime scene obliterated a bloody fingerprint which was on a button to operate the gate at the property entrance. He did this by pushing the button and superimposing his own print on the bloody one.

- During the course of the investigation, evidence at the crime scene was unaccountably moved: horn-rimmed glasses seen by the first three officers to arrive somehow shifted from a site near two trunks to the top of a desk six feet away; two pieces of a gun grip originally seen near the entryway somehow moved to the living room, under a chair.

- The officers at the scene tracked blood from the inside of the house to the front porch and walkway.

- The SID forensic chemist collecting blood at the crime scenes, Joe Granado, failed to collect samples from all the stained areas. For example, to the right side of the Tate front porch were several pools of blood, but Granado took a sample from only one of these pools. Granado did not observe blood spatters in the nearby bushes. He did not take blood samples from the pools of blood near Sharon Tate and Jay Sebring, the two victims found in the living room, or from blood stains in the vicinity of Abigail Folger and Voytek Frykowski, the two victims found on the lawn. Granado collected forty-five samples, but failed to conduct subtyping tests on twenty-one of those samples, seriously hampering efforts to re-create the crime. This blood was typed long before the introduction of forensic DNA tests, so lack of subtyping meant that information from those stains was extremely limited.

- When he came to testify at the trial, Granado's first visit to the witness stand was extremely brief because he forgot to bring his notes and he had to leave and retrieve them. When he returned to testify he was disorganized and frequently provided vague answers.

- Dr. Katsuyama, who performed the LaBianca autopsies, did not measure the dimensions of the wounds and the investigating detectives did not ask for these measurements.

- Dr. Noguchi, performing the autopsies on the Tate victims, incorrectly identified the number of times two victims were shot, in one case overcounting the number of times a victim was shot and in another case undercounting the number of times a victim was shot.

- A young boy who found a gun used in the commission of some of the murders was careful to touch it as little as possible, having learned the importance of this from watching *Dragnet*. When an officer came to collect the gun, the policeman touched it "with both hands, all over the gun". Adding insult to injury, the gun lay in an evidence room for months before it was connected to the Manson killings.

- Detectives were routinely slow in following up on investigative requests by the prosecutor.

Prosecutor Bugliosi, in discussing the errors, wrote "As much as possible, I tried to avoid embarrassing LAPD. It wasn't always possible."[13]

The fact that criminal investigations may regularly be conducted in less than exemplary fashion does not justify such practices. But some of the problems experienced in the Manson case make the defense complaints in the Simpson trial seem trivial. The doctor performing autopsies on Nicole and Ron did make errors, including the failure to observe a bruise to Nicole's head. But this, and the failure to save the stomach contents of Nicole, pale in comparison to autopsies unable to properly count bullet wounds or even measure stab wounds. Detective Ron Phillips left his own fingerprint at the Bundy murder scene, but he didn't superimpose it over one which might have proven highly useful. In spite of all the blood at Bundy and the number of police officers who were in or near the scene, there was no evidence that any of them stepped in blood and left their own shoe impressions. (Dr. Lee did testify for the defense regarding a bloody shoe impression on the Bundy walkway, far from the bodies, which the police ignored. But in rebuttal, FBI expert William Bodziak produced photos taken on June 13th which showed that the impression Lee had identified had not been there during the investigation.) There were numerous criticisms of evidence collection in the Simpson case, including some evidence not collected. But none of these omissions were as glaring as the errors made by Granado in the Manson investigation.

As in the case of O.J. Simpson, the Manson case had its charges of conspiracy, frame-ups, and planting. In the Simpson trial, references to prosecutorial involvement in a conspiracy were oblique. The attorneys for Manson and his co-defendants argued that the conspiracy against their clients included prosecutor Bugliosi as a prominent participant.

The Manson jury had similarities to the Simpson jury, most notably that they are the two longest sequestered juries in California history. The Simpson panel exceeded their Manson counterparts in time sequestered. Much was made of the interest in Simpson jurors in writing books, but no commentator pointed out that twenty-five years earlier one of the Manson jurors, while sitting on the case, had indicated that he wanted to write a book.[14]

The Jeffrey MacDonald Trial

Jeffrey MacDonald was a graduate of Princeton University, a respected and successful doctor, and a Green Beret. In February of 1970 his wife and two young daughters were murdered in their home. MacDonald was home at the time and maintained that drug-crazed hippies had perpetrated the murders, and attacked him as well. MacDonald sustained very few injuries (only one of which was arguably serious), while the murder victims had been stabbed or clubbed or both numerous times. After nearly a decade, MacDonald was brought to trial for the three murders.

The defense emphasized the numerous investigative errors: a single bloody footprint was observed in the house, but was destroyed during the investigation; the fingerprints of the two murdered children were never taken, other fingerprints were poorly documented, and some fingerprints destroyed; a woman reported to have been seen standing nearby in the shadows was never sought out by police; the telephone in the bedroom was handled; MacDonald's wallet was stolen during the time the military police had taken possession of his home; a flowerpot which MacDonald alleged was overturned during the struggle with his attackers was set upright by a military policeman; the garbage in MacDonald's home was not saved for investigation; the toilet was flushed even though the bathroom was one of the scenes important to the investigation; an *Esquire* magazine was handled and read even though it turned out to be an important piece of evidence in the case; MacDonald was interviewed by investigators at the hospital while he was under heavy sedation; MacDonald's pajama bottoms, worn at the time of the murders and his alleged struggle with the perpetrators, were discarded; evidence marked as a known sample of MacDonald's hair was actually hair of a pony.[15]

The defense, however, was unable to explain the evidence that was properly collected and duly scrutinized which pointed to MacDonald's guilt. MacDonald elected to testify in his own defense. Among other things, he told the jury that he took a knife out of his wife's chest. When asked on cross-examination why there was so little blood on the knife, he said "I don't know". He was asked if he could explain various pieces of physical evidence which were at odds with his story and he repeatedly answered "no". In closing argument, prosecutor James Blackburn told the jury:

> Ladies and gentlemen, I am not about to suggest that the burden of proof ever shifts to the defendant, because it doesn't. It stays with us.
>
> But you will recall on cross-examination that we asked the defendant a lot of questions—that if the jury should find this and that,

did he have an explanation. And you recall essentially his testimony: 'It would be pure conjecture,' or 'No,' or 'I can't recall.' Perhaps he does not have to explain, but think for a moment if you were on trial for your life and the only thing that made your story perhaps not believable was its inconsistency with the physical evidence.

Don't you think if you *could* explain it, you *would?*[16]

Simpson case followers may find something interesting in this approach, which seems relevant to some of the Simpson case issues. The defense brought some of O.J. Simpson's June 12th luggage into court. But they didn't bring the knapsack which the prosecution argued has disappeared and contained the murder weapon. The defense never explained why this bag was missing. If they *could* explain that, *wouldn't* they have done so? What about the missing clothes Simpson wore the night of the murders? What about the gloves Simpson was shown wearing at football games? If they *could* explain those things, *wouldn't* they have done so?

Motive is an important aspect in murder. Prosecutors are not required to prove motive. But when they can prove motive, they do, because a jury understandably wants to know why someone would commit the crime they are charged with, particularly when the crime is murder. In some cases it can be difficult to establish motive, if the precipitating cause is an argument between the victim and murderer, unwitnessed by anyone else. In the MacDonald case, the prosecution could not establish any clear motive, but suggested that the murders might have happened as a result of an argument which got out of hand. In closing argument, prosecutor Blackburn told the jury, "if we convince you by the evidence that he *did* it, we don't have to show you that he is the sort of person that *could* have done it."[17] In the Simpson case the prosecution introduced domestic violence as a motive (and as evidence of the identity of the perpetrator). But this seems to have been among the least persuasive evidence to the jury. One is forced to ask, if the physical evidence against Simpson shows that he did commit the crimes, is any motive necessary? Can we reasonably expect that the precise cause of every murderer's actions can be discovered by police or prosecutors? In the Simpson case, the motive evidence showed Simpson's proclivity to use violence against Nicole. The fact that no *exact* cause could be proven for the night of June 12th, 1994, does not diminish the fact that the prosecutors established much more than the

MacDonald prosecutors, who offered no motive whatever.

MacDonald, as observed by writer Joe McGinniss during the course of the trial and afterward, seemed to concentrate his anger more powerfully on the prosecution than on anything else, including the unknown people he accused of committing the murders. O.J. Simpson, since being acquitted, has similarly focused himself publicly on the prosecution and has shown no evidence of his resolve to seek out 'the real killers'. Worse, Simpson is a convicted wife-beater and a man accused of having no respect for women, yet he has generally directed his attacks on the primary woman involved in his prosecution, Marcia Clark. Repeated derisive remarks about "Marcia" were shown over a period of days in mid-January 1996 on the television tabloid show *Hard Copy*, which aired videotape recorded during the making of Simpson's commercial video.

The Rabbi Meir Kahane murder trial

Another trial with similarities to the Simpson case was the 1991 trial of El Sayyid Nosair, charged with murdering Rabbi Meir Kahane, an extreme Israeli nationalist and the founder of the Jewish Defense League. Just minutes after the murder, Nosair was apprehended but only after he had wounded a postal officer. Both the dead rabbi and wounded postal employee were shot with bullets which came from the gun held by Nosair at the time he was arrested. The evidence against Nosair was so strong that his attorney, William Kunstler, advised him to employ an insanity defense. When Nosair refused, Kunstler used the next best defense when the evidence against a client is overwhelming: argue that he was framed. Kunstler used his own version of the "rush to judgment" refrain by suggesting there was something suspicious in Nosair's arrest, that the police simply apprehended the first Arab they found near the scene—not even a literal smoking gun deterred Kunstler. He argued further that the Jewish Defense League were responsible for Rabbi Kahane's death and subsequent frame-up of his client.

Kunstler concentrated on eliminating whites from the jury and tried particularly hard to disqualify Jews. But where Ito rolled over and played dead for the Simpson lawyers, the judge presiding over Nosair's trial was firm during *voir dire*. He ruled that querying whether a potential juror was Jewish was a "gross invasion of privacy".

The impaneled jury had five blacks, six whites, and one

Hispanic. They found Nosair not guilty of the murder of Kahane but—strangely inconsistent with the defense theory—guilty of lesser charges including possession of the murder gun in the assault of the postal worker.

Learning a Lesson

Even this cursory examination of a small number of other trials provides some insight into the Simpson case. A frame-up may regularly be alleged in cases where the evidence against a defendant is particularly strong. The fact that a defense may be commonly employed doesn't make it untrue. But knowing that conspiracy claims are not unique to the Simpson case can help the careful observer realize that the evidence for and against such a charge should be examined carefully.

Police errors are not uncommon. But mistakes don't automatically make the evidence which is collected false or misleading.

Many defendants have been convicted in cases with errors similar to those found in the Simpson case, and with considerably less evidence. After Charles Manson's arraignment, his lawyer said, "There's no case against Manson and these defendants. All the prosecution has are two fingerprints and Vincent Bugliosi."[18] That was enough.

CHAPTER 17

The Truth, the Media, and Unreasonable Doubt

... the power of ignoring facts which are obvious and unalterable, and which will have to be faced sooner or later.

—George Orwell, "In Front of Your Nose"
Tribune, 22 March 1946

Ten thousand difficulties do not make one doubt.
—Cardinal Newman, *Position of my Mind since 1845*

Entire books could be written on the media coverage of the O.J. Simpson trial, and undoubtedly several will be. Numerous important issues are raised by media coverage of trials. Since this book is concerned with an analysis of the issues presented during the trial of O.J. Simpson, I will address briefly only one question: Did the media coverage of the trial help us understand the important issues and aid us in reaching a reasonable conclusion about the facts? Did the media help us discover the truth?

Rivera Live is a nationwide hour-long evening TV program on CNBC. The show is on almost every weeknight, and some of the week's shows are repeated on weekends. While the criminal trial of O.J. Simpson was in progress, *Rivera Live* devoted the great majority of its time to the trial. Geraldo Rivera himself has repeatedly claimed—and there is every reason to accept his claim—that very large numbers of people who had never before taken a special interest in a criminal trial became regular watchers of *Rivera Live*, both during and after the trial.

In many ways these shows were exemplary. They featured serious debates between knowledgeable people on many aspects of the trial as it unfolded. Some of the regular personalities, like James Curtis, Victoria Toensing, and Stan Goldman, were impressive for their knowledge and shrewd judgment. Yet there were some peculiarities in the show's coverage which, upon reflection, are strangely disconcerting.

Nearly everyone on the show was a lawyer. This is all the more remarkable because a large amount of time was devoted to the Simpson case by Court TV, the network entirely devoted to courtroom matters, whose viewership exploded because of the Simpson trial. It is, perhaps, natural to expect Court TV to look at almost everything from the lawyer's angle, and this was certainly what they did. You might have expected that *Rivera Live* would try to offer something a bit different.

Most conspicuously, the Simpson trial neglected the scientific issues. Out of the hundreds or thousands of hours of Simpson programming, scant minutes from time to time were allocated to contributions from non-lawyers who were forensic scientists, criminalists, doctors, or biologists. And don't forget that this was among the *best* the mainstream media had to offer. Most TV shows or magazines paid even less attention, proportionately, to scientific issues.

It might be supposed that it would be impossible to explain the scientific issues to the public, but this is a misunderstanding. It certainly takes years of study to become a competent forensic scientist, but it equally takes years of study to become a competent criminal attorney or law professor. If you invited the first couple of forensics experts you thought of to appear on a TV discussion, they might be boring and inarticulate, but so might many lawyers. All branches of science have their colorful, even flamboyant, characters, some of whom delight in explaining their science to ordinary people in pithy and entertaining terms.

But next we observe that the lawyers on *Rivera Live* were not there primarily to discuss the law; they were there to discuss (or to display) emotions. Although a legal background gave these experts some familiarity with the issues, and gave them an air of authority, the focus of their attention was on courtroom dynamics: how this or that would play to the jury, and the public.

This seems to be the key to the overwhelming preponderance

of lawyers on *Rivera Live* and elsewhere. It was not chiefly that they were legal experts. It was that their courtroom experience gave them a nose for what would go down well with juries. Whereas it would be difficult to stop a scientist from sliding dangerously into a discussion of *which point of view is objectively correct*, it is usually quite simple to tug lawyers back from such questions, which media people tend to view as remote, colorless, and unappetizing, to the 'real' issue: *which point of view can be persuasively sold?*

There were many issues in the Simpson case where expert was pitted against expert. Martz tested the blood on the socks and said this blood definitely did not come from a purple-top tube. Rieders looked at Martz's tests and said this blood might possibly have come from such a tube. Here we have two incompatible points of view. As a matter of objective truth, one of them must be wrong and one of them must be right. Furthermore, it is possible (and in this case it happens to be the case) that there is an overwhelming scientific consensus that one is wrong and one is right. It does not take a Ph.D. in analytical chemistry to ask around among those knowledgeable in the relevant areas, and find, that Rieders is wrong and Martz is right. I am not suggesting that it is sufficient *merely* to take a poll of scientific specialists. One can also ask these specialists for the basis of their judgments. It's not necessary to master chemistry to understand how deeply rooted in existing theoretical knowledge is the basis for a decision one way or the other.

Any journalist could have done as much when this issue arose during the trial, or could at least have taken the preliminary step of asking two or three experts. But it seems that none did. The presumption that such issues are too dry and abstract for the masses, who must be jostled along from one 'human' emotional stimulus to another, is self-fulfilling. One way in which the public could be educated in the outlines of some of these scientific areas is by bringing them to bear on current controversies where they are relevant.

Instead, there is a tendency to abandon any discussion once two 'experts' have been found to disagree. Many members of the public, and perhaps the jury, once they had learned that Martz and Rieders disagreed on the possible presence of substantial amounts of EDTA in the blood on the socks, assumed that they were entitled to regard this issue as a wash. The non-scientist could regard it as unsettled, or as something to be settled by comparing the engaging personalities of Martz and Rieders. But disagreement between Martz and Rieders should have been merely the beginning. *One of them was wrong and one of them was right.* It was the jury's job to spend the time necessary to determine which of these two experts was right. Simpson trial watchers, many of whom might never have cared about chemistry, would have benefited from a discussion of this issue and many would have watched eagerly.

There is a more general reason for the media's tendency to agnosticism. It is natural for journalists, who have to develop and sell news day by day, to accept certain opinions and points of view as more or less fixed, and not to question them. Much as people who play the financial markets may easily become fixated upon minor short-term adjustments, nuances of timing, and lose any appreciation for enduring fundamentals, so people who present news and commentary to the public every day may lose any sense of what is important in major clashes of opinion. They tend to divide all opinions into acceptable opinions, which it is not profitable to challenge, and odd-ball opinions, which are worth exposing because they may be offensive and hence are newsworthy. This leads many journalists to prefer to talk about other people's opinions rather than directly about the factual issues which are the subject matter of such opinions. For example, political commentators are often far more comfortable talking about whether protectionism will appeal to blue-collar workers than about the arguments for and against protectionism. So the commentator who says we should have protective tariffs against Japanese cars might be thought of as biased, while the commentator who says that such tariffs strike a chord among blue-collar workers afflicted by job insecurity can make the same point, while appearing to be reporting a fact about political opinions. The prevalence of this kind of disingenuousness favors a general prejudice that many kinds of differences of opinion are not to be criticized but merely acknowledged. Across a whole range of issues, it comes to be seen as a sort of *gaucherie* to directly mount a fundamental criticism of a 'legitimate' viewpoint. Habituated to this climate, the journalist will probably respond to a disagreement between two accredited scientists with a strong determination not to be seen as in any way favoring one side or the other.

Perhaps a remedy for this state of affairs is at hand with the new media, cyberspace, where people have individual input in discussions and can affect the course of debate directly.

The O.J. Phenomenon in Cyberspace

Traditional media sources were not the only places the O.J. Simpson case was hotly discussed. Soon after the murders the on-line computer world was abuzz with discussion, commentary, questions, and information—both true and false.

Even people who have never been near a computer know that the world of computer networks is large and growing rapidly. These networks are used for a vast array of purposes ranging from selling flowers to rapidly communicating the latest developments in high-energy physics. One of the most popular uses of the on-line world is for recreation. Simpson case junkies with no sympathetic friends, family, or co-workers to share their interest could turn to cyberspace and find countless others discussing the particular aspects of the case they found most intriguing.

Of course the on-line Simpson discussion shared many of the failings of the more established media sources: name-calling, trite observations, arguments based on inaccurate data, and so on. But cyberspace did have things not found anywhere else, most notably a vast amount of both primary and secondary information and some very high-quality discussions.

There was more than one place where a computer user could obtain the daily transcripts of the trial, often within just a few days. (One of these sources is listed in appendix 4.) Many other official documents, such as motions and rulings, were available. Some commercial sources, like Court TV, provided background material on some of the trial participants in their on-line forums. Many World-Wide Web sites published color photos of the evidence or exhibits. Sound files were widely distributed and there were even a few video clips available for downloading.

Coupled with this activity was a group of people who used the information to carefully argue the issues in the case. An Internet discussion group known as alt.fan.oj-simpson was quickly formed. Unlike the rest of the media commentators who were almost exclusively discussing events which had just happened, on-line discussions included arguments based on evidence which might have been days or weeks or months old. Many people used the actual transcripts to support their conclusions, quoting them liberally to establish a point. Dense testimony was studied closely over a period of time in order to glean subtle meanings and significance. Some of the participants in the on-line discussions were specialists of all kinds; most were amateurs who nonetheless contributed to the understanding of the case by careful argument. Other on-line forums quickly developed, some on the commercial computer on-line services, some privately arranged, some wide in scope, others narrow.

Interestingly, one of the regular topics of discussion in many such forums was the coverage of the trial in the 'old media'. Arguments heard on television by lawyer-commentators might be elaborated more fully by one on-line contributor and then critically exposed as in error by another.

Thus, even though the traditional media failed at presenting the kind of detailed, sometimes technical, issue-related analysis which many trial followers wanted, the gap was filled in part by the on-line media.

But not all the blame for the media's failures in the Simpson case can be laid at the door of the journalists themselves. After all, these people live or die by their ratings; they are powerfully driven to give the customers what the customers want. Nonetheless, the almost complete preoccupation of the media with how various stratagems would *play* reflects a number of common misconceptions, prevalent among press and public alike.

The Jury Crutch

The most prevalent of these preoccupations concerned the jury. Throughout the trial, commentators frequently discussed the competing testimony or theories of the case by restating the arguments of either side or both, usually passing some observations on how these would impress the jury, refraining from critical evaluation of the arguments, and then saying, in effect, "now it's up to the jury."

It is, of course, obvious and undisputed that the jury actually determines legal guilt or absence of guilt. The jury is empowered to arrive at a verdict. But it is quite silly to infer from this that other people are not fully entitled to have an opinion, to state their opinion, and to conduct vigorous arguments independently of what the jury decides.

Congress is empowered by the Constitution to enact new laws, but clearly this doesn't mean that you and I can't debate the merits of legislation, both before and after it has gone through Congress. A difference here is that it is quite proper for the debate outside Congress to influence Congress's decisions; it would be ominous if this did not occur. In the case of a jury decision, however, the jury is not supposed to be swayed by the views expressed in the public arena. But this is not to say that such views should not be expressed.

According to the principles embodied in our system of government, the citizenry ought to be informed about such matters as the workings of the courts. But if people don't debate the merits of a legal case, they can have little basis for any judgment with respect to the efficacy of the system of law enforcement. Ordinary citizens cannot decide whether juries are doing a good job without deciding whether juries make mistakes, and they can only decide that by forming opinions about trials independently of jury verdicts. Or take the question of police conspiracies to pervert justice. Such conspiracies sometimes occur, but opinions vary about how common they are. It is not possible to reach a sensible conclusion on this topic without looking at particular trials where a police conspiracy is alleged.

Once the jury returned a verdict of Not Guilty in the Simpson trial, the theory of "it's up to the jury" took a different and even stranger turn. Now some people declared that since the jury had spoken, it was improper to continue discussions of Simpson's possible guilt. This line of thinking embodies a simple confusion. The jury was entitled to find Simpson Not Guilty and did so find him. This means, in the Anglo-Saxon legal tradition, that Simpson cannot be tried again for this particular crime, and cannot be punished by the courts for this crime. He cannot be imprisoned for the murders of Nicole Brown Simpson and Ronald Goldman.

It is the extraordinarily rare Simpson trial watcher who wants to change this legal position as it relates to Simpson. In that sense, there is well-nigh unanimous agreement that the jury was empowered to make the decision and that this decision is final and irreversible. But it is quite a different question whether Simpson, as a matter of fact, committed those murders. It is another different question whether the jury decided rightly on the evidence available to them. It is yet another question whether the jury discharged their most elementary responsibilities, for example, by carefully considering the evidence. These three sorts of questions can be debated and should be debated; it would be a dereliction if they were not debated. Many of the people who claim that since the jury has spoken all discussion of Simpson's possible guilt should cease would be outraged if this principle were applied to a verdict of Guilty. If someone is wrongfully convicted, the verdict can be overturned. If someone is mistakenly acquitted, that verdict can never be overturned under our existing legal rules, but people are free to form the opinion that a mistake was made. And they are free to withdraw their patronage from someone they believe to be an evil-doer.

Life Experiences as a Source of Truth

When commentators did present brief arguments concerning the case, it was frequently followed by the disclaimer that whether or not the jury accepted the argument would be influenced or even determined by their 'life experiences'. Debates over issues often moved quickly from the issues themselves to discussion of the life experiences of jurors. Inner-city blacks, it was widely stated, would be more sympathetic to charges of police tampering than, say, suburban whites.

Remarkably, the whole idea of life experiences being a valid basis for judging the evidence of conspiracy in the case was widely accepted and rarely challenged, although such an idea clearly implies that there are multiple truths and the one which the jury delivers may be different from the one seen by someone else. It is not that life experience is irrelevant, but it is merely a starting point.

Philosopher David Detmer examined this tendency to rely on life experience as a means of analyzing the trial and concluded:

> ... how can anyone's thinking about the crimes, after the fact, affect what had already taken place? What we need to be able to figure out is what really happened. If the response is that the embeddedness of reason in diverse experiential contingencies rules out *a priori* any possibility of determining what really happened, or renders the very concept of "what really happened" incoherent, we should realize that we have arrived at a disabling skepticism, not a robust, exciting alternative to outworn notions of "truth." If the best evidence and arguments suggest that such a conclusion is warranted, then so be it, but we should recognize that it is nothing to celebrate. For we would then have to acknowledge, not only our inability to determine who has and has not committed a murder, a matter of no small moral seriousness, but also that we can never figure out what anyone has ever done. What then becomes of the notion of responsibility?[1]

Is it appropriate to decide the facts of any case based solely on our own personal experience, no matter how limited or unusual it may be? Don't we have a duty to put our biases aside in a search for truth? Can we use our life experience as a starting point but still evaluate all of the evidence fairly and in context? Is it really the case that truth is in the eye of the beholder?

Many media commentators regularly spoke of the Simpson trial as a great opportunity for the public to learn about the American judicial system. Unfortunately, this amounted to regular lessons on matters like the hearsay rule with virtually no time devoted to a discussion of how we might, as potential jurors in some future case, become better at critically but fairly appraising evidence, even if the facts of the case put before us are contrary to our personal experience. This was one valuable learning opportunity which was squandered by the people who seemed so intent on educating us.

Reasonable and Unreasonable Doubt

In the immediate aftermath of the 1995 verdict in the criminal case there was much talk about 'reasonable doubt', and it soon became clear that misconceptions abounded.

It was very commonly held that a person was the sole arbiter of whether there was reasonable doubt. This misunderstanding was sometimes betrayed by the use of the verb *have*, as in 'they had a reasonable doubt'. A doubt is a subjective feeling or attitude—one can simply 'have' a doubt. But whether the doubt is reasonable or not is independent of one's feelings. Marcia Clark had it right when she referred to "a doubt that is founded in reason":

> The question is whether you have a doubt that is founded in reason, so beware of the efforts to get you to accept the unreasonable, be distracted by the irrelevant and to base your decision on speculation, on mere possibilities with no hard evidence to show that any of them really occurred.[2]

It follows that a person could be mistaken about the status of their doubt—could harbor an unreasonable doubt and wrongly believe it to be reasonable. This suggests that the inquirer, for example the juror, has a responsibility to investigate whether any doubt is, as a matter of objective fact, reasonable. In the context of the Simpson case, the only alternative to Simpson's guilt is a police conspiracy, and therefore a reasonable doubt about Simpson's guilt must imply that it is reasonable to entertain the possibility of a police conspiracy.

This misunderstanding about reasonable doubt was compounded by a kind of psychological conjuring trick. To see how this trick works, imagine that you have before you enough evidence to convince you that X is guilty. Given that evidence alone, you would vote for X's guilt. Now imagine that this evidence is multiplied tenfold. Any tenth of the evidence you have would be enough for a Guilty verdict. Next, you come to entertain a significant doubt about five-tenths of the evidence. By rights, you ought now to vote Guilty without hesitation, for after all, you have five times as much unquestioned evidence as would be necessary for such a decision. In practice, many people in this situation will feel in their guts that the doubt attached to the five-tenths travels by osmosis into the other five-tenths. All their certainty becomes tainted by the doubt which ought to be confined to certain specific areas.

Given this human propensity, it is welcome to the defense, in an objectively 'hopeless' position, to complicate matters, to quibble over tangential issues, to raise doubts about inessential details. There is always the chance that the jury will actually be muddled, and not understand the limits of these doubts. But even if they understand the issues, the doubts about some little bits of the case may subtly influence their evaluation of the unquestioned parts of the evidence. Some of the remarks made by jurors since the 1995 verdict do indeed suggest that they believed that if they thought there was a reasonable doubt about *any part* of the prosecution case, they were obliged to acquit. But, naturally, the appropriate response to doubt about some part of the evidence is to ask: if we take away that part of the evidence, what is then implied by the totality of the evidence which remains?

In some areas, the prosecution performed better than they have been given credit for, if we judge them by whether they literally answered various defense assertions. But (although they were not helped by an overindulgent judge) they did a very poor job of avoiding unnecessary complications and keeping the essentials of their case as stark and simple as possible. By mounting an unnecessarily elaborate and detailed case, they invited speculative fishing expeditions which are always bound to turn up seeming anomalies that take a while to explain. It then becomes easy for an alert defense to drag red herrings through the evidence until it all smells fishy.

POSTSCRIPT

If O.J. Were Innocent

Why, sometimes I've believed as many as six impossible things before breakfast.
— Lewis Carroll, *Through the Looking Glass*

I f O.J. Simpson did not commit the brutal murders of Nicole Brown Simpson and Ronald Goldman, then the following must be true:

- It is just a coincidence that Simpson cut himself at his home, leaving blood in his Bronco, his driveway, his foyer, and his bathroom at about the time the murders occurred.

- There is an innocent explanation for how, after he cut himself at his Rockingham home, he could not recall how he did this when he spoke to police only about fifteen hours later.

- It is a coincidence that Simpson cut himself on his left hand and that there are drops of blood to the left of bloody footprints leaving the murder scene.

- Simpson then cut himself again on the same hand at a hotel room in Chicago only a few hours later.

- It is just a coincidence that the bloody shoe impressions walking away from the murder scene were in O.J.'s size and that the shoes which made them were quite expensive—$160 a pair. It is just another coincidence that he regularly purchased size 12 shoes at one of only forty stores in the U.S. which sold these expensive shoes.

- The bloody impression on the Bronco carpet, while consistent with the Bruno Magli shoe impressions left at the murder scene, was not made by a Bruno Magli shoe. If it was left by Fuhrman, then he somehow stepped in blood at the murder scene and left no record of it there. Sometime later, after at least forty-five minutes, he rewetted his shoes—perhaps by stepping in wet grass—and left the impression in the Bronco without leaving any grass or dirt.

- There is an innocent explanation for why Simpson failed to answer the limousine driver's buzz for twenty minutes and a similarly good explanation for why several seemingly conflicting alibis have been offered by Simpson and his lawyers.

- The thumps which frightened Kato had nothing to do with the murders or with O.J. Simpson or with the glove being dropped near the source of the thumps and there is another explanation for these occurrences, although no one has yet managed to guess what that explanation might be. The fact that Kato reached the front of the Rockingham estate to investigate these thumps at about the same time Simpson reached the front of his house is a coincidence.

- While Allan Park, the limousine driver, did not see the Bronco on Rockingham when he first arrived at Simpson's home, it was nonetheless there.

- It is mere coincidence that defense witness Robert Heidstra saw a white sports utility vehicle with tinted windows near the murder scene at a time which could coincide with the aftermath of the murders and that Simpson drives a white sports utility vehicle with tinted windows. It is also mere coincidence that Heidstra overheard two raised voices, one of which he described as that of a black man.

- There is an innocent explanation for why Simpson's defense lawyers brought all his luggage from the night of the murders to court except the knapsack he wouldn't let anyone else carry.

- The hat found at the murder scene containing hairs consistent with Simpson's can be attributed to cross-contamination, coincidental matching, or the fact that Simpson might have left it there days or weeks in advance of the murders.

- It is a coincidence that the murderer left blue-black cotton fibers on his victims and Simpson was seen wearing dark blue or black clothing the night of the murders.

- There is nothing significant in the fact that the bed Simpson slept in while in Chicago has blood on both the lower and upper sheets while there is no blood on the bathroom counter or in the sink full of the broken glass on which he cut his finger.

- The fact that the doctor Simpson went to a few days after the murders (at the behest of his lawyer) found numerous cuts and abrasions on his left hand is of no significance.

- It is nothing more than an unfortunate coincidence that on the day of the murders Paula Barbieri broke up with Simpson and that Nicole would not save him a seat at their daughter's dance recital.

- Many women like Nicole have safety deposit boxes and there isn't any particular significance to the fact that she kept photos there depicting her beaten body.

- The reason the Bundy blood drops matched Simpson with various DNA tests at various laboratories is because they were somehow contaminated with his own blood or his own blood was purposely planted.

- The reason the Rockingham glove was shown to have some of Simpson's blood on it is because Collin Yamauchi was very sloppy the day he handled and tested it.

- The reason Ron Goldman's blood was found in the Bronco just after the murders is because it was planted or because the DNA tests were contaminated. Even if the explanation is contamination, it is still true that Fuhrman made the Bronco footprint, and the contaminated results showing Ron's alleles in the Bronco was a stroke of good luck for the prosecution and the cops.

- The reason the blood on the back gate matched Simpson is because it was planted almost three weeks after the murders. The numerous police officers who saw that blood just after the murders are deluded or lying, or the blood they saw was carefully removed by the conspirators before being replaced with Simpson's.

- The reason Nicole's blood was found on Simpson's socks is because it was planted.

- Later, the conspirators put more blood in the Bronco, but were careful to plant so little that there was a danger that it could not be typed using DNA tests.

- Simpson fled from the police five days after the murders with a passport, a cheap disguise, some $8,000, and a gun, even though he was innocent.

- It is an astounding coincidence that the killer wore gloves from a batch of only a few hundred, of which Nicole purchased two pairs and Simpson has been depicted wearing two pairs.

- The Rockingham glove found on Simpson's property contained rare fibers matching the carpet in Simpson's Bronco either through unfortunate coincidence or because a conspirator used the glove inside Simpson's Bronco.

- It is just Simpson's extraordinary bad luck that the woman he beat, threatened, stalked, and terrorized was killed by someone else, for a completely unknown and unfathomable motive, under circumstances where Simpson had opportunity and no good alibi.

- Numerous police officers collaborated in a conspiracy to frame this popular celebrity, and although some of these officers were occasionally sloppy in following police procedures, they were always conscientious, and often brilliant, in executing their conspiracy, so that not a single scrap of evidence definitely indicating a frame-up attempt exists.

APPENDIX 1

DNA Evidence

This is a complete list of all 45 bloodstains subjected to DNA analysis and introduced in evidence at trial.[1]

Item	Description	Number of tested loci RFLP	PCR	Not Excluded	
6	Rockingham trail	0	2	OS	
7	Rockingham trail	0	5	OS	
12	Rockingham foyer	5	6	OS	
14	R'm master bathroom floor	0	1	OS	

At Bundy

42	Blood pool, Nicole	0	1	NB *	
47	1st blood drop by victims	0	7	OS	
48	Bundy walk blood drop	0	7	OS	
49	Bundy walk blood drop	0	6	OS	
50	Bundy walk blood drop	0	7	OS	
52	Bundy walk last drop	5	7	OS	
56	Shoe impression	0	5	NB	
78	Ron, boot blood drop	5	6	NB	RG
84	NB fingernails	0	7	NB	
115	Back gate	0	2	OS	
116	Back gate	0	2	OS	
117	Back gate	9	2	OS	

* The results of this test were not presented to the jury because the C dot was too faint to be identified, but the test itself was mentioned in testimony.

OS = O.J. Simpson
NB = Nicole Brown Simpson
RG = Ronald Goldman

Rockingham Glove, Item 9

9	Inside/back of wrist	0	1		NB	RG
G1	Inside/back index finger	5	2		NB	RG
G2	Inside/side middle finger	5	2		NB	RG
G3	Inside-back ring finger	8	2			RG
G4	Inside-back of hand	5	2		NB	RG
G9	Inside-by wrist notch	0	2			RG
G10	Inside-by wrist notch	0	2	OS		RG
G11	Outside-near wrist notch	0	1	OS	NB	RG
G12	Outside-near wrist notch	0	1		NB	RG
G13	Stitching, wrist notch	0	1	OS	NB	RG
G14	Inside-back of cuff	0	1		NB	RG

(The G-subdesignations refer to the Rockingham glove, Item 9)

Rockingham Socks, Item 13

42A-1	Ankle area	14	7		NB
42A-2	Leg opposite	0	2	OS	
42A-3	Leg same side	9	2	OS	
42A-4	Upper toe region	0	2	OS	
42B-1	Near ankle	0	2		NB
42B-2	Near ankle	0	2		NB

(All 42-subdesignations refer to the socks, Item 13)

The Bronco

23	Driver door interior	0	1	OS		
24	Instrument panel	0	1	OS		
25	Driver side carpet	0	2	OS		
29	Steering wheel	0	6	OS	NB	
30	Center console	0	2	OS		
31	Center console	0	2	OS		RG
34	Driver side wall	0	1	OS		
293	Driver side carpet	0	2		NB	
303	Center console	*	2	OS	NB	RG
304	Center console	*	2	OS	NB	RG
305	Center console	*	2	OS	NB	RG
C*	Center console	4	*	OS		RG

* Refers to the combination of 303, 304, and 305 for RFLP testing

APPENDIX 2

DNA Typing

DNA typing is a process of determining what DNA looks like at specific locations on the chromosome. Each chromosome is a long string of genes. The genes on the chromosome determine particular characteristics of our bodies, such as eye color. There may be several different versions of any particular gene, such as brown or blue or hazel eyes. Each different version of a gene is called an allele. In its simplest form, DNA typing is the process of determining which version or versions of a particular gene or genes are present in a sample of DNA.

Each particular chromosome is present in essentially every cell in our body as two versions. One version is inherited from our father and one version is inherited from our mother. Thus we each have two versions of each gene in our genome. Our genome is all the DNA which we have inherited from both our parents. These two versions for each gene will in general be different from each other in ways which are distinguishable by the DNA typing tests outlined below. (Sometimes we inherit the same allele from each parent.) The sum of the alleles present at each gene is called our genotype.

The process of determining a person's DNA type is particularly simple if one has the actual person present. In this case an abundance of tissue can be easily obtained (sometimes without even recourse to a syringe), and can be obtained under controlled conditions. DNA can be extracted from numerous sources, including blood, saliva, sperm, skin (epithelial cells), hair roots, and snot. The analysis of DNA from dried bloodstains—a common DNA source at crime scenes—is a far cry from the ideal situation. Depending on the age of the bloodstain, what it was found on (known as the substrate), and the environmental conditions it has endured before it was collected, the amount and quality of the DNA will vary. The effect of such variations should be compared with the extreme durability of DNA when it is dry, and the fact that DNA can be obtained and analyzed from fossil specimens millions of years old.

RFLP

If a sufficient amount of DNA of suitable quality (that is, it is not very degraded) is obtained from a bloodstain, then it can be typed using restriction fragment length polymorphisms (or RFLP). In this method of analysis, the DNA is cut by an enzyme called a restriction endonuclease which recognizes specific short sequences of DNA and cuts the DNA at such locations. Genomic DNA which has been digested by a restriction endonuclease will be cut into millions of pieces which will all vary in size (the size of each piece is determined by the DNA sequence of that piece). The different sized DNA fragments are separated on a gel by electrophoresis. The gel is a matrix with the consistency of gelatin, through which DNA must pass. The effect is similar to passing objects through a sieve in which smaller objects will pass more rapidly than larger ones. The DNA is forced through this gel by an electric current. Thus, smaller fragments in the gel will move further than larger fragments over a given time, and so the fragments are separated by size. The separated DNA is then fixed to a membrane in such a way that the precise position of each DNA fragment is retained on the membrane. This is called blotting. The DNA is blotted from the gel onto the membrane. The membrane is similar to a piece of paper, and the DNA is fixed onto it. Now, a fragment of a particular gene of interest can be hybridized to the DNA fixed on the membrane.

DNA consists of two strands wrapped around each other in the form of a helix. The two strands may be thought of as a plus and a minus strand. Separating the strands is called denaturing (the separated strands of DNA are called single-stranded DNA) whereas hybridizing the strands is a process of putting together the plus and minus strands which correspond to each other (when the two strands are bound to each other the DNA is said to be double-stranded). Corresponding strands are said to be complementary to each other. A cloned fragment is a piece of DNA which is a copy of DNA from our genome, and thus, it has a plus and a minus strand which will correspond to plus and minus strands in our DNA. So the clone will hybridize to those pieces of DNA which match it, and in this way the clone too will become affixed to the membrane. When a cloned piece of DNA is hybridized to a membrane with DNA affixed to it, the clone is referred to as a probe. The precise sizes of the fragments which have DNA that matches the clone will be revealed by the locations on the membrane where the clone is detected. The clone can be detected because it is made radioactive, and it will therefore expose a piece of film which is placed against the membrane.

The size of the genomic DNA fragments which hybridize to the clone is determined by the location of the restriction enzyme sites cleaved on either side of the region matching the clone. Thus, the size of the fragment can be any value. This is the discriminatory power of the RFLP typing test: the fragment lengths are continuously variable, whereas the differences detected by PCR can fall only in a set of discrete types. Moreover, the clone which was hybridized to the membrane can be removed after the film has been developed, and the membrane can be tested with many different cloned fragments. The most significant limitation in the RFLP test is simply the time the investigator has to perform the test, because this limits the number of different clones he or she may use.

The RFLP procedure requires enough DNA that an observable signal can be obtained from the radioactive clone which is hybridized to it. If only a tiny amount of DNA, or DNA which has already been broken into small pieces, is obtained, then a different approach is required.

The PCR Process

Specific regions of the DNA corresponding to any gene of interest, can be amplified, or increased in number, somewhat like a Xerox machine might copy a piece of paper over and over again. This will produce a large amount of DNA, large enough to be analyzed and typed. This amplification of specific genes is done by a process called the polymerase chain reaction (PCR). So, if only a small amount of DNA is extracted from a bloodstain, part of the DNA is amplified in amount, and then that amplified DNA is analyzed and typed.

PCR amplification and typing is relatively simple to employ and interpret, even though it is based on sophisticated scientific technology.[1] A scientist begins with a cloth swatch containing blood (or other source of DNA). The swatch is placed in a Chelex solution and boiled to remove the DNA from the swatch. Chelex is an inhibitor of proteins which might degrade DNA, use of Chelex stops degradation of DNA. This liquid solution is then put in a centrifuge. Very rapid spinning separates the liquid into two parts: the pellet (consisting of the swatch and the Chelex), and the DNA in a water solution. A small amount of the DNA in solution is removed and placed into a test tube. This test tube is prepared in advance, and contains the chemicals needed for the PCR reaction. Next the DNA polymerase is added. DNA Polymerase is an enzyme which synthesizes DNA. Now the sample is ready to be amplified using PCR. The amplification of the DNA samples occurs by repeating a series of steps called a cycle. Each cycle has three steps:

1. Denaturation. The tube is placed in a thermal cycler which raises the temperature to 94 degrees Celsius (slightly below the boiling temperature of water). The heat causes the double-stranded molecules of DNA to melt apart.

2. Annealing. Primers, small synthetic pieces of DNA, attach to specific points on the single-stranded DNA after the thermal cycler lowers the temperature enough to allow the primers to stick to DNA which is complementary to them. The primers chosen confer the specificity to the amplification—the primers 'program' the reaction and determine what gene portion gets amplified.

3. Extension. The polymerase reacts with the primers and begins to synthesize a DNA strand which is complementary to the single strands in the test tube.

Each step occurs at a different temperature, thus the thermal cycler machine merely cycles between the denaturation temperature, the annealing temperature, and the extension temperature. The DNA polymerase and the primers do the rest. Each PCR cycle results in twice as many double-stranded DNA molecules as before the cycle began. This cycle is repeated thirty-two times, resulting in millions more DNA molecules than what was initially put into the reaction.

PCR Product Typing

After the PCR amplification has been completed, the typing of the evidentiary DNA is ready to occur. It is at this stage in the analysis that the different DNA typing kits display many of their most significant differences. There are two basic categories into which forensic DNA testing may be said to fall. In the first, group, differences in the DNA sequence of alleles at a particular locus can be screened using an allele specific oligonucleotide (or ASO). An oligonucleotide is just like a primer, it is a small synthetic piece of DNA. So, in the PCR reaction, general primers are used which will amplify all the alleles which can be present and amplified at a gene, and then in the typing, ASOs are used to identify the particular alleles which were present in the evidentiary DNA. The second group uses loci which have a region containing a variable number of tandemly repeated sequences (called a VNTR), and this can then be typed based on the length of the PCR products which are produced (The length of DNA is measured in base pairs). This second group is similar in some ways to RFLP analysis.

The D1S80 locus falls into the second category. The AmpliFLP D1S80 PCR Amplification Kit uses primers which are specific to regions on either side of a repeat for the PCR amplification, and then determines the number of times the repeat unit (a 16 base pair DNA sequence) is present at each allele by comparing the PCR products to known size standards. The number of sixteen base pair repeats found in a particular allele at the D1S80 gene is the name of that allele. To determine this number, the PCR products are electrophoresed on a gel. After electrophoresis, the gel is stained using an extremely sensitive silver staining solution, and the bands produced from the evidentiary DNA are compared to an allelic ladder which contains bands corresponding to all the possible number of repeats found at the D1S80 gene. Thus, unlike the case in RFLP, the VNTR alleles detected by PCR must correspond in size to one of the standards.

The Polymarker test and the AmpliType HLA DQ-alpha PCR Amplification and Typing Kit are examples in the first category. In these kits after the loci are amplified by PCR using locus specific primers, the PCR products are hybridized to test strips which have immobilized on them a series of ASOs allowing identification of the particular alleles present in the evidentiary DNA. The hybridization of PCR products to the typing strip with it's immobilized ASO's (or probes) is called a reverse dot-blot.[2]

The typing procedures of the AmpliType HLA DQ-alpha PCR amplification and typing kit and the Polymarker kit are fairly similar and here the DQ-alpha typing is described in detail. The PCR products are removed from the test tube, and heated once again to denature them into single stranded DNA molecules. They are then placed with a DQ-alpha typing strip and a small amount of hybridization buffer. A hybridization buffer is a salt solution designed to cause the PCR products to bind themselves to the probes affixed to the test strip. There are nine probes on the DQ-alpha test strip, placed individually in each of nine dots on the strip itself. Each probe is a small piece of single-stranded DNA. The probes are made up of all the possible complementary DNA molecules for the DQ-alpha gene.[3] So the single-stranded DNA from the PCR reaction binds to the probes which are complementary to it.

The dots on the DQ-alpha typing strip are of three types:

1. The main typing dots. The 1 dot; 2 dot; 3 dot; and the 4 dot.

2. The allele subtyping dots. The 1.1 dot; the 1.2, 1.3, 4 dot; the 1.3 dot; and the all but 1.3 dot.

3. The control dot. This is generally called the C dot.

The first two types of dots are for distinguishing the different DQ-alpha alleles.

For the DQ-alpha gene there are four main alleles which are designated 1, 2, 3, and 4. There are three subtypes of the 1 allele, designated 1.1, 1.2, and 1.3.

After the hybridization process is complete, the hybridization buffer is replaced with a wash solution which has a lower salt concentration. The salt helps remove PCR products not tightly bound to any of the probes on the typing strip. This is to ensure that only PCR products which exactly or almost exactly match the probe bind to that probe. The temperature and timing of this wash are critical to achieving accurate results.

The wash solution is then replaced with a color development solution. PCR product bound to a dot causes the dot to turn blue in the presence of the color development solution. The developed strip is photographed. The strip or the photograph is then interpreted by analysts.

The analyst examines all the dots which 'light up' on the strip. The following general rules apply:

The C dot is designed to be the lightest dot on the strip. This is because a smaller amount of probe is affixed to this dot. If the C dot is not visible, the result is said to be uninterpretable. Lack of a C dot means there hasn't been enough amplification to ensure that all the alleles which are present will light up the relevant probes.

All of the 1 allele subtypes should light up the 1 dot as well as the appropriate subtype dot.

Notice that the 1.2 allele does not have a dot specific for it on the strip. The 1.2 allele is distinguishable from the 1.3 allele because it will also light up the all but 1.3 dot, as well as the 1.2, 1.3, 4 dot.

The 4 allele will light up the 4 dot, the 1.2, 1.3, 4 dot, and the all but 1.3 dot.

APPENDIX 3

Witness List

The witness list for *The People of the State of California vs. Orenthal James Simpson,* Case No. BA097211. Opening statements began on January 24th, 1995 and closing arguments concluded on September 29th, 1995. The first witness testified on January 31st, 1995; the last witness testified on September 20th, 1995.

Date	Witness	Description	Testimony	Direct	Cross
			**The Prosecution's Case in Chief**		
31 Jan	Sharyn Gilbert	LAPD 911 Dispatcher	Nicole's 911 call of 1 Jan 1989	Chris Darden	Johnnie Cochran
31 Jan	Det John Edwards	LAPD	Responded to 911 call of 1 Jan 1989	Chris Darden	Johnnie Cochran
31 Jan	Det Mike Farrell	LAPD	Investigated 1 Jan 1989 beating	Chris Darden	Johnnie Cochran
1–2 Feb	Ron Shipp	Friend of Nicole and O.J.; at O.J.'s home 13 June 1994	Knew of domestic violence between O.J. & Nicole; O.J. told him of murder dream	Chris Darden	Carl Douglas
2 Feb	Mike Stevens	Senior investigator, LA County DA's office	Retrieved contents of Nicole's safe deposit box, including photos showing her beaten	Chris Darden	Johnnie Cochran
2 Feb	Terri Moore	LAPD 911 Dispatcher	Nicole's 911 call of 25 Oct 93	Chris Darden	Johnnie Cochran
3 Feb	Sgt Robert Lerner	LAPD	Responded to 911 call of 25 Oct 93	Chris Darden	Johnnie Cochran
3 Feb	Catherine Boe	Next-door Neighbor of Nicole in 1993	O.J. told her how upset he was when he couldn't see Nicole	Chris Darden	Robert Shapiro
3 Feb	Carl Colby	Nicole's neighbor, husband of Boe	Saw O.J. staring at and walking around Nicole's house.	Chris Darden	Robert Shapiro
3, 6 Feb	Denise Brown	Sister of Nicole	Observed instances of abuse of Nicole by O.J.	Chris Darden	Robert Shapiro

6 Feb	Cynthia Shahian	Friend of Nicole	Nicole devastated by threatening legal letter from O.J. on 6 Jun 1994	Chris Darden	Johnnie Cochran
7 Feb	Tia Gavin	Mezzaluna waitress	Saw both victims at Mezzaluna	Marcia Clark	Robert Shapiro
7 Feb	Stewart Tanner	Mezzaluna bartender	Ron left Mezzaluna at about 9:50pm	Marcia Clark	Robert Shapiro
7 Feb	Karen Crawford	Mezzaluna manager	Retrieved Juditha's glasses, gave them to Ron	Marcia Clark	Robert Shapiro
7 Feb	Kim Goldman	Sister of Ron	Found waiter uniform draped carelessly over door in Ron's apartment	Marcia Clark	Johnnie Cochran (no questions)
7 Feb	Pablo Fenjves	Neighbor of Nicole	Heard plaintive wail of a dog at about 10:15 or 10:20	Marcia Clark	Johnnie Cochran
8 Feb	Eva Stein	Neighbor of Nicole	Heard dog barking	Marcia Clark	Johnnie Cochran
8 Feb	Louis Karpf	Neighbor of Nicole, lives with Eva Stein	Saw Kato-the-dog barking on the street at 10:45 P.M.	Marcia Clark	Johnnie Cochran
8 Feb	Steven Schwab	Brentwood resident	Found Kato-the-dog at 10:55 P.M. at Dorothy & Bundy	Marcia Clark	Carl Douglas
8 Feb	Sukru Boztepe	Brentwood resident	Kato-the-dog led him to Nicole's body	Marcia Clark	Johnnie Cochran
8 Feb	Elsie Tistaert	Brentwood resident	Heard barking, called police	Marcia Clark	Johnnie Cochran
9, 14 Feb	Officer Robert Riske	LAPD	Responded to Tistaert; 1st policeman to see Nicole, discovered Ron	Marcia Clark	Johnnie Cochran
14–15 Feb	Sgt David Rossi	LAPD	Watch commander who responded to Bundy scene	Marcia Clark	F. Lee Bailey
15–17 Feb	Det Ronald Phillips	LAPD	West LA cop who responded to Bundy scene	Marcia Clark	Johnnie Cochran
17, 21 – 22 Feb, 6 –9 Mar	Det Tom Lange	LAPD	Co-lead detective on case; in charge of Bundy crime scene	Marcia Clark	Johnnie Cochran
6 Mar	Mark Storfer	Brentwood Resident	Heard a dog barking at about 10:20 P.M.	Marcia Clark	Johnnie Cochran
9 Mar	Patti Goldman	Ron's stepmother	Her shopping list was in bag with Ron's clothes	Marcia Clark	Johnnie Cochran
9–10, 13–16 Mar	Det Mark Fuhrman	LAPD	Found the glove behind Kato's room and will regret it the rest of his life	Marcia Clark	F. Lee Bailey
16 Mar	Lt Frank Spangler	LAPD	Fuhrman wasn't alone	Marcia Clark	F. Lee Bailey

16 Mar	Darryl Smith	Freelance videographer	His film shows cops in blood *after* crime tape removed	Marcia Clark	Johnnie Cochran
16–17, 20–21 Mar	Det Philip Vannatter	LAPD	Co-lead investigator; in charge of Rockingham crime scene	Chris Darden	Robert Shapiro
21–23, 27–28 Mar	Brian "Kato" Kaelin	O.J.'s houseguest, formerly Nicole's tenant	Heard thumps, no sign of O.J. from 9:36 to 10:54	Marcia Clark	Robert Shapiro
28 Mar	Rachel Ferrara	Friend of Kaelin	On phone with Kato when he heard the three thumps	Marcia Clark	Johnnie Cochran
28–29 Mar	Allan Park	Limo driver	Drove O.J. to airport; saw black person enter house	Marcia Clark	Johnnie Cochran
29 Mar	Judge Delbert Wong	Special Master	Fetched luggage from O.J.'s & Kardashian's homes	Chris Darden	Johnnie Cochran
29 Mar	James Williams	LAX skycap	Checked O.J.'s bags, saw O.J. near rubbish bin	Marcia Clark	Carl Douglas
30 Mar	Sue Silva	Westec Security Inc.	Described O.J.'s security system	Chris Darden	Shawn Chapman
31 Mar	Charles Cale	Neighbor of O.J.	No Bronco Sunday night, Bronco askew Monday morning	Chris Darden	Robert Shapiro
3–5, 11–14, 17–18 Apr	Dennis Fung	LAPD criminalist	Collected evidence at Bundy & Rockingham	Hank Goldberg	Barry Scheck
20, 25–27 Apr	Andrea Mazzola	LAPD criminalist	Worked with Fung, had never heard of O.J. Simpson	Hank Goldberg	Peter Neufeld
1–5 May	Gregory Matheson	Chief chemist, LAPD	Tested some blood evidence	Hank Goldberg	Robert Blasier
8 May	Bernie Douroux	Towtruck driver	Towed Bronco from Rockingham	Chris Darden	Johnnie Cochran
8–15 May	Dr. Robin Cotton	Lab director, Cellmark Diagnostics	DNA evidence, both PCR and RFLP	George Clarke	Peter Neufeld
16–19, 22, 31 May–1 Jun	Gary Sims	California Dept of Justice	DNA evidence	Rockne Harmon	Barry Scheck
23–24 May	Renee Montgomery	Criminalist, CA DOJ	DNA evidence	Rockne Harmon	Robert Blasier
24–31 May	Collin Yamauchi	LAPD criminalist	Handled evidence, did PCR	Rockne Harmon	Barry Scheck
2–15 Jun	Dr. Lakshmanan Sathyavagisw aran	LA County Coroner	Cause & manner of death	Brian Kelberg	Robert Shapiro

15 Jun	Brenda Vemich	Merchandise buyer, Bloomingdale's	Nicole bought gloves the week before Xmas in 1990	Chris Darden	Johnnie Cochran
15 Jun	Richard Rubin	Former Isotoner VP & General Manager	The gloves were distinctive & only sold by Bloomies; O.J. tries on gloves	Chris Darden	Johnnie Cochran
16 Jun	Richard Rubin (resworn as witness)	Former Isotoner VP & General Manager	The gloves in original condition would easily fit O.J.; liquid causes shrinkage	Chris Darden	Johnnie Cochran
19 Jun	William J Bodziak	FBI shoeprint expert	Bloody Bundy prints: size 12, Bruno Magli, $160 a pair	Hank Goldberg	F. Lee Bailey
20 Jun	Samuel Poser	Shoe dept manager, Bloomingdale's	Sold O.J. shoes 4 or 5 times, all size 12; Bloomies stocks Bruno Magli	Hank Goldberg	F. Lee Bailey
20 Jun	Gary Sims (resumes testimony)	California DOJ	RFLP: rear gate, Bronco, socks all match O.J.	Rockne Harmon	Barry Scheck
21 Jun	Richard Rubin (resworn)	Former Isotoner VP & GM	O.J. tries on new pair of gloves and "they fit quite well"	Chris Darden	Johnnie Cochran
21 Jun	LuEllen Robertson	Custodian of records, Airtouch Cellular	O.J. rang Nicole at 2:18pm; rang Paula at 10:03 & :04 P.M.	Marcia Clark	Johnnie Cochran
21 Jun	Kathleen Delaney	Lawyer for Mirage Hotel, Las Vegas	Paula Barbieri in Las Vegas night of murders, guest of Michael Bolton	Marcia Clark	Johnnie Cochran
22–23, 26 Jun	Bruce Weir	Professor of statistics	Astronomical statistics for mixed samples	George Clarke	Peter Neufeld
26–27 Jun	Denise Lewis	LAPD criminalist	Recovered hair & trace evidence from victim's clothes	Marcia Clark	Robert Blasier
27–28 Jun	Susan Brockbank	LAPD criminalist	Recovered hair & trace evidence from crime scene stuff	Marcia Clark	Robert Blasier
29 Jun–6 Jul	Douglas Deedrick	FBI hair & fiber expert	Hair at crime scene matches O.J., fibers left by killer distinct	Marcia Clark	F. Lee Bailey

The Defense's Case in Chief

10 Jul	Arnelle Simpson	O.J.'s daughter (from first marriage)	Shipp was drinking and not alone with her father	Johnnie Cochran	Marcia Clark
10 Jul	Carmelita Simpson-Durio	O.J.'s sister	Shipp was drinking and not alone with her brother	Robert Shapiro	Chris Darden

10 Jul	Eunice Simpson	O.J.'s mother	Shipp was drinking and not alone with her son	Johnnie Cochran	Chris Darden (no questions)
10 Jul	Carol Conner	Song writer	Saw O.J. & Paula the evening before the murders	Robert Shapiro	Chris Darden
10 Jul	Mary Collins	O.J.'s longtime interior designer	Week before murders, discussed redecorating with O.J. & Paula	Johnnie Cochran	Marcia Clark
11 Jul	Mattie Shirley Simpson Baker	O.J.'s elder sister	Shipp was drinking and not alone with her brother	Robert Shapiro	Marcia Clark
11 Jul	Jack McKay	CFO, American Psychological Assn	Played golf with O.J. on 8 June 94	Johnnie Cochran	Marcia Clark
11 Jul	Danny Mandel	Aaronson's blind date (see below)	Walked by scene near time of murders; saw no bodies	Robert Shapiro	Marcia Clark
11 Jul	Ellen Aaronson	Brentwood resident	Walked with Danny, saw no bodies	Johnnie Cochran	Marcia Clark
11 Jul	Francesca Harman	Dinner party guest in Brentwood murder night	Left dinner party near Nicole's at 10:15; heard no dog	Robert Shapiro	Chris Darden
11 Jul	Denise Pilnak	Nicole's neighbor (900 block of Bundy)	Remembered 8 months after the murders that she heard no dog	Johnnie Cochran	Marcia Clark
11 Jul	Judy Telander	Friend of Pilnak	With Pilnak night of murders; didn't hear dog	Robert Shapiro	Marcia Clark
11 Jul	Robert Heidstra	Neighbor of Nicole	Heard "Hey, hey, hey" at 10:40. Saw a bronco-like vehicle near murder scene	Johnnie Cochran	Chris Darden
12 Jul	Wayne Stanfield	American Airlines captain	Flew plane O.J. took to O'Hare, saw O.J. staring into space	F. Lee Bailey	Chris Darden
12 Jul	Michael Norris	Network Courier employee	O.J. was friendly as he exited limo. Norris saw no cut.	Robert Shapiro	Marcia Clark
12–13 Jul	Michael Gladden	Network Courier employee	Got autograph from O.J. at LAX. O.J. calm and friendly.	Johnnie Cochran	Chris Darden
13 Jul	Howard Bingham	Professional photographer	On flight to Chicago; O.J. had pleasant demeanor, no cut	Johnnie Cochran	Marcia Clark
13 Jul	Stephen Valerie	Passenger to Chicago	Saw no cut on finger	Johnnie Cochran	Chris Darden
13 Jul	Jim Merrill	Hertz employee	Collected O.J. at O'Hare	Carl Douglas	Marcia Clark

13 Jul	Raymond Kilduff	Hertz vice president	Saw O.J. outside Chi hotel with bloody finger	Robert Shapiro	Chris Darden
13 Jul	Mark Partridge	Intellectual property lawyer; passenger to LAX	Sat next to O.J., copyrighted his notes then forgot the contents	Johnnie Cochran	Marcia Clark
14, 17–18 Jul	Dr. Robert Huizenga	Beverly Hills private physician, Harvard trained	O.J. walked like Tarzan's grandfather, but physically capable of murder	Robert Shapiro	Brian Kelberg
18 Jul	Juanita Moore	O.J.'s longtime barber	O.J. had dandruff in summer	Johnnie Cochran	Marcia Clark
18 Jul	Officer Donald Thompson	LAPD	Cuffed O.J. the afternoon of 13 June 1994	Johnnie Cochran	Chris Darden
18–19 Jul	John Meraz	Viertel's employee	Towed Bronco, saw no blood, stole papers from Bronco	Johnnie Cochran	Marcia Clark
19 Jul	Richard Walsh	Fitness trainer in O.J. video	Heard O.J. make wife hitting remarks; surprised O.J. could work hard for hours & hours	Johnnie Cochran	Chris Darden
19–20 Jul	Willie Ford	Videographer, LAPD	Video of O.J.'s home day after murders did not include the socks	Johnnie Cochran	Chris Darden
20 Jul	Josephine "Gigi" Guarin	O.J.'s housekeeper	O.J. is very tidy, doesn't leave clothes laying around; let her stay away Sun. night	Johnnie Cochran	Chris Darden
20 Jul	Det Kelly Mulldorfer	LAPD, Legal Affairs Division	Investigated the storage of the Bronco at Viertel's	Barry Scheck	Chris Darden
20 Jul	Det Adalberto Luper	LAPD	Witnesses Fung collecting socks from bedroom	Johnnie Cochran	Chris Darden
24 Jul	Dr. Fredric Rieders	Forensic toxicologist	EDTA present in the stains on the socks and back gate; did not conduct tests	Robert Blasier	Marcia Clark
25–26 Jul	Roger Martz	FBI Special Agent	No EDTA present in the stains on the socks and the back gate; conducted tests	Robert Blasier	Marcia Clark
27, 31 Jul, 1 Aug	Herbert MacDonell	Blood splatter expert	Sock stains not spatter, but smear; stains were made when no foot in sock	Peter Neufeld	Marcia Clark
1 Aug	Thano Peratis, RN	LAPD jail nurse	Took O.J.'s blood, put in EDTA tube. (Taped and read testimony)	Marcia Clark	(video tape & Qs read by C Douglas

2–4, 7 Aug	John Gerdes Ph.D.	Clinical Lab Director	LAPD lab contaminated; evidence may be contaminated	Barry Scheck	George Clarke
7–8 Aug	Terence Speed Ph.D.	Professor of Statistics	Common-mode errors are relevant for making statistical judgments	Peter Neufeld	Rockne Harmon
10–11 Aug	Dr. Michael Baden	Forensic pathologist	The victims put up a hard struggle for non-trivial amount of time	Robert Shapiro	Brian Kelberg
14 Aug	Dr. Fredric Rieders (resumed)	Forensic toxicologist	Rieders may have misdiagnosed the cause of death in another case	Robert Blasier	Marcia Clark
14, 16 Aug	Michelle Kestler	Director, LAPD crime lab	LAPD lab's collection and handling methods	Peter Neufeld	Chris Darden
17 Aug	Gilbert Aguilar	LAPD fingerprint specialist	No O.J. prints at murder scene; some unidentified prints	Johnnie Cochran	Chris Darden
21 Aug	John Larry Ragle	former director, Orange County Crime lab	Investigation in the Simpson case was below minimum standard	Robert Blasier	Hank Goldberg
22 Aug	Christian Reichardt	O.J.'s friend, ex-boyfriend of Faye Resnick	O.J. happy during a 9 P.M. phone conversation the night of the murders	Johnnie Cochran	Chris Darden
22 Aug	Det Kenneth Berris	Chicago Police Dept	Involved in the Chicago investigation	Johnnie Cochran	Chris Darden
22–23, 25, 28 Aug	Dr. Henry Lee	Chief criminalist, state of Connecticut	Parallel line imprints at Bundy; "something wrong" with Item #47	Barry Scheck	Hank Goldberg
5 Sep	Kathleen Bell	Acquaintance of Mark Fuhrman in 1985 or 86	Heard Fuhrman say he wanted to "burn niggers"	F. Lee Bailey	Chris Darden
5 Sep	Natalie Singer	Acquaintance of Mark Fuhrman in 1987	Heard Fuhrman say "the only good nigger is a dead nigger"	F. Lee Bailey	Marcia Clark
5 Sep	William Blasini, Jr.	Frequents Viertel's tow yard	Bronco was unlocked, no blood seen on the console	Johnnie Cochran	Marcia Clark
5 Sep	Rolf Rokahr	LAPD photographer	Took the photos at both crime scenes	Peter Neufeld	Chris Darden
5–6 Sep	Laura Hart McKinny	Freelance writer	Made tapes of Fuhrman wherein he said "nigger" at least 42 times	Johnnie Cochran	Chris Darden
6 Sep	Roderic Hodge	Man arrested by Mark Fuhrman	Fuhrman said to him "I told you I'd get you, nigger."	Johnnie Cochran	Chris Darden
Even though prosecution begins rebuttal now, defense hasn't rested					

18 Sep	Herbert MacDonell	Blood splatter expert	Lots of blood does not shrink brand new Aris Leather Lights	Peter Neufeld	Marcia Clark
19 Sep	Michael Wacks	FBI special agent	Overheard Vanatter's conversation with Fiato brothers	Johnnie Cochran	Brian Kelberg
19 Sep	Larry Fiato	Organized crime informant	Vannatter told him that Simpson was a suspect	Robert Shapiro	Brian Kelberg
19 Sep	Craig Fiato	Organized crime informant	Vannatter said "the husband is always the suspect"	Johnnie Cochran	Brian Kelberg
19 Sep	Det Philip Vannatter	LAPD	Did not recall making the statements attributed to him by Fiato brothers	Robert Shapiro	Brian Kelberg

The Prosecution's Rebuttal Case

11 Sep	Mark Krueger	Amateur photographer	O.J. photo w/ black gloves; 29 Dec 1990 Bears–Chiefs, Soldier Field	Marcia Clark	Robert Blasier
11 Sep	Bill Renken	Professional photographer	O.J. photo & video w/ gloves; 6 Jan 1991 Oilers–Bengals, Cincinnati	Marcia Clark	Robert Blasier
11 Sep	Kevin Schott	Photography teacher	O.J. photo w/ gloves; 21 Nov 1993 Colts–Bills, Buffalo, NY	Marcia Clark	Robert Blasier
11 Sep	Stewart West	Professional photographer	O.J. photo w/ gloves; Dec 93, Oilers–49ers Candlestick Park	Marcia Clark	Robert Blasier
11 Sep	Michael Romano	Freelance photographer	O.J. photo w/ gloves; 15 Jan 1994, Raiders–Bills, Buffalo	Marcia Clark	Robert Blasier
11 Sep	Debra Guidera	Photo messenger (& amateur photographer)	O.J. photo w/ gloves; 12 Dec 1993, Colts–Giants, E. Rutherford, NJ	Marcia Clark	Robert Blasier
12 Sep	Richard Rubin (yes, again)	Glove expert	The photo gloves are Aris Leather Lights, size XL	Chris Darden	Robert Blasier
13 Sep	Gary Sims	DOJ	3 combined Bronco console bloodstains match OJS and RG at 4 RFLP probes	Rockne Harmon	Barry Scheck
13 Sep	Stephen Oppler	DA's investigator	Peratis video	Marcia Clark	Peter Neufeld
13 Sep	Theresa Ramirez	DA's photographer	Peratis video	Marcia Clark	Peter Neufeld
14 Sep	Douglas Deedrick	FBI fiber expert	Bloody impressions on jeans and paper likely came from shirt and jeans	Marcia Clark	Barry Scheck

| 14 Sep | William Bodziak | FBI foot impressions expert | There was only one set of foot impressions at Bundy | Marcia Clark | Barry Scheck |
| 20 Sep | Keith Bushey | Commander, LAPD | Ordered detectives to notify OJS of murders | Marcia Clark | Johnnie Cochran |

APPENDIX 4

Simpson Trial Web Pages

The O.J. Simpson Trial Court Transcripts

http://www.islandnet.com/~walraven/simpson.html

This web site provides a complete set of trial transcripts (most of which have been edited to remove the jarring ALL-CAPS formatting provided by court reporters) as well as excerpts from Jack Walraven's fun book *We Are at Sidebar*, a collection of trial sidebar transcripts.

Dmitri's O.J. Simpson Trial Center

http://www.cs.indiana.edu/hyplan/dmiguse/oj.html

A site jam-packed with interesting and informative material: photos, archived articles, court documents as well as dozens of links to other sites concerned with the Simpson case.

The O.J. Simpson Poetry Corner

http://www.cco.caltech.edu/~ekrider/OJPoetry/ojpoetry.html

A beautifully designed page of original poetry on the Simpson case. It begins with a photo of Shakespeare with the caption "bard" and includes the world's most famous police booking photo with the palindrome caption "drab". Poetry includes limericks, haiku, Dr. Seuss parody, and more.

LSI Scan Report of O.J. Simpson's Letter

http://www.getnet.com:80/~lsiscan/oj2.html

Scientific Content Analysis (SCAN) of the language used by Simpson in his so-called suicide letter. A fascinating read.

O.J. Simpson Trial Trivia Quiz

http://www.physics.unlv.edu/~farley/humor/OJ.html

Lots of interesting questions about the O.J. case, with answers provided on separate pages.

Simpson: Trial & Trivia

http://140.175.5.92/misc/oj.html

Interesting collection of facts regarding the O.J. case, for example, the jurors spent six one hundredths of one percent of their entire time in sequestration in deliberations.

'da O.J. Scoop!

http://ucsub.colorado.edu/~enger/oj.html

Lots of photos, some sound files, addresses, trial statistics, and one man's essay on the trial.

The 'Lectric Law Library™ Alcove for the "Trial of the Century"

http://www.inter-law.com/oj.html

Modest site worth visiting for its poetic tribute to Marcia Clark. A few court documents are available.

The Unofficial O.J. Simpson Boycott Page

http://sidewalk.com/boycott/

A page providing information on how to boycott Simpson and companies who may employ him. This page has been mentioned in the *Los Angeles Times*, *Washington Post*, *New York Times*, and on "This Week with David Brinkley".

I Want to Tell You

http://pathfinder.com/@@qL1NXAEYYAIAQlIL/twep/Focus/OJ/OJ.html

Page by Little, Brown promoting Simpson's book. Includes audio excerpts, photos, and passages. Tells how to order the book or get further information from Little, Brown.

Tracie Savage's Home Page

http://www.knbc4la.com/cast/savage.html

Notable because Savage may be the only witness in the Simpson case to actually have her own home page. Includes her photo and a resume of her career in television broadcasting. No actual reference to the Simpson case is made.

APPENDIX 5

O.J. Haiku

A few weeks after the October 1995 verdict, someone began a thread on the Internet suggesting a contest for the best haiku on the Simpson case. With the permission of the authors, I present my favorites here.

911 phone call
"His name is O.J. Simpson"
They did not listen

—Laura Beth Weiss,
university secretary

Barking dog alerts
Something bad has happened here
In darkness blood flows

—J. Montgomery,
associate systems analyst

Slick eel tries to make
a home in a glove at pond's
bottom, but ... too small

—Lee J. Merkel,
news editor for a daily newspaper

Newest Mega-Star
Lack of talent—no problem!
He's Kato Kaelin

—Peter Benjamin Swank,
investment advisor and strategist

White Bronco escape
O.J. cannot flee justice
Justice has fled us
—David P. Mikkelson

I wear two watches.
When I heard, I was in shock.
Figuratively.

—Tom McLoughlin,
financial analyst

Marcia bungles case:
Jury nullification.
The Juice squeezes free.

—Ian Munro,
literature student

National Rorschach:
Simpson, silent, served justice.
Blacks and whites estranged.

—John R. Kender,
professor of computer science

I did not watch it.
Apparently many did.
What will they do now?

—Craig S. Thom,
office automation support
specialist

APPENDIX 6

Simpson Trial Trivia Quiz

Answers on page 238

1. How did Lance Ito meet his wife Peggy York?

2. Who gave O.J. a Chia Pet as a Christmas gift in 1993?

3. Which witness was nominated for an Academy Award?

4. Which nonlawyer associate of O.J. Simpson has also been associated with convicted and executed murderer Gary Gilmore, Charles Manson co-defendant Susan Atkins, and Lee Harvey Oswald?

5. What confession did Christopher Darden claim O.J. Simpson had made to Candace Garvey in church?

6. Which witness's testimony in another case once caused defendants to come to court without any shoes?

7. What was Marcia Clark talking about when she said at sidebar, "if it were my husband I couldn't identify him"?

8. Who asked Johnnie Cochran why he wanted to beat up on a kid and an 85-year-old woman?

9. In a different case, one of the Simpson prosecutors argued in favor of the death penalty by waving a bible in front of the jury and saying "God recognized there would be people like Mr. Wash. That's why those commandments were delivered." Who said this?

10. Who incorrectly suggested that the value of pi is 3.1214?

11. During cross-examination, Johnnie Cochran brought up more than once where Detective Lange lived. Where was that?

12. Who did David Margolick, covering the case for the *New York Times*, describe as "a man with a hundred facial expressions for disgust"?

13. How many jurors were dismissed before opening statements even began?

14. Who suggested he might call a dead man as a witness?

15. Who used the expression "plaintive wail" at the preliminary hearing and was inclined not to repeat it again at the trial?

16. Of a prosecution witness, Johnnie Cochran said at sidebar "She is an alien from another planet". Who was he talking about?

17. In his 1967 interview with *Playboy*, F. Lee Bailey said "... a criminal lawyer who doesn't hold his booze well and goes jabberwocky can't have clients very long". Bailey had Lewis Carroll thrown back at him in the Simpson trial. Who did it and what prompted it?

18. When a Special Master was needed to fetch to court luggage from Rockingham and Robert Kardashian's home, Ito selected retired Judge Delbert Wong. How did Ito first meet Wong?

19. Allan Park's mother is an attorney. She advised her son not to do something before he testified. What was that?

20. Which two witnesses were asked no questions whatever on cross-examination?

21. To whom was Marcia Clark referring when she said "She is a known liar and a Simpson case groupie?"

22. On August 14th the following exchange occurred between Hank Goldberg and Judge Ito:

Mr. Goldberg: Kind of reminded here of one of those monster movies that we've all seen where the monster is impaled and burned and stabbed and just when you think it's finally going to rest, it rises up again out of the ashes.
The Court: You're probably speaking of Friday the 13th.
Mr. Goldberg: Yeah. I think so. I'm referring of course now to the matter before the court, not Professor Uelmen.

What was the matter before the court?

23. What happened on December 12th, 1968?

24. Who cross-examined Sue Silva, the Westec Security employee who described O.J.'s security system?

25. What was Lance Ito's license plate when he was a prosecutor?

26. What was on the license plate of Nicole's Ferrari?

27. How many times was Richard Rubin, former executive for Aris who testified as a glove expert, sworn in as a witness?

28. Who suggested that the water available outside the courtroom is toxic?

29. Who swore in FBI special agent Douglas Deedrick when he testified in the prosecution rebuttal case on September 14th?

30. Which witness, crucial to the defense conspiracy-planting theory, said in front of the jury "I don't take myself that importantly"?

31. Which relative of an important trial witness once represented one of Charles Manson's co-defendants?

32. Who said "It's a naked grab for people's wallets. It's a mercenary act, not publishing. It compounds the charge of homicide with a literary mugging" and what was he talking about?

33. Which television station advertised "We're the only ... network that is one hundred percent O.J.-free"?

34. Which witness mentioned the use of a space suit?

35. In the preliminary hearing, what was Detective Fuhrman's answer to Gerald Uelmen's question "Well, does dried blood look any different than dried taco sauce?"

36. Simpson's first wife, now Marguerite Simpson Thomas, denied that Simpson beat her during their marriage. One of Simpson's lawyers, however, had a first wife who did claim spousal battery. Which lawyer was this?

37. What did Judge Ito say to Court Reporter Olson at a March 8th sidebar when she told him "I'm sorry, judge. I can't make a record when counsel are both speaking at the same time"?

38. Who described whom with these words: "His eyes bulged almost out of their sockets as he directed a Bela Lugosi gaze on his prey"?

39. Marcia Clark asked the defense toxicology expert, Dr. Rieders, "And if you drink alcohol, you will become inebriated, correct?" What did Rieders say in reply?

40. Who compared the evidence collection techniques of Dennis Fung and Andrea Mazzola to that of a house cat?

41. How are the numbers 6–12–1994 and 32 related?

42. One of the lawyers for O.J. Simpson shares the first and last name of the one of the lawyers who worked on behalf of Sacco and Vanzetti. Name the lawyer.

43. Marcia Clark accused the defense of being greedy beyond belief on March 9th. What was Johnnie Cochran's reply?

44. Who was talking about whom: "I think the evidence at this point, you know, may establish that he is some form of a jerk. And what kind of jerk he is, I don't know ..."?

45. Which non-Simpson lawyer composed four poems he called "The Simpson Sonnets"?

46. What is located at 11663 Gorham Avenue?

47. Whom did Dominick Dunn describe as "Eve Harrington in grunge"?

48. Which author of a Simpson-related book claimed to have been inspired by the absurdly implausible film *The Pelican Brief*?

49. When Mike Walker, co-author with Faye Resnick of *Nicole Brown Simpson: Diary of a Life Interrupted*, was asked by Jeffrey Toobin "why, for example, he felt it necessary for the book to recount Nicole's supposed enthusiasm for fellatio with virtual strangers" what was Walker's reply?

50. Which juror sometimes wore to court an eye-catching "perfectly tailored tomato-red gabardine suit, with red shoes and a red tie"?

51. What happened after Marcia Clark asked Detective Lange on re-direct examination if he was "a human being"?

52. Who was F. Lee Bailey talking about when he said "the focal point of this witness' testimony ... is presently opposed by a dog"?

53. How much time did Christopher Darden and F. Lee Bailey estimate the conditional examination of Rosa Lopez would take?

54. How much time did the conditional examination of Rosa Lopez actually take?

55. Who said at sidebar "if there was an objection for gross insensitivity, that would be it?"

56. Who did Johnnie Cochran say Marcia Clark had portrayed as "the greatest sleuth since Sherlock Holmes?

57. The "mystery envelope" became famous at the preliminary hearing. Later it was disclosed (although never to the jury at trial) that the envelope contained a knife like the one the police searched for in vain at Simpson's home. Who actually searched Rockingham on June 28th looking for this knife and failed to find it?

58. Which lawyer said during testimony before the jury "I object to that objection"?

59. Which lawyer asked if he could be marked as an exhibit?

60. Who said of whom, "I don't have him on a leash either. He is a capable man. He is capable of walking around"?

61. Which detective refused to compare himself to Sherlock Holmes?

62. What did Barry Scheck say when Judge Ito jokingly suggested that a defense DNA expert had spit on the evidence?

63. What request did William Hodgman make of both Vincent Bugliosi, the Charles Manson prosecutor, and Marc Eliot, author of *Kato Kaelin: The Whole Truth*?

64. A large poster of Jim Morrison is on the wall of which lawyer's office?

65. What did Herbert MacDonell say when asked by Marcia Clark if he owned any gloves which cost $77 a pair?

66. Who is Holina Phipps?

67. Which participant in the Simpson trial, L.A. county's second most expensive trial, also participated in the county's most costly trial? What was the most costly trial in L.A. county?

68. Which reporter wrote about what group of people when he observed, "not since the Mona Lisa have people appeared so enigmatic"?

69. Which trial participant has run in the Los Angeles marathon three times?

70. Who said "my wife has an expression, 'you need to get outside and get the stink blowed off you'"?

71. Which juror said to Judge Ito "this is—as you mentioned earlier, before the case started, probably the most high-profile case that will probably ever be tried in history. There are a lot of people who like to secure a place for themselves as far as notoriety is concerned."

72. Who said to whom "Come on, young man. It is taught in interrogation school when you ask a question and the answer is 'I'm shocked to hear that,' that is not a no"?

73. What caused Judge Ito to suggest as a sanction that Johnnie Cochran pay for Christopher Darden's next shoe shine?

74. Who described whom as a "sick little puppy"?

75. On April 13th, which lawyers accused each other of being childish?

76. What two frequent commentators on the Simpson trial prosecuted Charles Manson?

77. In direct examination, witness Ellen Aaronson testified that she had once met Johnnie Cochran socially, during the course of the trial. When Cochran asked Aaronson if he had been with his wife at the time, what was Marcia Clark's objection?

78. Who said on June 16th, 1995 that Paula Barbieri's relationship with O.J. Simpson was "every bit as strong [now] as it was on June 12, 1994"?

79. Who pointed out that the Germans call the Neckar Valley River the "Romantic Highway"?

80. What caused Judge Ito to advise the jury to disregard banter?

81. Who said to whom: "This is your first case in a long time. You have been an administrator, we can tell"?

82. Who spoke of why men go on the left side of the road so that their sword hands are free?

83. One of the prosecution witnesses was once a student of one of the defense witnesses. The defense witness nicknamed his student "Lucky". Who are these two witnesses?

84. What was described as "waved around the scene like a matador

would in an arena"?

85. Which O.J. Simpson associate was called by the defense as a witness in the Charles Manson murder trial?

86. Which lawyer agreed that his own question was unintelligible?

87. Who suggested in a sidebar that O.J. Simpson hadn't "seen the bottom of his shoes in a while"?

88. Early on in the trial, Peter Neufeld had a conflict—both the Simpson trial and the trial of a different client (in New York) were going to be conducted simultaneously. Neufeld retained legal counsel who requested that Neufeld be permitted to argue in the Simpson case. Whom did he retain?

89. Who said of whom, she wanted to "come over here to stand close to me"?

90. Which witness helped to convict a streaker?

91. Who left a fingerprint, identified in court as lift number ten, by the outside gated entrance door bar in front of Nicole's home?

92. Who spoke of eighteen pairs of feet?

93. Who said that planting evidence wasn't part of his training?

94. Who first made reference to DNA being happy?

95. What do James Woods, Anita Hill, Steve Garvey, Geraldo Rivera, and Richard Dreyfuss have in common?

96. Who lost a son in a civil war?

97. Which lawyer said to Judge Ito at the side bar "you're my bud"?

98. What did Johnnie Cochran say at a March 7th sidebar that caused Marcia Clark to accuse of him going off on wild tangents?

99. Who suggested that Kato Kaelin didn't look "like a fellow who rode around in limousines"?

100. Which British knight was mentioned in trial testimony?

101. What was being referred to in these words: "it is like Lay's Potato Chips, you can't put them down and you can't eat just one"?

Trivia Quiz Answers

1. Over a dead body. Before becoming a judge, Ito was a deputy district attorney in Los Angeles. One night he got a phone call asking him to come to a crime scene. Near the corpse of a gang victim he was introduced to Margaret York, a detective on the case. York, now a captain and the highest-ranking woman in the LAPD, became a focal point of the trial for a brief period when there was a possibility that she would testify thus requiring Ito to recuse himself.

2. Kato Kaelin

3. Defense witness Carol Conner, who co-wrote the theme to *Rocky* with Bill Conty and Ann Robbins. The year she was nominated for the song-writing award, the Oscar went to Barbara Streisand. Connor was at a charity event the night before the murders and saw O.J. and Paula Barbieri there.

4. Lawrence Schiller. Schiller spent quite a while in Utah before Gilmore's execution. As in the Simpson case, he regularly visited Gilmore in prison. His tapes of conversations with Gilmore were the basis of Norman Mailer's book *The Executioner's Song* (Mailer and Schiller share the copyright for this work). Schiller obtained and sold Susan Atkins's story—although he never met her—and contracted to receive 25 percent of the proceeds of sale. The story was somehow obtained by the *Los Angeles Times* before it was published in the British and European outlets with whom Schiller had contracted. Schiller teamed up again with Mailer for a book on Oswald, again someone he had never met. Schiller assisted Mailer in establishing contacts in the Soviet Union with people Oswald had known during his stay in that country.

5. That he had cheated on Nicole. From a February 6th discussion held outside the presence of the jury:

Mr. Cochran: The next witness is Cindy Garvey?
Mr. Darden: Candace Garvey.
Mr. Cochran: I want to make sure we have it clear where counsel is going to go, because each time they don't talk to their witnesses and we get a lot of extra stuff in, and I want to try to avoid just that. You said that is permissible, so

maybe if we could have an offer of proof.

The Court: Which incidents? She is just for the recital, too, isn't she?...

Mr. Darden: This is a search for the truth. She may, you know, testify to something else, Judge.

Mr. Cochran: What if he kept it out? Does that bother you at all?

The Court: All right. Come on. Counsel, counsel. The offer of proof is that she is going to testify to the afternoon or the evening recital? Was she one of the people who went to dinner?

Ms. Clark: No, she didn't go.

The Court: All right.

Mr. Darden: We are not going to ask her about, you know, him telling her in church that he cheated on his wife and all that other—

Mr. Cochran: This is part of the record. If you don't mind, your honor, would you—

[discussion between lawyers from both sides goes off the record]

6. **William Bodziak, the FBI shoe impression expert. He was questioned by F. Lee Bailey on June 19th:**

Q   ... you would assume that somewhere along the line, the defendant who got caught because of his own shoeprints was made aware of that fact?

A   They are, yeah. I mean they would—they'll sit and watch my testimony, and I've even had one case where they came in the next day without their shoes on. So they certainly are aware of that, yes.

7. **The fact that Cochran wanted to show the witness, Officer Robert Riske, a photograph which Clark said was very unclear:**

The Court: ... from these three photographs can you identify this officer?

Mr. Cochran: Yes.

Ms. Clark: Obviously no one can. This is so disingenuous. This is so disingenuous. Look at this.

Mr. Cochran: I showed it to them first. That is not disingenuous.

Ms. Clark: This is extremely highly and completely disingenuous. There is no way that anyone could identify who this is. If it were my husband I couldn't identify him.

8. **Christopher Darden. At a February 9th sidebar the prosecution argued that to question Officer Riske about the criminalists' procedure for numbering pieces of evidence was beating up on a young witness who was not involved in the numbering process. The day before, Cochran had cross-examined 85-year-old Elsie Tistaert who lived across the street from Nicole:**

Mr. Darden: Why do you want to beat up on a kid? On [an] 85-year old women and a kid.

Mr. Cochran: I was so nice to that lady yesterday and she was tuning me out.

Ms. Clark: We all wanted to.

9. **Rockne Harmon in 1993. The jury had already found defendant Jeffrey Dean Wash guilty of murdering two women after raping one of them in Livermore in 1984. Wash appealed and Harmon's language in**

his closing was upheld in People v. Wash, 6 Cal.4th 215.

10. Judge Ito. Robert Blasier, cross-examining FBI special agent Martz, wanted the witness to show how he computed the minimum size of a swatch needed to detect blood with the preservative EDTA in it:

Q   Can you calculate the area of a circle with a five-millimeter diameter?
A   I mean I could. I don't — math — I don't — I don't know right now what it is.
Q   Well, what is the formula for the area of a circle?
A   Pi r squared.
Q   What is pi?
A   Boy, you are really testing me. 2.12, 2.17.
The Court: How about 3.1214.
Q   By Mr. Blasier: Isn't pi kind of essential to being a scientist knowing what it is?
A   I haven't used pi since I guess I was in high school.
Q   Let's try 3.12.
A   Is that what it is? There is an easier way to do —
Q   Let's try 3.14.

11. Simi Valley, site of the first Rodney King trial.

12. Barry Scheck. Early on in the trial, Margolick had compared Scheck to Nathan Detroit, a character in stories by Damon Runyon and in the musical based on them, *Guys and Dolls*.

13. Two, a man who worked for Hertz and who may have previously met Simpson and a woman who had personally experienced domestic violence.

14. Johnnie Cochran, who in a January 26th discussion with Judge Ito did not appear to recognize that double–Noble Prize winner Linus Pauling is dead:

Mr. Cochran: The same thing with Kary Mullis. If he wins the Nobel Peace Prize and they don't have him, they may not like that, but that doesn't level the playing field, Judge. They know about it.
The Court: I don't think he won the Peace Prize. I think that was—
Mr. Cochran: You know, Judge, I said that. I'm going to make that clear. The Noble Prize for chemistry. I had Dr. King on the mind yesterday when I was saying that who did win the Nobel Peace Prize.
The Court: Linus Pauling won those. Never mind. Never mind.
Mr. Cochran: Now, you would know those facts, too. I'm not surprised, Judge. Is he on our witness list yet?
Mr. Douglas: Not yet.
Mr. Cochran: Okay. We put him on our list. I will let you know—if we put him on your list, Judge, I'll let you know.
The Court: If he appears, I will be amazed.
Mr. Cochran: Then you will be amazed. ...

15. Pablo Fenjves. He is a writer and he thought that the expression might seem clichéd if repeated in his trial testimony. The prosecutors convinced him otherwise.

16. Catherine Boe, once a neighbor of Nicole.

17. In open court Bailey told the judge he had spoken with potential witness Max Cordoba "marine to marine." On national television, Cordoba denied having spoken with Bailey. The next day (15th March) Marcia Clark brought up the issue. Bailey tried to explain and Clark then gave the following speech:

> This is the kind of nonsense that gives lawyers a bad name, Your Honor. You know, it is very clear what he said to the court and what he was intending to convey. He was intending to convey to the court that he had personal knowledge of what this man said because this man said it to him personally marine to marine, and now he is standing up and hair splitting with us.
>
> I never said he said this to me, I just said he spoke to me personally. That is nonsense. That shows you what kind — what we have over here in the way of ethics on this side of the table. They get up and they will misrepresent to their heart's content, until they caught, and then they have excuses.
>
> And then they start splitting hairs and then, well, this means this, and no, that means that, that I felt like Alice in Wonderland. We have got Jabberwocky here. Nothing means what it says it does. "no" means I don't remember. "I don't remember" means no. Same thing.

18. Ito met Wong as child, when Ito was a boy scout and Wong was his scoutmaster.

19. She urged him not to drink soda before testifying because it might make him burp.

20. Kim Goldman (Ron's sister) was asked no questions by Johnnie Cochran on cross-examination. Eunice Simpson (O.J.'s mother) was asked no questions by Christopher Darden on cross-examination.

21. Mary Anne Gerchas, a witness mentioned by Johnnie Cochran in his opening statement, but never called to testify before the jury.

22. Whether the leaking of information concerning the DNA tests on Simpson's socks was relevant to the case. The defense argued that the leak came from the LAPD.

23. O.J. won the Heisman trophy and his daughter Arnelle was born.

24. Shawn Chapman; it was her only speaking appearance before the jury. She was the youngest attorney to question a witness.

25. 7 BOZOS (referring to the California Supreme Court). He changed his license plate when he was elevated to the bench.

26. L84AD8 (read as "Late for a Date").

27. Four times, more than any other witness. On June 15th he testified that the gloves were distinctive and O.J. tried on the gloves while Rubin was on the stand. On June 16th he testified that the gloves in original condition would easily have fit Simpson and that liquid could cause the

gloves to shrink. On June 21st O.J. tried on new pair of gloves and Rubin testified that "they fit quite well". On September 12th he testified that the gloves worn by O.J. in various evidence photos and videos were Aris Leather Lights, size XL. After each time he testified, he was excused as a witness and therefore had to be sworn again.

28. The testimony of LAX skycap James Williams is most famous for the fact that defense attorney Carl Douglas elicited the damaging testimony that Simpson was near a trash bin (where he might have disposed of a bag containing bloody clothes and a weapon). But Williams's testimony, with questioning by Marcia Clark, began with a discussion of water and a strange observation by Ito:

Q   Good afternoon, Mr. Williams.
A   Good afternoon.
Q   A little bit nervous?
A   Yes.
Q   Would you like some water?
A   Is the water fresh?
Q   Is it someone else's?
A   I'm thirsty. The water out there is hot.
The Court: It is not hot, it is toxic.
The Witness: It tastes like metal. It tastes like metal.

Later, Williams asked for more water, and at the beginning of re-direct examination, he said:

The Witness: You have some good water here, beats that stuff outside.
Ms. Clark: Don't drink that stuff outside. Skull and cross bones over that.

And when Ito excused Williams as a witness, the following exchange took place:

The Court: Mr. Williams, I am going to excuse you as a witness. Thank you very much for coming in, sir.
The Witness: All right. I have to come back tomorrow?
The Court: You are out of here.
The Witness: Oh, okay. Not like it was a problem. Thanks for the water.
The Court: Sure thing. Take the water with you.

29. Judge Ito. Apparently his clerk, Mrs. Robertson, was out of the courtroom at the time.

30. Frederic Rieders, who testified that FBI Agent Martz's tests revealed the presence of EDTA in the socks and the Bundy back gate stains, even though Martz had said those tests revealed the same level of EDTA as he found in his own, unpreserved blood.

31. Allan Park's mother, an attorney, represented Patricia Krenwinkel in her most recent parole hearing. Krenwinkel, originally sentenced to death, has served 25 years thus far for her participation in the murders at Sharon Tate's home.

32. Steve Wasserman, editorial director of Random House's Times Books

division, commenting on O.J. Simpson's book, *I Want to Tell You.*

33. Nick at Nite. Ironically, witness Stephen Schwab, who found Kato the Akita wandering the street and took him home, timed his evening dog walks around Nick at Nite programming. The dog Kato led Schwab's neighbors to the bodies.

34. Henry Lee. On August 23rd he testified concerning the examination of the socks found at Rockingham: "I wasn't provide [sic] with a lab coat nor a hair net. After I look, these both socks already put in one envelope. Doesn't matter what I wear, space suit, body armor. Still contaminated."

35. "I don't take much note of dried taco sauce too many times, so I wouldn't know."

36. Johnnie Cochran's first wife, Barbara Cochran, claimed that Johnnie twice assaulted her: once in 1967 and again in 1977.

37. "Just put attorneys ignore court's order to talk one at a time, there is no record to report."

38. Dominick Dunn writing about Carl Douglas's cross-examination of Ron Shipp, the prosecution witness who said that Simpson had told him the night following the murders that he had had dreams of killing Nicole. Dunn also wrote: "I think I have never seen a meaner face than Carl Douglas's when he went after Shipp in his cross-examination. ... From a showbiz point of view, it was a great scene, brilliantly acted. Legally, it was less than great. Douglas's attack went on much too long, and it allowed the prosecution to ask Shipp for more and more details about family life in the Simpson household, which in no manner enhanced O.J.'s already tarnished image. Before Shipp's testimony, I hadn't known that O.J. had a life-size statue of himself in his garden, which his son Jason, from his first marriage, once tried to destroy with a baseball bat. (I wonder if that's the same baseball bat that O.J. used when he smashed the windshield of Nicole's Mercedes.)" Dominick Dunn, *Vanity Fair*, April 1995, p. 90.

39. "You will. I won't. I won't drink that much."

40. Hank Goldberg.

41. 6–12–1994 is the date of the murders and 32 was O.J.'s number while a football player. When the individual digits of the date are added together, they equal 32.

42. William C. Thompson worked closely with Scheck and Neufeld on DNA issues. It was Thompson who discovered that prosecution witness Professor Bruce Weir had made an error in calculating some of his probabilities. William G. Thompson worked for Sacco and Vanzetti.

43. He questioned the appropriateness of the objection. The conflict was over the car Ron Goldman drove to Nicole's condo the night he was murdered:

Ms. Clark: But now they want to play fast and loose even more. There was nothing wrong with asking a question that had only one logical inference. Let him go and prove otherwise. Everyone knows how that car got there. Everyone knows how keys—those are the technical objections just to break the people's stride and break up the case, I understand, but to now complain about this after all they have gotten away with is greedy beyond belief.

Mr. Cochran: That is an objection, greedy beyond belief?

44. Christopher Darden was referring to juror Tracy Kennedy, later dismissed.

45. William Kuntsler, who died before the trial concluded.

46. Ron Goldman's apartment.

47. Kato Kaelin. Dunn says one his own detractors calls him "Judith Krantz in pants".

48. Faye Resnick. Jeffrey Toobin wrote in the February 6th, 1995 issue of *The New Yorker*: "I asked her if she had any literary influences. 'I wasn't inspired by a book to do this,' she said. 'The movie that inspired me was *The Pelican Brief*.'"

49. "You could have left out a few things," he said. "But my training is to write stories that grab you by the throat."

50. A. Michael Knox, dismissed before deliberations.

51. Cochran objected, saying, "that is self-serving. We can all see him". After Cochran was overruled, he made some comment, unrecorded in the record, which upset Judge Ito. From the transcript of March 7th, Marcia Clark questioning Detective Lange:

Q   Now, it was indicated in your notes that you saw two dimes and two pennies at the rear driveway of 875 South Bundy. Do you recall that, sir?

A   Yes.

Q   You also reviewed all the photographs, did you?

A   Yes.

Q   In any of the photographs did you see two dimes and two pennies?

A   No, that is a mistake, and I erred in writing two down.

Q   So that was a mistake you made in your notes?

A   That's correct.

Q   All right. You are a human being?

Mr. Cochran: Your Honor, that is self-serving. We can all see him.

The Court: Overruled. Overruled.

The Witness: I do make mistakes.

Q   Now, you indicated that you booked the change and that—

The Court: Mr. Cochran, I heard the comment.

Mr. Cochran: What comment? I didn't say anything.

The Court: I heard the comment.

Mr. Cochran: I didn't make any comment, Your Honor.

The Court: I heard the comment. Proceed.

52. Rosa Lopez. In arguing before Judge Ito on February 21st for a conditional examination of Rosa Lopez, Bailey argued:

> Now, the focal point of this witness' testimony, as I'm sure Your Honor understands, is presently opposed by a dog. A dog has announced that murder was occurring at 10:15, if I understand the prosecution's opening and its evidence so far. This witness says at 10:15 this man's automobile, which is cast as an instrument of murder in this case, and they are locked in, they can't separate O.J. Simpson, that Bronco in their evidence, it is too late. That car was where it is usually parked when it is at home, and that is right outside the Rockingham entrance and she saw it there as she routinely walked a path. That is pretty simple evidence.

53. Bailey said half-an-hour and Darden said three hours.

54. It consumed most of the week beginning February 27th. The time spent included questioning as well as wrangling over legal matters related to Lopez.

55. Johnnie Cochran on February 16th, regarding Detective Phillips's testimony concerning his notifying O.J. Simpson of Nicole's death.

56. Officer Robert Riske, the first officer on the scene at 875 South Bundy. From a sidebar in the February 9th transcript concerning how the criminalists numbered evidence at the scene:

Mr. Cochran: ... we will be able to demonstrate this in an offer of proof. These guys mislabeled everything. First of all, let me tell you the offer of proof.

The Court: But for this guy to tell you this? Is a brand new police officer who doesn't know how they do this stuff. To ask him how—if it makes any sense, it is a meaningless answer.

Mr. Cochran: He is the first guy at the scene and he is the guy who is in charge until the other guys get there. He may be a new officer, but these jurors don't know that, and Marcia has him as the greatest sleuth since Sherlock Holmes. She builds this guy up. And you tell me he is a new guy. That was about a hundred questions ago.

57. Dennis Fung.

58. Barry Scheck, during his cross-examination of Dennis Fung on April 12th:

Q By Mr. Scheck: Let me put it directly to you, sir. On June 14th, when you examined the Bronco, did you see four red stains on the door sill of the Bronco?

Mr. Goldberg: Your Honor, I object to counsel's tone of voice. I also object because this does not refer to the area that was related to the testimony by Fuhrman.

Mr. Scheck: I object to that objection.

The Court: Overruled.

Mr. Scheck: It's a speaking objection.

The Court: It is a speaking objection. Proceed.

59. Robert Shapiro during his recross-examination of Detective Vannatter, on March 21st:

Q   And you can tell a defensive wound from an offensive wound?

A   Well, normally—normally, defensive wounds occur to the hands and arms, yes.

Mr. Shapiro: May I approach the witness for a moment, Your Honor?

The Court: You may.

Mr. Shapiro: I have a bruise on my hand.

Mr. Darden: I object, Your Honor.

The Court: We'll have Mr. Shapiro marked as—

Mr. Shapiro: Can I be marked as an exhibit?

I would like—I mean, can I ask him if he has an opinion as to whether this is an offensive or defensive wound?

Mr. Darden: This is absurd, Your Honor.

The Court: I agree.

60. Philip Vannatter during cross-examination by Robert Shapiro, talking about Detective Fuhrman:

Q   Did you hear him [Fuhrman] testify that while you guys were ringing the door he decided just to take a walk down Rockingham?

A   Yes.

Q   Was that something that you asked him to do?

A   No, but I don't have him on a leash either. He is a capable man. He is capable of walking around and I don't follow him at all times.

61. Philip Vannatter. From the March 20th transcript, during cross-examination by Robert Shapiro:

Q   But you're the one who's walking by with a magnifying glass saying, "this is what I want to preserve."

A   Like Sherlock Holmes with a magnifying glass? No. Yes, I go into the crime scene to acclimate myself to the scene to know what's there so I can direct the criminalist when he gets there for the search for obvious evidence as well as latent evidence that may be there.

62. Scheck added that he sneezed and flaked dandruff on it, too:

Mr. Clarke: ... I was going to ask the witness if Dr. Blake did anything to contaminate any of the samples in the witness' opinion in the course of this cutting process. ... And then, lastly, were—

Mr. Scheck: You will say no, right?

Mr. Clarke: —were all of the raw data—

The Court: He spit on it.

Mr. Scheck: He sneezed on it. He flaked dandruff on that.

Mr. Shapiro: We have another term for that.

63. He asked each of them to autograph a book they had written.

64. Marcia Clark.

65. "No. I'm Scottish. No."

Judge Ito pointed out to Clark that the $77 referred to two pairs of gloves at a thirty percent discount. So Clark asked MacDonell if he owned any gloves which cost $55 a pair and he responded, "I hope not. I don't know. My wife frequently buys gloves for Christmas and I hope she doesn't spend that much."

66. The Bloomingdales employee who sold Nicole gloves on December 18th, 1990. While present at the courthouse when Brenda Vemich testified and when Richard Rubin testified the first time, she was not called as a witness.

67. Jo-Ellan Dimitrius. She was a defense jury consultant in both the O.J. Simpson trial, and in the McMartin child abuse trial, the latter being the most expensive ever conducted by L.A. county.

68. David Margolick on the jury, the day before the verdict, in his article "Reading Simpson's Hard-to-Read Jury" for the *New York Times*.

69. Judge Ito

70. Judge Ito.

71. Michael Knox.

72. F. Lee Bailey to Christopher Darden, in discussing alternative juror 353 on February 7th.

73. Darden's complaint that Cochran stepped on his shoes during a January 31st sidebar:

Mr. Darden: Are we going to talk about the terms of his probation?
       Your Honor, I object. He has stepped on my shined Ferragamo's. You know, I think he should have to buy me another pair of Ferragamo's.
The Court: Come on guys. ...
Mr. Darden: I have about one more question. Then we can wrap this up.
The Court: And I'll direct counsel to pay for your next shoe shine as a sanction.
Mr. Darden: Shoe shine? He should buy me a new pair of shoes.

74. F. Lee Bailey called Robert Shapiro a "sick little puppy", speaking after the verdict.

75. Christopher Darden and Johnnie Cochran, at a sidebar:

Mr. Darden: How many lawyers get to talk on this issue?
Mr. Cochran: Maybe if the other side would abide by your rulings. As I was going to point out to you—
The Court: Please, Mr. Cochran, one lawyer at a time.
Mr. Scheck: I'm going to move on, but I think we should be allowed cross-examination.
The Court: Counsel, I understand it's cross-examination. But I don't know if you're watching the jury, but they've stopped paying attention.
Mr. Cochran: We think they are going to pay attention—
Mr. Darden: I think they have had enough smooth defense tactics for the day.
Mr. Cochran: I resent that. I resent that remark, smooth defense tactics. What

they've got—

The Court: Don't spit at me, Mr. Cochran.

Mr. Cochran: We're being killed in these ridiculous.

Mr. Darden: He is testifying to the best he can, and that's all he can do.

Mr. Cochran: Be a lawyer. Stop acting like a child.

Mr. Darden: Such he is with minutiae.

The Court: Mr. Darden.

Mr. Darden: You are a child, Mr. Cochran.

The Court: Mr. Darden, when you talk when Mr. Cochran talks, the court reporter doesn't get down any of our record here.

Mr. Darden: It is difficult for any of us to get another word in when Mr. Cochran is talking.

76. Vincent Bugliosi and Burton Katz. Bugliosi got the first convictions against Manson for the Tate–LaBianca murders. Less famous is the conviction of Manson for the Hinman–Shea murders, where Burton Katz was the prosecutor.

77. "Calls for speculation." The exchange occurred on July 11th:

Q   You happened to see me at a place?

A   Yes.

Mr. Cochran: My wife may be watching.

Q   You saw me someplace socially?

A   I saw you someplace where we were both at, not together.

Q   Okay. Separately? I was with my wife, right?

A   Yes, you were.

Q   Okay. Good.

Ms. Clark: Objection. Calls for speculation.

Mr. Cochran: I'll take the stand. I'll take the stand. I was with my wife. No speculation.

78. F. Lee Bailey, in open court without the jury present:

> If it please the court, a little before ten o'clock central daylight time this morning Officer Rodney Tilley of the Panama City Police Department approached Marianne Barbieri, the mother of Paula Barbieri whose name has surfaced in this case, and as a messenger, allegedly for Detective Tom Lange, said, "now that the relationship between Mr. Simpson and your daughter has changed, would you find out if she would like to talk to us?"
>
> Miss Barbieri has hired a lawyer, made it known to the prosecution that she can be reached through her lawyer, and only that way, and we would like to make this a matter of record, because if it happens again, we will ask for sanctions. I am in touch with her on a regular basis. There is no change in the relationship. It is every bit as strong as it was on June 12, 1994, and we would ask that she not be surreptitiously approached by the police.

79. Judge Ito. From the July 24th transcript:

The Court: What form of EDTA was used—is used in the purple vials?

Mr. Blasier: Well, actually it is—do you want me to answer?

The Court: Yes, I would like to know.

Mr. Blasier: It can be there in several forms; iron EDTA, calcium EDTA, several others.

The Court: What was used here?

Mr. Blasier: I don't know. I mean it can—it picks up iron is what it does.

The Court: I understand that, but the one article you have talks about the water quality in the Neckar Valley River.

Mr. Blasier: Uh-huh.

The Court: A delightful place. That is why the Germans call it the Romantic Highway, but it doesn't tell me a lot about this case.

80. Barry Scheck's comments immediately following a sidebar on April 5th:

Mr. Scheck: New Yorkers, we talk fast, we move fast.

The Court: Not fast enough.

Mr. Scheck: Not fast enough, I know. I'm trying, Your Honor.

The Court: Ladies and gentlemen, please disregard any banter.

81. Johnnie Cochran to Marcia Clark. During a February 21st sidebar Clark told the judge that Detective Lange should be able to testify to his conclusion that the finding of the keys next to Ron Goldman's body, rather than in his pocket, indicated that Goldman was taken by surprise:

Mr. Cochran: Back up here again, your honor. What happened is that you asked him "when did you join the LAPD, how long have you been a detective, how long have you been a homicide detective," but you never asked him "how many homicides have you investigated?"

Mr. Cochran: I would love to hear that now.

Ms. Clark: Standard routine stuff. I just didn't believe it.

Mr. Cochran: This is your first case in a long time. You have been an administrator, we can tell.

82. Judge Ito. The sidebar quoted in the previous question continued:

The Court: Counsel, assuming that she gets the appropriate answers, I'm going to allow the question and answer because I think he can opine that based upon his experience, assuming it is there.

Mr. Cochran: May I be heard, Your Honor?

The Court: Sure.

Mr. Cochran: Your Honor, surprise? How can he opine that? He didn't have a vote. I mean, what are we going to do—I mean, that is preposterous for him to understand that he could say whether he was taken by surprise. What does it say that? How do we know? How do you separate that out? We need a further foundation.

The Court: Counsel, counsel, it goes to why men shake hands, it goes to why men go on the left side of the road instead of the right side of the road, so that you have your sword hand free. If you have your keys in your sword hand—

Mr. Cochran: Judge, I don't think—

The Court: I know Mr. Bailey can appreciate this kind of stuff.

83. Dr. Michael Baden calls his former student Dr. Lakshmanan

Sathyavagiswaran "Lucky".

84. The blanket put over Nicole's body. Marcia Clark ridiculed the defense theory in an argument before the judge on April 17th:

> Nevertheless, the defense has attempted to sell to this jury through their hypotheticals that this blanket was waved around the scene like a matador would in an arena and that somehow particles flew off of that blanket and magically landed one on Ron Goldman and another on the cap and I mean kind of crazy stuff. But that's what they've been trying to do and they've been doing it repeatedly, specifically with respect to the defendant's hair could have been on the blanket, the Bronco fibers could have been on the blanket and they could have wound up here and they could have wound up there because of this, that and the other.
>
> So the defense has done that very thing. Now when we come back and in the most mild and muted form come back with a hypothetical concerning this witness' handling of the crime scene collection procedures used, they're screaming bloody murder, and it's not appropriate. They don't have the right to—

The Court: Bad—

Ms. Clark: Bad choice of words. [bloody murder]

85. Lawrence Schiller, who co-wrote with Simpson *I Want to Tell You*. Schiller had sold the story of Susan Atkins, one of Charles Manson's co-defendants in the Tate–LaBianca case. He was questioned in detail about the events surrounding the sale of the story during the penalty phase of that case.

86. Barry Scheck, during his questioning of Dennis Fung on April 11th:

Q   Okay. And would you not agree, sir, that when biological material such as wet bloodstains begin to degrade through bacterial contamination, that there is greater danger of cross-contaminating those degraded samples than if the samples had not been degraded?

Mr. Goldberg: Unintelligible, Your Honor.

Mr. Scheck: Let me rephrase that because it is unintelligible.

The Court: Sustained.

Mr. Scheck: Sustained and self-censured.

The Court: Yes. Sustained.

87. Marcia Clark. While FBI shoe impression expert William Bodziak was on the witness stand, the following took place at a sidebar:

Mr. Cochran: Whenever you decide to break, I just want to be able to show these various things to the client.

The Court: Yes.

Mr. Cochran: I looked at them for the first time. Okay.

The Court: Yes.

Ms. Clark: Because he hasn't seen the bottom of his shoes in a while.

Mr. Cochran: I'm not commenting on any personal comments, judge.

The Court: Would you advise your co-counsel?

Mr. Cochran: I will.

88. William Kunstler and Ron Kuby.

89. Johnnie Cochran of Marcia Clark, at a sidebar on March 28th:

The Court: Want to show me the transcript? What line?

Mr. Cochran: Beginning line 15. She'll agree she just wanted to come over here to stand close to me.

Ms. Clark: True. You're so hard to resist.

90. Remarkably enough, William Bodziak, the FBI shoe impression expert. He explained this during cross-examination by F. Lee Bailey on June 19th:

The Witness: We're having a hard time educating the police forces of all of the possibilities with shoes. Most people are totally unaware of the footprints they leave. And perhaps the best example I could give on this is, maybe 15 years ago, there was a fad called streaking, and I had a case involving some streaking in a hotel up in the northeast part of the country. And ironically, the only part of clothing that the person ever wore and what convicted the person was the shoes. So I use that as a good example of how persons are just unaware of the prints they leave, which we discussed earlier, and they are even more unaware of the kind of hypothetical that you're suggesting. And not only are they unaware of that evidence and how to use the evidence in the manner you suggested, but the possibility or the likelihood of them going to the extreme that they would have to find this shoe, I just—I don't believe in my opinion that that could possibly happen.

The Court: So the FBI investigates streaking.

The Witness: We conduct comparisons of evidence that are submitted to us by any law enforcement agency. We don't decide what's important or not.

91. Detective Ron Phillips

92. F. Lee Bailey, during his March 13th cross-examination of Detective Furhman concerning the number of people who walked in the area where the Rockingham glove was found:

Q   Did you then cause eighteen pairs of feet to trample that area before any criminalist could get to it?

A   Eighteen pairs of feet?

Q   Eighteen pairs of feet. Two Fuhrman, four Fuhrman and Phillips, four Fuhrman and Vannatter, four Fuhrman and Lange and four Fuhrman and Rokahr? Did you do that?

A   Yes, sir.

93. Detective Fuhrman, during cross-examination by F. Lee Bailey on March 13th:

Q   ... Now, would you agree that when there is delay in a homicide investigation, number one, the perpetrators or perpetrator, as the case may be, have a chance to get further and further away from the scene, correct?

A   Well, I think that would be common sense, yes.

Q   They have the opportunity perhaps to plant evidence, to mislead the detectives as time goes by?

A   I couldn't answer that, sir.
Q   They have time—this is no part of your training I take it?
A   Planting evidence? No, it isn't.

94. While Dr. Cotton did talk about DNA being happy, it was Mr. Clark who introduced the concept in a question on May 8th:

Q   So therefore DNA is at its happiest, would that be correct to say, when the pairs match up correctly?
A   Yes. It is happy and it is stable when they are paired up correctly. It is pretty happy when they are completely separate, but not as happy as when they are together.

95. They all made visits to the courtroom to observe the trial.

96. Rosa Lopez.

97. Christopher Darden, at a February 1st sidebar:

The Court: Mr. Darden, this is your witness. It's your presentation —
Mr. Darden: I'm not criticizing you, judge. You're my bud.
Mr. Cochran: Wait a minute. I resent that.
Mr. Darden: I'm trying to cover myself.
Mr. Cochran: It's not a question of him being your bud. I move to strike that.

98. Cochran complained about Darden calling Ito "my bud":

Mr. Cochran: I asked him was it Vannatter and I backed up. I didn't try to come up with some other wild theory to change your mind. You ruled on this and I was just saying that my objection from the standpoint of my client and our side, that we don't ask for any suggestions, we don't need any help. And I would just ask the court not to give them any help either. I think that is the appropriate way of doing it. Judge, we have Mr. Darden on national T.V. saying the judge is my bud.
Ms. Clark: What is the relevance of this? What is the relevance of this?
Mr. Cochran: I think—
Ms. Clark: What does this have to do with what we are up here for? Mr. Cochran is going off on wild tangents.
The Court: Hold on.
Mr. Cochran: Mr. Darden is saying on national T.V. the Judge is my bud and The Court suggests to him—and that is all I'm saying. He did say that.
Ms. Clark: I don't know what counsel is referring to. Could we just discuss the issue at hand here?
Mr. Darden: By the way, I also said I loved Mr. Cochran.
Mr. Cochran: He has always said that.

99. F. Lee Bailey, during his cross-examination of Detective Fuhrman:

Q   And you didn't ask him why the limousine was there?
A   No.
Q   And you didn't ask him if Mr. Simpson had been the one using the limousine?
A   No, I didn't.

Q   Kato Kaelin didn't look to you like a fellow who rode around in limousines, did he?
A   (no audible response.)
Q   Did he?
A   In this area of Los Angeles, I don't think could you say that.

100. A. Sir Alec Jeffreys, who did pioneering work in the use of DNA analysis for identification in criminal cases. Dr. Cotton spent a short amount of time in Dr. Jeffreys's lab to learn certain forensic PCR techniques.

101. Laura Hart McKinny's tapes of Mark Fuhrman, in a remark made by Johnnie Cochran to Judge Ito.

Notes

Preface

1. Vincent Bugliosi with Curt Gentry, *Helter Skelter* (New York: Bantam Books, 1974; Afterword 1994), p. 24.

2. Transcript, 27 September 1995.

Chapter 1
Facts and Theories

1. In her preliminary hearing testimony, Bettina Rasmussen described the blood she saw around Nicole: "I was remembering is like it was coming down like a river. I mean I saw it, and then I saw the body, and I remember—like I saw—like it didn't flow, but it looked like it was on the way down the walkway." Preliminary Hearing Transcript, 1 July 1994.

2. Transcript, 11 January 1995.

3. Transcript, 30 January 1995.

4. Since the 1995 verdict, Simpson has publicly denied ever striking Nicole, in spite of the evidence presented at the criminal trial.

Chapter 2
A School of Red Herrings

1. Transcript, 28 August 1995.

2. Transcript, 31 July 1995.

3. Transcript, 1 August 1995.

4. Transcript, 13 March 1995.

5. Transcript, 14 March 1995.

6. Transcript, 15 March 1995.

7. Transcript, 16 June 1995.

8. Transcript, 16 June 1995.

9. Transcript, 2 August 1995.

10. Transcript, 31 May 1995.

11. Transcript, 31 May 1995.

12. Transcript, 31 May 1995.

13. Transcript, 31 May 1995.

14. Transcript, 31 May 1995.

15. Transcript, 31 May 1995.

16. Transcript, 31 May 1995.

17. DNA extracted from stains placed outdoors through three weeks amplified and typed correctly according to Catherine Theisen Comey and Bruce Budowle, "Validation Studies on the Analysis of the HLA DQα Locus Using the Polymerase Chain Reaction", *Journal of Forensic Sciences*, vol. 36, no. 6, November 1991, p. 1641.

For a discussion of the durability of serological protein markers, see G.C. Denault, H.H. Takimoto, Q.Y. Kwan, and Andrew Pallos, "Detectability of Selected Genetic Markers in Dried Blood on Aging", *Journal of Forensic Sciences,* vol. 25, no. 3, July 1980, pp. 479–498.

18. Transcript, 29 September 1995.

19. I.J. Good, "When Batterer Turns Murderer", *Nature*, vol. 375, 15 June 1995, p. 541.

20. Good, p. 541. He concludes, "I have sent a copy of this note to both

Professor Dershowitz and the Los Angeles Police Department."

Since the verdict in the criminal case, Dershowitz has written, "It is, of course, also true that a high proportion of women who have been battered by their husbands or boyfriends and are then found dead were killed by these batterers, but it is equally true that a high proportion of women who have not been battered and are found dead were killed by their husbands or boyfriends. The reality is that a majority of women who are killed are killed by men with whom they have had a relationship, *regardless of whether their men previously battered them.*" Alan Dershowitz, *Reasonable Doubts* (New York: Simon & Schuster, 1996) p. 105.

So Dershowitz now seems to concede Good's point. Compare Dershowitz's conclusion with domestic violence expert Donald Dutton, who testified outside the presence of the jury on January 12th:

Q   In regard to the studies of spousal homicide, is there any one motive that has come out as predominant?

A   Well, the main precipitating factor— in fact, there is six different studies that have been done. The first one was Martin Wolfgang, did a study in Philadelphia, which is still a classic in 1948, but the two main things that come out is, first of all, estrangement, jealousy, a history of physical abuse and/or jealousy in the relationship and recent estrangement between the perpetrator and victim.

21. Transcript, 13 April 1995.
22. Transcript, 13 April 1995.
23. Transcript, 13 April 1995.
24. Transcript, 13 April 1995.
25. Transcript, 14 April 1995.

Chapter 3
Dogs that Didn't Bark

1. Transcript, 29 March 1995.
2. Transcript, 29 March 1995.
3. Transcript, 29 March 1995.
4. Transcript, 29 March 1995.
5. Transcript, 27 September 1995.
6. Transcript, 27 September 1995.
7. Transcript, 28 August 1995. For example, in some cases blood group antigens can be identified testing human hair shafts, see Henry Lee, Robert Gaensslen, and Beryl Novitch, "A Review of ABH Blood Group Antigen Determinations in Human Hair and some Further Studies on its Relaiability", Crime Laboratory Digest, vol. 12, no.4, October 1985, pp. 83–89.
8. Transcript, 19 June 1995. I have not been able to make sense of "daylight inchoata".
9. Transcript, 19 June 1995. Note that the court reporter should have written "officers'" and not "officer's". Bodziak was talking about the shoes of multiple people.
10. Transcript, 14 February 1995.
11. Transcript, 28 September 1995.
12. Transcript, 14 February 1995.
13. Transcript, 14 February 1995.
14. Some conspiracy theorists (unconnected with the defense) have argued that perhaps the blood Blasier was talking about came from a source other than an EDTA vial. For example, at autopsy blood from the victims was placed in two different kind of vials, only one of which was treated with EDTA. Conspirators might have snatched blood from these test tubes. Or perhaps they stole blood off of the Rockingham swatches. But it was the defense who claimed in opening argument that the blood missing from the EDTA vial was the

smoking gun of the conspiracy. To suppose that Vannatter used different blood seems very strange indeed since the defense also claimed that Vannatter's possession of the EDTA vial for a few hours was so sinister, and since to extract blood from the Rockingham swatches to plant elsewhere is a complicated matter.

15. Transcript, 14 February 1995.

16. Transcript, 2 August 1995:

Q And is there a particular kit that is used with that PCR application [a test for chlamydia used in Gerdes's lab]?
A Yes.
Q And who approved that kit?
A Well, it is a FDA-approved kit.
Q What is the FDA?
A The Food and Drug Administration, and for clinical testing, if you use a kit, it has to be approved by that organization...

17. Transcript, 15 February 1995.

Chapter 4
The Beast with Five Fingers

1. Jeffrey Toobin, "Annals of Law: An Incendiary Defense", *The New Yorker*, 25 July 1994, pp. 56–59.

2. Transcript, 13 and 14 March 1995.

3. Transcript, 16 March 1995.

4. Transcript, 10 March 1995.

5. Transcript, 22 March 1995.

6. Transcript, 22 March 1995.

Chapter 5
If the Glove Fits ...

1. Transcript, 27 and 28 September 1995.

2. Transcript, 15 June 1995.

3. Transcript, 15 June 1995.

4. Transcript, 16 June 1995.

5. Transcript, 16 June 1995.

6. Transcript, 31 July 1995.

7. Transcript, 31 July 1995.

8. Transcript, 18 September 1995.

9. Transcript, 31 July 1995.

10. Transcript, 16 June 1995.

11. Transcript, 15 June 1995.

12. Transcript, 16 June 1995.

13. Transcript, 15 June 1995.

14. Personal communication.

15. James Thacker. "Re: Toobin Article in New Yorker" article posted to the internet newsgroup alt.fan.oj-simpson, 1 November 1995.

16. Transcript, 21 June 1995.

17. Transcript, 21 June 1995.

18. Transcript, 19 June 1995.

19. Transcript, 15 June 1995.

20. Transcript, 15 June 1995.

21. Transcript, 15 June 1995.

22. Transcript, 15 June 1995.

23. Transcript, 21 June 1995.

24. Transcript, 16 June 1995.

25. Transcript, 16 June 1995.

26. Transcript, 27 September 1995.

27. Transcript, 16 June 1995.

Chapter 6
Vannatter and the Vial

1. Transcript, 28 September 1995.

2. Transcript, 12 April 1995.

3. Transcript, 5 April 1995.

4. Transcript, 28 September 1995.

5. Transcript, 17 March 1995.

Chapter 7
The Case of the Bloodstained Bindle

1. Transcript, 25 August 1995.

2. For example, Scheck questioned Gary Sims on this issue, specifically comparing the DNA content of the back gate stains to Item 47:

Q Now, with respect to 115 and 116 [blood from the Bundy back gate], same

comparison, 115 and 116 have about two times as much DNA as No. 6 [a Rockingham blood drop]?
A Yes.
Q 15 times as much DNA as No. 47, a Bundy blood drop?
A Yes
Transcript, 31 May 1995.

3. Arnold V. Lesikar, "Thoughts on the Item 47—Planting Degraded Material?" article posted to the internet newsgroup alt.fan.oj-simpson, 28 August 1995.

4. This analysis draws heavily on the discussion of Item 56 by Lesikar.

5. Catherine Theisen Comey and Bruce Budowle, "Validation Studies on the Analysis of the HLA DQα Locus Using the Polymerase Chain Reaction", *Journal of Forensic Sciences*, vol. 36, no. 6, November 1991, pp. 1636, 1641.

6. Transcript, 25 August 1995.

7. Transcript, 28 August 1995.

8. Transcript, 28 August 1995.

Chapter 8
Blood on the Back Gate

1. Transcript, 28 September 1995.
2. Transcript, 28 September 1995.
3. Transcript, 9 February 1995.
4. Transcript, 9 February 1995.
5. Transcript, 9 February 1995.
6. Transcript, 9 February 1995.
7. Transcript, 9 February 1995.
8. Transcript, 9 February 1995.
9. Transcript, 9 February 1995.
10. Transcript, 9 February 1995.
11. Transcript, 9 February 1995.
12. Transcript, 9 February 1995.
13. Transcript, 14 February 1995.
14. Transcript, 15 February 1995.
15. Transcript, 15 February 1995.
16. Transcript, 17 February 1995.

17. Transcript, 21 February 1995.
18. Transcript, 21 February 1995.
19. Transcript, 22 February 1995.
20. Transcript, 22 February 1995.
21. Transcript, 22 February 1995.
22. Transcript, 22 February 1995.
23. Transcript, 6 March 1995.
24. Transcript, 7 March 1995.
25. Transcript, 6 March 1995.
26. Transcript, 7 March 1995.
27. Transcript, 8 March 1995.
28. Transcript, 8 March 1995.
29. Transcript, 9 March 1995.
30. Transcript, 9 and 10 March 1995.
31. Transcript, 13 March 1995.
32. Transcript, 13 March 1995.
33. Transcript, 13 March 1995.
34. Transcript, 13 March 1995.
35. Transcript, 16 March 1995.
36. Transcript, 16 March 1995.
37. Transcript, 16 March 1995.
38. Transcript, 20 March 1995.
39. Transcript, 27 September 1995.
40. Transcript, 27 September 1995.
41. Transcript, 27 September 1995.
42. Transcript, 27 September 1995.
43. Transcript, 28 September 1995
44. Mark Miller, "Justice: The Road to Panama City", *Newsweek*, 30 October 1995, p. 84.

Chapter 9
DNA on Trial

1. A few weeks after the verdict Gerdes attended his first scientific conference, the Annual Symposium on Human Identification sponsored by the Promega corporation, held in Scottsdale, Arizona. Many of the participants in the DNA aspects of the Simpson trial spoke at this meeting.

2. For an excellent short history of DNA typing, see Keith Inman and Norah Rudin, *DNA Demystified: Solving Crimes in the '90s*, NR Biocom, 1994.

3. Transcript, 2 August 1995.

4. The DX artifact causes the 1.1 dot to hybridize faintly even though the 1 dot does not hybridize. A strip with a 1 dot and a faint 1.1 dot could be a DX and Gerdes admits this.

5. Some of the causes of faint dots are listed in the *AmpliType User Guide* in section 4, p. 1 and are explained throughout section 4.

6. See, for example, Catherine Theisen Comey and Bruce Budowle, "Validation Studies on the Analysis of the HLA DQα Locus Using the Polymerase Chain Reaction", *Journal of Forensic Sciences*, vol. 36, no. 6, November 1991, p. 1641; and Henry A. Erlich and Teodorica L. Bugawan, "HLA DNA Typing", *PCR Protocols, A Guide to Methods and Applications,* Academic Press, Inc., 1990, pp. 270–71.

7. *AmpliType User Guide*, Section 4, p. 7.

8. Comey and Budowle, pp. 1636, 1641.

9. Gerdes testified that for the 1.3 dot to appear as an artifact "you need greater than 6 nanograms of DNA". Transcript, 2 August 1995. In fact, this kind of artifact applies to many of the other dots on the DQ-alpha strip as well. *AmpliType User Guide*, Section 6, p. 5. These artifacts are due to nonspecific cross-hybridization.

10. *AmpliType User Guide*, Section 4, p. 1.

11. *People v. McIntosh & Schlaepfer*, testimony of Dr. Kary Mullis, quoted in "Motion to Exclude DNA Evidence" submitted by the defense in *People of the State of California vs. Orenthal James Simpson*, dated 4 October 1994.

12. Gerdes could have isolated a contaminant allele by cloning the PCR products and then screening them for the presence of the putative contaminant. Stephen J. Scharf, Glenn T. Horn, Henry A. Erlich, "Direct Cloning and Sequence Analysis of Enzymatically Amplified Genomic Sequences", *Science*, vol. 233, 5 September 1986, pp.1076–78.

Alternatively, Gerdes could have specifically amplified only the suspected contaminant using allele specific primers and PCR. Such a procedure is reported to be capable of detecting alleles representing less than 0.0001 of the background genotype, and is 1,000 times more sensitive than the AmpliType DQα test. U.B. Gyllensten et al., "DNA Typing of Forensic Material with Mixed Genotypes Using Allele-Specific Enzymatic Amplification (Polymerase Chain Reaction)", *Forensic Science International,* vol. 52, 1992, pp. 149–160.

Or Gerdes could have simply repeated the PCR analysis using the DQα or D1S80 kits. If he had shown that he got faint dots consistently each time he repeated the analysis, this too would more persuasively demonstrate that there was contamination.

Yet another possibility is employing standardized tests for mitochondrial DNA typing. Mitochondrial DNA is interesting because we inherit it just from our mothers and so we have only a single allele for each mitochondrial gene. Thus, if more than one allele is observed this is unequivocal proof that there is a mixture of more than one individual's blood in the sample. See, for example, C.F. Aquadro, D.B.

Greenberg, "Human Mitochondrial DNA Variation and Evolution, Analysis of Nucleotide Sequences form Seven Individuals", *Genetics*, vol. 103, 1983, pp. 287–312.

13. A literature search conducted by Arthur J. Milgram, using Biological Abstracts, MedLine, and the Science Citation Index, covering 1965 through 1995 found no publications attributable to Dr. Gerdes. (There were numerous papers written by various people named John Gerdes or J. Gerdes, but these all appear to be written by Europeans or are on subjects unrelated to the defense witness's background or work.)

14. Comey and Budowle, pp. 1633–1648.

15. Transcript, 3 August 1995.

16. Transcript, 3 August 1995.

17. Transcript, 3 August 1995.

18. Transcript, 3 August 1995.

19. Transcript, 3 August 1995.

20. Transcript, 3 August 1995.

21. Generally, if the number of sperm observed are under one hundred, analysts do not even try to type the sample. Edward Blake, Jennifer Mihalovich, Russell Higuchi, P. Sean Walsh, and Henry Erlich, "Polymerase Chain Reaction (PCR) Amplification and Human Leukocyte Antigen (HLA)-DQα Oligonucleotides Typing on Biological Evidence Samples: Casework Experience", *Journal of Forensic Sciences*, vol. 37, no. 3, May 1992, p. 719.

22. Transcript, 3 August 1995.

23. Blake considers information from the shaft to be vital precisely *because* DNA typed from the shaft is often not from the person from whom the hair originated. For example, it can help an analyst distinguish between two genotypes found at the hair root in cases where bloody hair roots type as a mixture and where no reference sample for the root exists. Blake et al., pp. 708–09.

24. Gerdes admits a strip with a 1 dot and a faint 1.1 dot could be a DX. But if he found an unexplained 1 dot or a 1.1 dot on any typing strip or control strips done that same day or within a day, then he considered the faint 1.1 dot to be contamination and not a DX. This undercounts the actual DX artifacts because he has not logically excluded the possibility that these faint dots could in fact still be DX artifacts.

Gerdes also looks to the 1 dot to confirm the presence of a 1.3 allele or a 1.2 allele when he sees a faint 1.3 dot or a faint all but 1.3 dot. The presence of the 1 dot, for Gerdes, confirms the possibility of extra 1 alleles floating around. But one might wonder how a single 1 dot can legitimately be used to account for the presence of all the suballeles, 1.1, 1.2, 1.3, simultaneously.

25. In those instances, Gerdes examined the strips relating directly to the case in question as well as controls run at about the same time.

26. For a readable discussion of the manipulation of statistics, see Darrell Huff, *How to Lie with Statistics* (New York: Norton, 1954). Graphs are discussed in chapter 5.

27. Another approach to Gerdes's data would be to arrange all the runs in order and then calculate a sliding average of contaminated runs moving from the first run to the last. (The first data point might be runs 1–5 with a contamination frequency computed, the second data point could be runs 2–6 with a

contamination frequency computed, and so on.) This method takes into account the interactions of adjacent runs—which is information Gerdes considers valuable for determining contamination—and because it avoids the problems of monthly aggregation and differing numbers of runs in a month, provides a more accurate measure of interaction through time than presented by Gerdes.

28. One of the developers of the DQ-alpha kit, Dr. Russell Higuchi, describes PCR carryover: "More unique to PCR is the possibility of carryover contamination from a completed PCR to another sample yet to be amplified. Because by the nature of PCR, PCR product will seed production of more PCR product, the sheer number of copies of PCR product after amplification can make the consequences of such contamination more dramatic. A typical PCR could have 10^{12} copies of an amplified gene. If a preparer inadvertently transfers, as before, $0.1 \, \mu l$ of PCR sample A into sample B, even though sample B has a relatively high concentration of human DNA, the number of copies of the target, single-locus gene that derive from sample A far outnumber the copies that actually stem from sample B. Thus, the DNA type obtained will be that of A and not B, and the relative amount of the B type is so small that it would not even show up in the test, eliminating the possibility that the presence of more than two alleles would flag the occurrence of the contamination." Russell Higuchi and Edward T. Blake, "PCR in Forensic Science, DNA Technology and Forensic Science", *Banbury Report*, Cold Spring Harbor Laboratory Press, 1989, p. 275, quoted in "Motion to Exclude DNA Evidence" submitted by the defense in *People of the State of California vs. Orenthal James Simpson*, dated 4 October 1994.

29. Transcript, 2 August 1995.

30. Transcript, 3 August 1995.

31. Transcript, 12 May 1995.

32. Transcript, 3 August 1995.

33. The *AmpliType User Guide* describes the precise procedure: "When pipetting Chelex solutions, the resin beads must be distributed evenly in solution; this can be achieved by gentle mixing with a stir bar in a beaker. Make 20% and 5% (w/v) stock solutions in sterile distilled water to a final volume of 100 to 300 ml. Add Chelex to individual samples as follows: For each set of samples, pour approximately 15 ml of Chelex stock solution into a 50 ml beaker containing a stir bar. Pipette the volume needed for each sample directly from the beaker while the stir bar is mixing. The pipette tip used must have a relatively large bore—1 ml pipetman tips are adequate." Section 3, p. 14.

34. Transcript, 2 August 1995.

35. Transcript, 3 August 1995.

36. Transcript, 3 August 1995.

37. Comey and Budowle, pp. 1636, 1641.

It should be noted that the *AmpliType User Guide* recommends periodically cleaning a lab bench with a very dilute solution of bleach, but makes no claim that this reduces cross-contamination of human DNA. *AmpliType User Guide*, Section 2, p. 4.

To the extent that any sort of cleaning of this type is useful, it is the liquid which is crucial. DNA is soluble in water so wiping the water off the bench will remove the DNA with it.

38. Transcript, 4 August 1995.

39. William C. Thompson, "Subjective Interpretation, Laboratory Error and the Value of Forensic DNA Evidence: Three Case Studies", *Genetica*, vol. 96, 1995, p. 154.

40. Bruce S. Weir, "DNA statistics in the Simpson matter", *Nature Genetics*, vol. 11, December 1995, p. 367.

41. Howard Coleman and Eric Swenson, *DNA in the Courtroom* (Seattle: GeneLex Press, 1994), p. 14.

42. Eric S. Lander and Bruce Budowle, "DNA Fingerprinting Dispute Laid to Rest", *Nature*, vol. 371, 27 October 1994, p. 735.

43. Lander and Budowle, p. 735.

44. Transcript, 3 August 1995.

45. Transcript, 3 August 1995.

46. Transcript, 3 August 1995.

47. See, for example, George Schiro, "Collection and Preservation of Blood Evidence from Crime Scenes", Paper presented at the Jefferson Parish Coroner's Office Eighth Annual Death Investigation Conference, 17 November 1995, p. 2.

48. Serologist Greg Matheson first testified to this match statistic at the preliminary hearing on 8 July 1994. He actually computed the match statistic to be 0.43, but rounded it off for ease of understanding. For a discussion of this particular statistic, see Donald A. Berry, "DNA, Statistics, and the Simpson Case", *Chance*, vol. 7, no. 4, 1994, pp. 9–12.

49. For example, one reason Gerdes rejected cross-contamination in Item 117 (one of the back gate stains) is precisely because the amount of DNA there is so large. This amount of DNA could have

only come from a quantity of blood too large to be inadvertently transferred.

Chapter 10
Shoes and Socks

1. Transcript, 19 June 1995.

2. Transcript, 19 June 1995.

3. Transcript, 19 June 1995.

4. Transcript, 19 June 1995.

5. Transcript, 19 June 1995.

6. Transcript, 19 June 1995.

7. Transcript, 24 January 1995.

8. Transcript, 31 July 1995.

9. Transcript, 28 August 1995.

10. Transcript, 28 September 1995.

11. Transcript, 28 September 1995.

12. Transcript, 28 August 1995.

13. Transcript, 28 September 1995.

14. Transcript, 28 September 1995.

15. Transcript, 1 August 1995.

16. Transcript, 23 August 1995.

17. Transcript, 28 September 1995.

18. Transcript, 23 August 1995.

19. Transcript, 1 August 1995.

Chapter 11
EDTA

1. EDTA stands for Ethylenediaminetetraacetic acid, defined as "A compound that acts as a chelating agent, reversibly binding with iron, magnesium, and other metal ions." *Concise Science Dictionary*, Second Edition (Oxford: Oxford University Press, 1991), p. 219.

2. Transcript, 25 and 26 July, 1995.

3. Transcript, 25 July 1995. It should also be noted that there are numerous compounds not even listed in the *Merck Index*.

4. Transcript, 24 July 1995.

5. Transcript, 25 July 1995.

6. It is also possible that a combination of these two factors could explain the results obtained by Martz.

Alternatively, it might be argued that the extraction efficiency of EDTA in evidence bloodstains was one thousand times less than the extraction from Martz's controls. But this assertion lacks merit since Martz testified that in validating the procedure he found he could extract EDTA from three-year-old preserved bloodstains and still distinguish the preserved blood from unpreserved blood.

There were also suggestions that instrumental variation might have affected Martz's findings. The machine Martz used gives slightly different results each time it is employed, so the standard had a four-fold difference in readings between runs. Even so, noise was noise, standard was standard, and EDTA was present in unequivocal abundance from the reference samples containing EDTA-preserved blood. Also, the ratio between the external standard which he used before each run and the reference blood samples remained constant. This is clearly visible on the chromatographs. Instrumental variation cannot explain Martz's results in favor of the defense.

Chapter 12
The Four Faces of Fung

1. Transcript, 12 April 1995.
2. Transcript, 12 April 1995.
3. Transcript, 11 April 1995.
4. Transcript, 11 April 1995.
5. Transcript, 11 April 1995.
6. Transcript, 13 April 1995.
7. Transcript, 12 April 1995.
8. Transcript, 12 April 1995.
9. Transcript, 12 April 1995.
10. Transcript, 12 April 1995.
11. Transcript, 12 April 1995.
12. Transcript, 11 April 1995.
13. Transcript, 22 May 1995.

Chapter 13
Fuhrman on Tape

1. According to the "Defense Amended Offer of Proof re: Fuhrman Tapes" dated 22 August, 1995, the dates of the twelve taped conversations between McKinny and Fuhrman were:
    1. April 2, 1985
    2. April 1985 (no day noted)
    3. April 15, 1985
    4. April 16, 1985
    5. August 20, 1985
    6. April 23, 1985
    7. May 23, 1986
    8. August 22, 1986
    9. April 7, 1987
    10. 1988 (no month or day noted)
    11. June 1993 (no day noted)
    12. July 28, 1994

2. Ito's ruling discusses forty-one times Fuhrman uttered the word 'nigger'. "Fuhrman Tapes", Judge Ito's ruling on the admissibility of the Fuhrman tapes, dated 31 August 1995. When she testified, McKinny said there were approximately forty-two uses of this word on the tapes. Transcript, 5 September 1995.

3. "Fuhrman Tapes", Judge Ito's ruling.

4. "Fuhrman Tapes", Judge Ito's ruling.

5. "Fuhrman Tapes", Judge Ito's ruling.

6. "Defense Amended Offer of Proof re: Fuhrman Tapes"

7. "Fuhrman Tapes", Judge Ito's ruling.

8. "Fuhrman Tapes", Judge Ito's ruling.

9. "Fuhrman Tapes", Judge Ito's ruling.

10. "Defense Amended Offer of Proof re: Fuhrman Tapes"

11. "Defense Amended Offer of Proof re: Fuhrman Tapes"

12. Transcript, 5 September 1995.

13. Transcript, 9 March 1995.

14. Transcript, 13 March 1995.

Chapter 14
The Fates Conspire

Chapter 15
The Jury

1. Michael Knox with Mike Walker. *The Private Diary of an O.J. Juror* (Beverly Hills: Dove Books, 1995), p. 57.

2. Jeffrey Toobin, "Annals of Law: Juries on Trial", *The New Yorker*, 13 October 1994, p. 44.

3. Gay Jervey, "The Seer", *The American Lawyer*, June 1993.

4. O.J. Simpson. *I Want to Tell You* (Boston: Little, Brown and Company, 1995), p. 86.

5. Stephen J. Adler, *The Jury* (New York: Doubleday, 1994), see chapter 3: "The Wizards of Odds", pp. 84–115.

6. Jeffrey Abramson, *We, The Jury* (New York: Basic Books, 1994), see chapter 4: "Scientific Jury Selection", pp. 143–76.

7. Abramson, pp. 155–59.

8. Abramson discusses the Mitchell–Stans Watergate trial (pp. 159–60); the Joan Little trial (pp. 160–62); the John DeLorean trial (pp. 162–65); the Lee Edward Harris trial (pp. 165–67), where scientific jury selection "did achieve positive, if still mixed, results" (p. 165); and the McMartin trial (pp. 167–70). His conclusions about the scientific selection are found in the chapter subsection "The Myth of Scientific Jury Selection", pp. 171–76.

9. Jervey quotes Powell as saying: "(Jo-Ellan could) step back and explain why certain organizations somebody belonged to would be good or bad for us, or tell us what questions to ask to probe further. Sometimes she would say, 'Look at his body language.' Or even, 'Look at his shoes!'" Powell is also quoted as saying "... she has extra credibility because she really cares." This conclusion seems all the more peculiar in light of her participation in the defense of those tried for their attacks on Reginald Denny, since such attacks arose from the Simi Valley verdict she is said to have helped create.

10. "I acknowledge all these legitimate uses of peremptory challenges. Yet I remain convinced that illegitimate uses for far outweigh proper ones that the time has come to eliminate peremptories or curtail drastically their number. ... *Batson* and its progeny have proven powerless to end racial, ethnic, religious, or sex discrimination during jury selection. ... *Batson* succeeded only in driving discrimination underground and into other channels." Abramson, p. 259. Adler discusses the value of eliminating peremptories on pp. 221–24, although he argues such a change may be hard to effect.

11. *Batson v. Kentucky*, 476 U.S. 79, 103, n. 3; 107 (Marshall concurring). Quoted by Adler, p. 223.

12. Adler, p. 113.

13. Quoted by Abramson, pp. 41–42.

14. Abramson, p. 43.

15. Quoted by Abramson, p. 50.

16. Armanda Cooley, Carrie Bess, and Marsha Rubin-Jackson, with a forum including Willie Cravin, Tracy Hampton, Jeanette Harris, Tracy Kennedy, and Michael Knox; as told to Tom Byrnes; with Mike Walker, *Madam Foreman: A Rush to Judgment?* (Beverly Hills, California: Dove Books, 1995).

17. Cooley, Bess, and Rubin-Jackson, p. 124.

18. Transcript, 26 September 1995.

19. Cooley, Bess, and Rubin-Jackson, pp. 118, 121, 162.

20. Cooley\ Bess, and Rubin-Jackson, pp. 120.

21. Here are Simpson's and Mazzola's genotypes for the seven different PCR tests employed in the Simpson case:

PCR Locus Tested	Simpson's Genotype	Mazzola's Genotype
DQ-alpha	1.1, 1.2	1.1, 1.2
D1S80	24, 25	31, 39
Polymarkers:		
LDLR	A, B	A, B
GYPA	B, B	A, B
HBGG	B, C	B, B
D7S8	A, B	A, B
Gc	B, C	A, C

22. Cooley, Bess, and Rubin-Jackson, p. 201.

23. Cooley, Bess, and Rubin-Jackson, p. 202.

24. Transcript, 29 September 1995.

25. Cooley, Bess, and Rubin-Jackson, p. 202.

26. Transcript, 3 April 1995.

27. Cooley, Bess, and Rubin-Jackson, p. 202.

28. Cooley, Bess, and Rubin-Jackson, p. 94

29. Cooley, Bess, and Rubin-Jackson, p. 95.

30. Transcript, 9 February 1995.

31. Transcript, 28 September 1995.

32. Cooley, Bess, and Rubin-Jackson, p. 101.

33. Cooley, Bess, and Rubin-Jackson, pp. 103–04.

34. Cooley, Bess, and Rubin-Jackson, pp. 160–61.

Chapter 16
Nothing New under the Sun

1. Stephen J. Adler, *The Jury: Disorder in the Courts* (New York: Doubleday, 1994), p. 51.

2. Adler, pp. 54–55.

3. F. Lee Bailey, *To be a Trial Lawyer* (New York: Wiley, 1985, 1994), p. 118. Bailey also writes: "The reason why strong-willed, educated, intelligent people are often removed from the jury box by the lawyers is disappointingly simple: To the fellow who believes that his case is weak, these human qualities spell 'enemy.'" p. 115.

4. Adler, p. 64.

5. Adler, p. 67.

6. Adler, p. 69.

7. Adler, p. 72.

8. Transcript, 28 September 1995.

9. Transcript, 27 September 1995.

10. Transcript, 28 September 1995.

11. Adler, p. 82.

12. Vincent Bugliosi with Curt Gentry, *Helter Skelter* (New York: Bantam Books, 1974, Afterword 1994), pp. 7, 14, 16–18, 63, 91, 257, 267, 459, and *passim*.

13. Bugliosi, p. 470.

14. Bugliosi, p. 554.

15. Joe McGinniss. *Fatal Vision*. (New York: Signet, 1983, Afterword 1985, Epilogue 1989), p. 491 and *passim*.

16. Quoted by McGinniss, pp. 561–62.

17. McGinniss, pp. 559–60.

18. Bugliosi, p. 256.

Chapter 17
The Truth, the Media, and Unreasonable Doubt

1. David Detmer, "The Limitations of Rationality and Science?—From Noam Chomsky to O.J. Simpson" (paper to be presented at the Central Division meeting of the American Philosophical Association, Chicago, Illinois, April 25–27, 1996), p. 22.

2. Transcript, 24 January 1995.

Appendix 1
The DNA Evidence

1. This information is summarized by Bruce S. Weir, "DNA Statistics in the Simpson Matter", *Nature Genetics*, vol. 11, December 1995, p. 366. Weir's tables contain a few typographical errors (several different sock stains are listed with identical numbers) and he doesn't point out that the PCR results for Item 42 were not actually presented to the jury.

Appendix 2
DNA Typing

1. The procedure outlined in this section is discussed in great detail in the *AmpliType User Guide*, Version 2, Perkin-Elmer Corp., 1993. This is a guide published by the company which manufactures and markets the AmpliType HLA DQα PCR Amplification and Typing Kit, the kit that was used for typing many evidence stains in the O.J. Simpson case.

2. The development of the reverse dot blot is discussed in Ernest Kawasaki, Randall Saiki, and Henry Erlich, "Genetic Analysis Using Polymerase Chain Reaction-Amplified DNA and Immobilized Oligonucleotide Probes: Reverse Dot-Blot Typing", *Methods in Enzymology,* vol. 218, 1993, pp. 369–381.

3. Actually, there is no probe for the 1.2 allele, but other probes on the strip make it possible to determine if the 1.2 allele is present.

All notes which say "transcript" refer to the unofficial trial transcripts which are available from numerous on-line computer sources. Quotations from the transcripts are verbatim, but the following changes have been made: while the transcripts are produced using only capital letters, I have converted my extracts to the proper mix of upper- and lower-case letters; minor typographical changes have been made, such as changing two hyphens ("--") to an m-dash ("—"); in a small number of cases, the text of multiple paragraphs has been converted into a single paragraph, that is, I have occasionally eliminated the court reporter's carriage returns; a few technical inclusions in the transcript have been eliminated without note, for example "Q: by [attorney's name]" is rendered simply as "Q:" and occasionally I have eliminated lines from the transcript unrelated to actual testimony, such as an indication that a discussion was held off the record, without inserting ellipses.

Index